THE BLUE CHIP STORE

THE BLUE CHIP STORE

How Bank Robbery Changed my Life

BY
CLAY TUMEY

LUCIDBOOKS

The Blue Chip Store

Published by Lucid Books in Houston, TX.
www.LucidBooks.net

ISBN 10: 1632960591
ISBN 13: 978-1-63296-059-7
eISBN 10: 1632960605
eISBN 13: 978-1-63296-060-3

Special Sales: Most Lucid Books titles are available in special quantity discounts. Custom imprinting or excerpting can also be done to fit special needs. Contact Lucid Books at info@lucidbooks.net.

DEDICATION

To my mother, Sherrie. You are love personified.
To anyone named Olesek, especially Rick and Susan.

*

To the incarcerated fathers, mothers, sons,
and daughters who are looking for a way out.

You have a voice in your destiny.
You have a say in your life.
You have a choice in the path you take.

–Max Lucado

TABLE OF CONTENTS

SPECIAL THANKS

To the editor, Laurie Waller. Your insight has been a blessing to me. Thank you for helping me transform a mere collection of stories into the message I most wanted to communicate.

Additionally, there were those who supported this endeavor in some exceptional way that warrants special recognition. Larry Smith. Russ Hudson. Lance, Diane, Ben, and Zach White. Claus Roager Olsen and Enneagramstedet Denmark. Marion Gilbert. Deborah Ooten. Gayle Scott. Susan & Rick Olesek. David & Sherrie Lee. Eric Schwandt. Maggie Simpson-Crabaugh. Maryanne Colter. Alexander Berezkin. Henriette Kildegaard Svenssen. Kim Bornstedt Væring.

To Joycelyn Jones, for never leaving me alone about finishing this book and for shamelessly promoting it anywhere and everywhere. To Roger Sanchez, for having an impact in my life on the inside and again on the outside. To Dave Ramsey, for exposing me to a whole new world of support and encouragement.

ACKNOWLEDGMENTS

First of all, I am thankful for Candice. In addition to being a complete godsend to our children, she's also the reason I was able to spend so much time at my desk writing this.

The book transitioned from a mere idea to a completed project thanks to the support of the following: Adam & Kim Stipanovich, Audrey Fernández, Bill Skaer & TJ Griffin, Brian Fong, Christi Wright Elkins, Dorothy Hatic, Hilary Langford, Jenny Campbell, Jeremy Gregg, Jillian Gilliam, Josh Kieschnick, Katherine Chernick Fauvre, Kathi Overheul, Kaye Bernard, Kristy Nissly, Kyle & Tara Copeland, Laura Valtonen, Laurens van Ovost, Lisa Phelan, Marcus Hill, Matthew Oastler, Michael Price, Michael Whitfield, Orlando & Gina De Dominicis, Patrick & Sara Henagar, Paulo & Alaina Franco, Sara Stockwell, Sarah-Anne Falcon, Sherry Pfaffenberg, Steve McGraw, TJ Dawe, Trina Anderson, and Zack Hill.

For the majority of my time writing this book, I listened to a repeating loop of a 28-song playlist consisting of music by The Illustrated Band, Victor Wooten, SRV, Yiruma, Mogwai, Richard Elliot & Rick Braun, Eric Johnson, and a 41-second version of Für Elise by Trans-Siberian Orchestra. During the editing process (which lasted two months, by the way), the repeating loop was reduced to two Grammatrain covers ("Wake Up" and "God").

AUTHOR'S NOTE

When Jett came to visit me, he was too young to know where I was. During the first four years of his life, I was incarcerated all but a few months. He loved Cool Ranch Doritos, but as a small toddler learning to talk, "Cool Ranch Doritos" can be a mouthful. Instead, he opted for the simpler term "blue chips" since they were chips that came in a blue bag.

For Jett, I'm sure part of the joy in visiting me was that he got to go to the vending machine and get those same blue chips over and over. Eventually, he determined that I actually lived at the blue chip store because that was the only place he ever saw me.

During the first few years following my release from prison, Jett never asked many questions about my time away. But at the age of seven, while munching on chips and salsa at a favorite restaurant of ours, Jett suddenly recalled the days when he came to see me at the blue chip store, and he asked me if I still worked there. I told him no and waited for his follow-up question.

Staring into the bowl of chips in front of him, he searched for the right words to ask what he really wanted to know. It was like watching a child prepare to ask if Santa Claus were real. I didn't want to rush the conversation, and I wasn't sure I even wanted him to ask, so I just waited silently.

After a few seconds, he finally looked up with a mixture of confusion and curiosity and asked me, "Daddy, what was that place really called?"

INTRODUCTION

Relatively speaking, I was not locked up for an unbearable amount of time—May 21, 2007 to August 31, 2010. In prison, some would call that short-timing. For me, though, those days were more than just squares on a calendar. For starters, I was not at the hospital to welcome my niece into the world. And I was not at the funeral home to say goodbye to my uncle who passed away just a few weeks before I got out.

I was not there when my son took his first steps. I had no part in teaching him how to talk. I still don't know what his first word was, but I know for certain it wasn't *Daddy*.

For that span of nearly 1200 days, I was not a part of my own family. Sure, they tried to include me—and that helped—but nothing can take the place of actually being there, and nothing will ever undo the pain of being absent for so many good memories that my family made without me.

As an inmate, you no longer get to choose when you wake up, eat, or go to sleep. You no longer get to choose what kind of clothes you wear or how often you go outside. The guards will open the rec yard when they're ready, not when you're ready. If you don't like it, so what? Nobody cares.

Under normal circumstances, freedom and prison are polar opposites. Basically, if you have one, you don't have the other. Simple enough, right?

IT'S A BOY!

Born on the Fourth of July, my birthday has never been my own. Perhaps being born in another nation would have allowed me to have that special day all to myself, but I had no such luck in The United States of America. In my country, I was born on the very day we celebrate our independence.

True freedom, however, was a concept that would take decades for me to understand.

Some of the tales told in my family are taller than Big Tex himself, so when I was born two weeks past my due date, I was basically a small toddler already, and I may or may not have taken my first steps right there in the nursery at Baylor Medical Center of Dallas. Rumor has it I even offered a polite *nice to meet you* to my fellow newborns before subsequently rolling my condescending eyes when I realized that the other babies could not yet speak.

Less than a day old, I was already a grumpy old man.

One of my grandfathers convinced me at an early age that the fireworks on Independence Day were specifically for me. He reinforced his outrageous claim by nicknaming me Firecracker. Yes, it seemed farfetched to me, but my skepticism was not fully developed at an early enough age to address Grandaddy's declaration. Or maybe it was just fun pretending that an entire nation celebrated my existence.

Like any other boy who was not yet old enough to be in school, my focus in life as a toddler was on fun and games, which were usually driven by imagination. Rarely did I enjoy activities that involved predetermined or rigid guidelines, and I was never a fan of anything not conducive to creativity. But with my first day of school fast approaching, I would soon learn that most other kids my age were good little boys and girls who were content to *sit down, be quiet, and do as you're told.*

Gross.

❧ ❧ ❧ ❧ ❧ ❧

Like any great mother, mine has quite the collection of artifacts from my childhood, things that have remained mostly untouched for decades. Photographs, drawings, and the obligatory tuft of hair are among those boxed remnants. There is also a large, nicely bound hardback book with blank pages that have been filled with my mother's handwritten account of my birth and early life, including this description of my first year in school as a kindergartner:

> *Clay was more than ready for school. He did very well. As the year went on though, he got into trouble quite a bit. He thinks his reasoning is as good as an adult's, and sometimes that means trouble for Clay.*

Some days were better than others, but overwhelmingly my years in school were nothing short of miserable. I never wanted to go because it was difficult for me to see the point in it all. My brother was two grades ahead of me and his textbooks seemed infinitely more interesting than mine, but in my own grade, I was bored and apathetic. From the beginning, my contempt for school was noticeable and severe. No teacher ever quite discovered the secret to making me work or behave in class on a regular basis, which frustrated them more because I was not a student who struggled academically. I learned and retained information with an ease that should have allowed me to excel in advanced classes.

Instead, I failed.

Again and again, I failed.

Early on, I possessed an interest in making other kids laugh. Everyone loves the funny kid, but for me being funny was not about acceptance or finding romance. It was about solving a puzzle. Humor was an interesting concept to me. Two kids could tell the same joke verbatim and one could be hilarious while another completely failed. It was odd to me that there was always that one person who could make anything funny. They could recite the alphabet and somehow make it hilarious. Likewise, there was always that person who botched every joke they attempted. Everyone knows someone like this. Their anecdotes start strong but invariably spiral downward to the anticlimactic *I guess you had to be there.*

Blessed—or perhaps cursed—with an infinite curiosity, I always wanted to know more. There was a reason why some kids were funny while others were not, and that reason is exactly what I wanted to discover. This book is not a guide on how to be funny, but suffice it to say that Clay Tumey was the kid you hoped to see in your class on the first day of school—unless you were the teacher of that class, of course. I was the class clown, but worse, I found a special joy in entertaining my classmates at the expense of the teacher's sanity. While class clowns usually just want to be funny, most of them settle down when they realize they have crossed the line and are at risk of getting into serious trouble, but for me that line was where the fun began. I was a particularly arrogant little bastard who rarely acknowledged any authority adults assumed to have over me, so the threat of trouble was rather ineffective. *Because I said so* was never a good enough reason for anything.

When a teacher spoke in class, I paid close attention, but my reasons were unique. Most likely, I already knew what was being taught. My interest in my older brother's textbooks ensured that my education usually happened long before I actually sat in class. My motivation for paying attention in class came instead from the great pleasure I took in correcting a teacher's errors in front of my classmates. Few things were more entertaining to me than watching a grown adult lose her mind after being corrected by a child. It makes sense that I have no memories of ever achieving my most desired reaction—a teacher admitting, *You're right, Clay*. Even when I was right, the ensuing conversation was less about my teacher's imperfection and more about my impending trip to the principal's office.

Going to the principal's office was always an interesting event. Growing up in the 1980s, corporal punishment was still a primary disciplinary tool. This method of punishment never did anything productive in my particular case. In school, threatening me with a trip to the principal's office was ineffective, at best. If anything, it was a relief being sent out of class because it was an escape, almost literally, from the painfully redundant classwork that I probably already knew how to do in the first place. Plus, the amount of physical pain I could withstand was a source of pride for me.

At home, there were times that I even reminded my dad to punish me. He almost never spanked me in public, but he would remind me *that's one...that's two...that's three,* referring to the number of swats he would give me later when we got home. On more than one occasion, though, he forgot about those swats, which was when I refreshed his memory. In my defense, there was good reasoning behind my odd choice to remind my father to punish me. First and most importantly, it was a way for me to control my own fate. *Yes, I misbehaved. Yes, you were supposed to punish me. Yes, I am reminding you to do that.* Second, I thought he would eventually remember anyway, which might create more trouble for me if he knew that I remembered and kept it to myself. *You knew I forgot to spank you and didn't tell me. That's the same as lying, so now you'll get more.* In my best-case fantasy, he would see my reminder as an indication that perhaps I did not need to be punished after all. It seemed logical to me that snitching on myself might reduce my sentence or even eliminate it altogether—a hypothesis that failed every single test, by the way.

My dad strongly believed in the power of spanking. At an early age, he also had the brilliant idea of doubling any punishment the school gave me. For example, if I was paddled at school and got two swats, my dad gave me four when I got home. My only benefit in this was learning how to multiply by two earlier than anyone else my age. It served no other purpose.

One would think—or at least hope—that the adults in my life would have realized sooner than later that this particular method of discipline was not making any progress with me, but until I was a teenager in high school, corporal punishment was just part of my routine, and there was never much reason to complain about it or try to stop it. Besides, my tolerance increased with my age, and physical pain dissipated exponentially faster than the pain of surrendering self-control. Perhaps an improvement in my behavior might have changed their minds, but it was not worth the effort to me.

Corporal punishment was not the only thing that failed to correct my behavior. After school detention was also quite a common occurrence for me, although it also showed no noticeable benefits. In fifth grade, my teacher almost never sent me to the principal's office because she preferred to administer discipline herself. God only knows how many times I stayed after school with my nose planted to the space on a wall where detentions were served in her class. There was literally a circle on the wall where the detainee was to put his or her nose for the duration of the detention. Above that circle was an unrelated poster with an assortment of vocabulary words far too big for fifth graders to use in their daily lives. To most, it probably looked like a giant bowl of alphabet soup, but I was fascinated with those words, and I loved that poster. Those words were unlike anything I could find in any fifth grade book. Adjectives like *ambidextrous, opulent,* and *phlegmatic* jumped from the poster and into my *lexicon.* I was *elated* to find such a collection of unfamiliar words. It was like learning an entirely new language. Seriously, this was not punishment at all! *I think I'll have another detention tomorrow, Mrs. Vasquez.*

Mrs. Vasquez was my fifth grade teacher. She was actually one of the few teachers that I would ever describe as mean. I got into trouble with literally every teacher (and probably every substitute teacher) who ever presided over me, but they were never mean to me. I was an obnoxious little twerp who brought out the worst in teachers, but Mrs. Vasquez needed no help from me to reveal her ugly side.

She had a jar, and in that jar were small pieces of paper. On each piece of paper was the name of a student in her class, so each student was represented in that jar. At the beginning of the school year, she explained to us that each week she would have an assistant who would basically be her helper. It was a coveted position because it often involved trips to the copy machine or other special privileges that basically translated to being exempt from whatever classwork the rest of the students were doing. She even had a title for the position: The Apprentice.

With about 25 kids in my class that year, some of the kids would get to be her apprentice twice, but Mrs. Vasquez explained very clearly that no student would have a second term as The Apprentice until each student had enjoyed their first.

Each week in that fifth grade class ended with the declaration of the following week's apprentice. The incumbent apprentice's final duty would be to pull a name from the jar to determine who would be the new apprentice when we returned to school the following week. This was the last thing that happened every Friday afternoon before we were dismissed for the weekend, and it never failed to create anticipation and excitement.

It was a big deal!

As the school year went on, it seemed that I would never be chosen. At the Christmas break, there had already been about 18 apprentices, but I was still waiting for my opportunity.

That January, after we came back from Christmas break, Mrs. Vasquez announced that she had misplaced her jar of names, which meant she had also lost track of who had been apprentices and who hadn't. Her only "fair" solution was to just start over and put everyone's name back into the jar. Obviously, this meant that there would no longer be a guarantee that everyone would have their chance to be an apprentice before the year was over.

Later in the school year, with only about four weeks remaining, I was the only kid in the class who had not been an apprentice. Even the worst kids in the class were pardoned from their "bad kid" labels for that one week. For those kids, the magic of being her apprentice was that she ignored your past and just allowed you to be her little helper for the week. For those five days, nothing from the past mattered.

I was so looking forward to that.

Then, it happened.

One Friday afternoon, as had been the case with every other Friday afternoon that year, it was time to find out who would be The Apprentice for the following week. With only four weeks left, it seemed to be an even more prestigious position for some reason, and to add to it all, everyone knew that I only had four chances left to have my name pulled from that magical jar.

The apprentice that week was my friend, and with my fifth grade logic, I thought it was likely that he would pull my name. For his final duty as The Apprentice, he reached into the jar and grabbed one of the few remaining pieces of wadded up paper. Mrs. Vasquez always instructed the apprentices to not look at the paper and to just hand it directly to her, so without knowing whose name he had drawn, my friend gave the piece of paper to our teacher.

Just imagine the scene for a moment, a class full of fifth grade kids who are already giddy because it's Friday afternoon with only about 10 minutes left in the day. On top of that, we're about to find out who one of the year's final apprentices will be! While she began to unravel the piece of paper, she dramatically announced, "Next week's apprentice is…"

Then, without any attempt at disguising her disgust, she said the name on the paper.

"Clay?!"

The class burst into laughter at my reaction because I was so excited that I just began fist pumping and silently screaming, "Yes! Yes! Yes!"

I wish I could say the story ended there. It would be a nice ending, and it might even leave you smiling as you remember something similar from your own elementary years. Unfortunately, the story continues, and what happened next left me crying and wondering what I had done to deserve to be humiliated so badly in front of all my friends.

"I don't think so," she said. "You don't deserve to be my apprentice."

She wasn't joking. She wasn't smiling. She wasn't even being nice about it. There was obviously no value in letting me down easily.

All sound left the room except for the slight buzz of the fluorescent lights and the sniffle of that one kid who always had a runny nose.

Some knew she was serious, but the rest of us thought maybe it was just a joke that she was pulling on me. Perhaps, it was her way of "getting me back" for talking in class so much. *Does she really have a sense of humor? Does she actually know how to be funny?*

Until that point, she had let every student be her apprentice when their name was chosen regardless of their previous behavior. Remember? Even the worst kids in the class were pardoned from their "bad kid" labels.

But when she reached into the jar and pulled out another name, it was official. She wasn't kidding. She wasn't being funny. She had no sense of humor, and she was not going to allow me to fill the position that I had so badly wanted to fill all year.

I was defeated, embarrassed, and worst of all...hurt. I just wanted to run home and cry, and that's exactly what I did as soon as school let out a few minutes later. To make matters worse, she hadn't even put my name back into the jar. She had just wadded it up and thrown it in the trash right there in front of everyone.

❧ ❧ ❧ ❧ ❧ ❧

My sixth grade teacher was definitely an upgrade from my fifth grade Faileducator. Mrs. Cerny was odd—equally obsessed with quilting, Egypt, and maintaining a colorful collection of reading glasses—but at least she was nice and professional. When she had been my brother's teacher two years earlier, I had once passed her in the hallway and asked if my brother ever got in trouble. Without breaking stride, she had simply replied, "I don't believe I'll be discussing that with you, young man."

For most of the school year, Mrs. Cerny kept my desk next to hers so she could keep an eye on me. She was far too supercilious to engage in any of my super silliness, but that never stopped me from trying. My behavior was mostly tolerable that year, but I still refused to do any normal amount of classwork.

As my sixth grade year went along, it progressively got better before it got worse. The work remained easy, but there was a sense of graduation approaching as we all prepared to leave elementary school for middle school. Though I did not struggle with reading or writing, English was among my least favorite subjects. *Why exactly do we need to study something that we should have naturally learned from our parents, families, and society in general anyway?* Not understanding that every person has unique strengths and weaknesses, I figured everyone else should be pretty much just like me and looked with arrogance at the kids around me who didn't excel at English. I despised them for not making the connection between the written and the spoken, and I was genuinely insulted that I had to be in class with them.

Regardless of feeling that I was above the rest of my class, I had no choice but to participate in the writing assignment given by Mrs. Cerny near the middle of my sixth grade year. Learning the art of choosing my battles served me well by the age of 11, and this particular task was graded solely on participation. In other words, it was a perfect 100 if I tried it and a big fat zero if I didn't.

Without much instruction, she only told us to write a poem with the phrase "If I had a wish. . ." in mind. With Christmas just around the corner, I immediately thought it was some lame attempt at getting us to write letters to Santa Claus. It was an easy grade, and I decided to just throw something on paper. After all, this was poetry, not rocket science.

It took a few minutes to come up with an appropriate subject to spend my imaginary wish on, and assuming that nobody other than my teacher would see the final product, I decided to write something serious that might appeal to her softer side and potentially garner some sort of sympathetic special treatment. I decided to write about the divorce of my parents. They'd divorced when I was seven years old, only to remarry each other on July 4, 1987—my eighth birthday. But their second marriage was considerably shorter than their first, and they were divorced for a second time when I was 11 years old. Just a few months after their second divorce, I wrote this poem:

If I had a wish
One real easy way
My parents would remarry
On this Christmas Day

The poem continued with the melancholy that a child typically expresses when parents stop being married to each other. The poem itself was forgettable to me because it was not genuine. It was fiction based on factual events—mere words on paper, thoughts I never had until our teacher gave us that assignment.

It was a hollow poem that I forgot as soon as I had written it. Months later though, it would be a poem that was no longer a simple daily assignment. Without my knowledge, and certainly without my consent, my teacher entered my poem into a district-wide cultural arts contest involving dozens of elementary schools. My other teachers, my principal, and even my classmates would all get to read those words I so haphazardly had thrown onto paper. Worst of all, my parents were notified and informed that their son had won first place in writing a poem about them that would receive district-wide attention.

Suddenly, I wanted my wish back. Fictitious or not, that poem was private and nobody ever told me that it would be shared with anyone, much less the entire universe. Nobody wanted to believe that it was total nonsense. Instead, I was showered with hugs and other unwanted attention. I even had to go accept my award at some sort of ceremony at one of the high schools.

Nightmare.

Fool me once, shame on you. Fool me twice, *shame on you again, and now I hate you. Next time, I'll just avoid the easy grade and take my big fat zero.*

Things went downhill for the rest of my sixth grade year. It's not like I was a model student prior to the poetry incident, but I certainly had no interest in cutting my teacher any slack after such treachery. She had obviously had good intentions, but that didn't undo the fact that my private thoughts were now on display for public consumption, and it angered me. Worse, they weren't even my actual thoughts. It didn't really matter to me whether or not my parents were married. It wasn't even the first time they'd been divorced. They were the ones struggling with their marriage, not me. All I wanted was to write a poem that might garner some sort of sympathy from my teacher. It was borderline fictional anyway, and I certainly didn't realize she was going to blast it to the entire world.

As the year wore on, my behavior declined beyond the point of simply being class clown. I was just a nuisance, and Mrs. Cerny eventually banned me from class altogether.

Literally, I was no longer allowed in class.

My desk was removed from its safe spot in the classroom next to the teacher's desk, and it was placed in the hallway. All my assignments were brought to me, and I completed them on my own. There's no telling who thought this would be construed as discipline, but it was heaven for me. I was completely alone except for the occasional passerby, and I could finally enjoy school.

However, with two weeks left in school, someone decided that it was no longer acceptable to keep me in the hallway. Apparently I was "distracting" people as they walked by. Apparently I was "disruptive" by not staring at the wall or pretending to be a statue when others were in the hallway. Call it what you wish, but they solved their problem when they moved my desk to a much more secluded area where no innocent passersby would run the risk of my saying hi. My school had a small stage in the cafeteria for plays, musicals, and other mind-numbing performances. Behind that stage was a small corridor that was only about three feet wide. Although I don't know the intended function of that tiny space, I can tell you that a desk fits perfectly there because that's where I spent the last two weeks of elementary school.

In fairness, the monsters in charge did not burden me with any more classwork. Instead, they allowed me to sit there in solitary confinement with little more than pen and paper. My lunch was brought to me, but I saw no other people at any point during the day except for the occasional headcount to make sure I had not escaped. They even took recess from me.

There I sat, at the age of 11, developing coping strategies that would vanish for decades only to come rushing back at warp speed 20 years later as I sat in a segregated prison cell with little more than pen and paper, eating meals that were given to me through a slot in a door that never opened, seeing no people at any point during the day except for the occasional headcount to make sure I had not escaped.

At least most prison cells have windows. My narrow space behind that stage did not.

I hated school.

FAMILIAR TERRITORY

The summer following my sixth grade year was great. Galloway Elementary was finally behind me, and as one might expect, it was quite a relief to rid myself of that school. They were probably just as excited to rid themselves of me. However, the relief of leaving one school was offset by the anxiety of going to a new one.

McDonald Middle School did not have the most pleasant reputation in the early 1990s and I fully expected it to be some type of inner-city, gang-infested school. Still, starting the year at a new school offered one particular benefit that would trump all of the downsides. Nobody there had ever even heard of Clay Tumey. Perhaps a few dozen students might remember me from elementary school, but the rest of them didn't know a thing about me and, more importantly, neither did the staff or faculty. This was the perfect chance to reinvent myself and maybe—just maybe—make my life easier by actually being a good student for once.

In middle school, we didn't have a homeroom teacher who kept us throughout the day. Instead, we had several different teachers who each taught a specific subject. At the end of each period, a bell would signal the end of one class, and five minutes later another class would begin somewhere else. It was awesome knowing that my days would now be broken up into segments. I was certain this would solve most of my problems. *If I screw up in first period, it'll be over soon enough and I'll have a clean slate in second period. If I screw up again in second period, I'll have a fresh start again in third period, fourth period, fifth period...I can do this!* Class would be more tolerable for me, which would make me more tolerable to my teachers. It seemed like a win/win situation for everyone involved!

If only things were as simple as they seemed.

Things were tolerable at best for the first few days of seventh grade, but I didn't even make it to the end of my first week at McDonald before being sent to the principal's office. It was one of the few times in my young life that I actually felt disappointed in myself. It was totally my fault and I knew it.

About halfway through that first week, I sat in math class wondering why we were being taught sixth grade math. *I already know this,* I thought. *Can you please teach us something new?!* The teacher seemed to have no problem talking to a class of unteachable bricks. I assumed she was either too ignorant to know how stupid her students were or was too lazy to care, so it never crossed my mind that some people actually forget stuff over the summer.

Annoyed, I rolled my eyes harder and harder each time someone asked a question that sixth-grade Clay could have answered. When I finally had enough, I simultaneously raised my hand and blurted out, "Can I go to eighth grade math?"

A few kids spun around with the curious glance of rubberneckers passing a minor traffic accident. One of the cheerleaders in class scrunched her face and punctuated it with an audible, "Ew." The rest of the class looked at the teacher with their wide-eyed *uh oh* faces and waited for her reaction.

The teacher responded as if she simply hadn't heard me. "Excuse me?"

"Oh, hi," I said with the friendliest furniture salesman voice I could muster. Smiling, I continued, "I just wanted to know if I could go to eighth grade math because I already know seventh grade math apparently. I learned all of this in sixth grade."

Visibly annoyed but maintaining her composure, she replied, "No, you cannot go to eighth grade math. We're just reviewing to make sure we're all on the same page before going forward. Please be patient and do not disrupt my class again Mister..."

"Tumey," I answered. "Clay. Tumey."

A few students giggled quietly, but my teacher chose to ignore my James Bond impression. She carried on with her lesson, of which I heard approximately not-a-damn-thing because I was fuming about how she had so effortlessly deflected my request to be in a class where I might learn something. *This is not a joke; I'm dying in here!*

Sarcasm hadn't worked in my first attempt to get out of class, so I decided to rephrase my question and ask again.

"Can I leave?"

"Oh, sure," she quipped. "You can leave and go straight to the principal's office." It was a threat dipped in her own sarcasm, but I thought it actually sounded like a great idea. My reply was immediate.

"Cool! Where's that?"

It was hard to know which made her angrier—my reply, or the collective outburst of laughter from the other students. Her frustration was obvious as she scribbled gibberish onto a yellow disciplinary slip like a doctor prescribing euthanasia to a hated patient. It was somehow calming to see my teacher lose control and turn to anger as she ripped the completed slip from its pad and handed it to me with a defeated, "Get out."

This was familiar territory for me, so I recognized the look on her face. As a child, it was empowering to see the energy drained from an adult all because of something I chose to do or say. I took pride in having that kind of control over someone else. The more distressed they got, the more content I was.

Leaving her class, my mind immediately went into instant replay mode. *Was it really so unreasonable for me to ask to change classes? How else could I have asked that would have had a better outcome? Why did she get so mad when the class laughed? Laughter is supposed to be a good thing.* It was interesting to me that she displayed such a variety of emotions in such a small amount of time. At my first interruption, she was patient and unruffled. With my second outburst, she was controlled and even witty. By the end of our last exchange, she was downright angry and just wanted to get rid of me.

Familiar territory, indeed.

While I had felt elated at seeing my teacher's reaction, as I moved slowly down the hallway toward the principal's office, my mind raced. I wondered why school had never worked for me and why it probably never would. My plan to reinvent myself in middle school had failed after just a few short days.

In reality, the review being taught in class that day was necessary for only a few students while the others enjoyed the opportunity to sit in class and do nothing. It was much easier to see the situation for what it was in retrospect, and it was clearly my fault. *Why can't you be like the other kids? Why can't you just sit and appreciate the fact that today will be easy? Who cares if you already know what's being taught? Why can't you just be normal?*

Those kinds of questions haunted me. I loved being unique, so it wasn't that I wanted to find a way to fit in and be like everybody else. The thought of being just another normal kid was actually repulsive, but it was also very stressful that there never seemed to be a normal day for me. There was never a day where I didn't ruffle somebody's feathers. At that point in my life, it wasn't that I felt bad about getting in trouble; I only felt bad about not being able to master my own behavior. It was frustrating to consider the possibility that I might not even be in control of my own mind. After all, I had a clear plan heading into middle school to avoid getting into trouble, yet there I was trying to match my teacher's wits for the sole purpose of... nothing.

Despite this inner conversation I was having, walking into the front office was completely shrugworthy for me. Again, familiar territory. I handed the yellow disciplinary referral slip to the secretary. She smiled and asked me to have a seat. Within a minute, the secretary returned with Mr. Spencer, one of two assistant principals who would soon become very familiar with me. In fact, much to my surprise, he was already familiar with me.

"I wondered how long it'd be before I got to meet you," Mr. Spencer said as he walked toward me smiling. "Come on back, let's have a chat." His smile was anything but friendly. He reminded me of every Tommy Lee Jones character I'd ever seen. The smile was not a reflection of inner peace. It was merely a warning that bad things were on the horizon.

In his office, he walked behind his desk and sat down. Motioning with his hand for me to have a seat in the opposing chair, he introduced himself and continued. Pleasantries and idle chat preceded the actual business, but Mr. Spencer soon got to the point and respectfully informed me, "We heard about you from the folks over at Galloway." Still smiling, he added, "We always appreciate a warning with kiddos like you because it prevents us from sitting on our hands too long."

Kids like me?

He continued, "But I think you're gonna do just fine here because we do things a little bit differently. You're a sharp kid, Tumey. I wanna see you succeed. I really do."

If ever there was a phrase I didn't trust, it was *I really do.* Even if I had believed every word he said—which I hadn't, by the way—I would have been immediately suspicious at *I really do.* Frivolous adverbs are red flags. I wondered how many eyebrows might be raised if a groom-to-be had ever answered *I really do* instead of the standard reply to the minister's inquisition regarding holy matrimony.

Unaware that I was daydreaming, Mr. Spencer went on. "But if you get out of line, we will help you get back in line by any means necessary. I hope I've made myself clear."

By any means necessary? My eyes rolled hard enough that I nearly required medical attention. Did this fool seriously expect me to believe that he really wanted me to succeed? His genteel tone did not mask the obvious message. *I'm the boss and you gon' do what I tell you, when I tell you, and how I tell you.*

Challenge accepted.

Since this was our first time meeting, he only gave me a warning and a promise that a second visit to his office would not be so pleasant. I fake-thanked him and feigned relief. He stood and walked around the desk to where I sat before offering a handshake to confirm whatever deal he thought we'd made.

When grown men treated me as a man—with their handshakes and formal dialogues—I no longer felt like a common child, and it was one of the things I enjoyed about being in trouble. Even though it was for the wrong reason, I existed in the adult world when I left the classroom and entered the principal's office.

After a firm handshake and a pat on the back, Mr. Spencer asked, "Any questions?"

"Actually, yes." I paused to make sure I chose the correct words for my question. "You said Galloway Elementary gave you a warning about me. Was that for real, or were you just kidding?"

He chuckled a subtle confirmation and asked why I looked surprised, but I didn't bother responding. *This is not my surprised face. This is my confused face.* It didn't seem fair to me that my reputation had preceded me at McDonald. While I completely understood the purpose of that kind of communication between schools, it still felt wrong to me, and it made me wonder how the hell I was supposed to ever have a second chance if my first chance followed me around everywhere I went.

He added the standard forgettable rhetoric about doing my best, a speech I had heard only a few million times by that point. I stood and was escorted out of his office, but I was not allowed back in math class that day. Instead, I sat in a chair near the secretary until the class period was over.

When I got to math class the following day, the teacher informed me that I was no longer in her class. She claimed this was due to overcrowding, but that didn't seem believable. She told me where my new class was, and as I walked down the hall I fantasized that they had actually put me in eighth grade math after all. Of course, when I got to the new class and recognized a few seventh grade faces, my fantasies were over. Worse, not only did they keep me in seventh grade math, but my new math teacher was a football coach who preferred talking about his college days rather than anything related to math.

My first week at McDonald Middle School turned out to be little more than a continuation of my days at Galloway Elementary. My intention to reinvent myself was worthless. There were a few times during those first couple of weeks at McDonald when I wondered what other information my old school had passed along to my new school. I was the center of a lot of negative attention when I was an elementary student, but I wondered what I had done that was so bad. *I never get in fights. I never destroy school property. I'm not a bad influence on my friends, and I learn everything I'm supposed to learn. Isn't that what school is for?*

Insubordination was my biggest problem. In fact, *insubordination* is actually one of the many words I learned as a result of being in trouble all the time. It was one of the options a teacher could select when filling out one of those yellow slips to send me to the principal's office. I finally took the time to find it in the dictionary one day and agreed that it was a fair and accurate description of my behavior most of the time.

insubordination
('insə-bôrdə' nā-shən)
Noun

1) defiance of authority; refusal to obey orders.

Yes, this was definitely me, and once it became clear to me exactly what insubordination was, I was arrogant enough to be proud of it. It was appalling to imagine submitting to teachers just for the sake of being a good little boy. To me, there was no reason to conform. *What kind of maniac would expect me to behave well when I get nothing in return?*

❧ ❧ ❧ ❧ ❧ ❧

By middle school, my parents had been divorced for a year. My brother and I spent equal amounts of time at each parent's house. My dad was remarried and lived in the same town where we grew up, and my mother still lived in our original home until about halfway through my seventh grade year when she moved a couple thousand miles away to Seattle to be with her new husband.

At first, I hated that my mom had moved away. My parents lived walking distance from each other, and I loved having two homes in the same neighborhood. When she moved to Seattle, it meant living with my dad full-time. It also meant that I would essentially be without a mom. To be fair, my mother returned to Dallas every month, so I still saw her quite a bit, but it was not the same. When she was in town, my brother and I would stay with her, but since she didn't have a home in the Dallas area, she stayed with family, which meant we would have a temporary home for the week or so that she was in town. While it was always great to see my mom and spend time with her, having her in town as a visitor just was not the same as spending a week at her house. The amount of time we spent with her might have been the same, but it was a completely different kind of visit altogether, and I hated it.

At school, things got progressively worse as my seventh grade year went along. In addition to my usual problems, there was the added stress of being surrounded by so many new people who were completely uninterested in me. Granted, most of them were just as boring to me, but that was beside the point. I was not used to feeling like an outcast, but I had managed to transition from class clown to problem child, and there was nothing fun about that shift.

Miraculously, I made it to the end of seventh grade without being killed by any of my teachers. I spent a fair amount of time in the principal's office and even more time in after school detention, and, of course, the paddling had also followed me from Galloway to McDonald.

By the end of my first year in middle school, I was just tired. Getting into trouble never bothered me much, but that year, I didn't even have the benefit of making anyone laugh along the way. Nobody liked me—not the other students and definitely not my teachers. It was an awful year altogether, and I could not have possibly been more relieved when summer vacation finally rolled around. But summer would pass quickly, as summers often do, and I would soon find myself forced into another school year.

❧ ❧ ❧ ❧ ❧ ❧

At the beginning of my eighth grade year at McDonald, Mr. Spencer called me to his office, but I hadn't done anything to get in trouble. I had at least made it past my first week of eighth grade without causing any problems, so *why in the world is he calling me to his office?* Reminiscent of our first meeting a year earlier, he shook my hand and motioned for me to have a seat as he sat down behind his desk. He apologized for letting the previous year get out of control, and he wanted to discuss a few options and suggestions about how to make eighth grade a little bit more enjoyable for me. More than simply telling me what was going to happen, he actually wanted my input on the matter.

Oh, I loved that conversation instantly. In addition to the handshakes and adult dialogue, he was now actually talking to me as though my opinion actually mattered. Furthermore, he wanted to use my expertise in a field where nobody on the planet was more qualified.

It was quite difficult, as it turned out, to explain what strategies might work best for me. First of all, school was monotonous and pointless to me, and since my behavior prevented me from being in advanced classes, my only option was to learn how to behave in normal classes. If I proved myself to be worthy over a long enough period of time, then we could discuss advanced classes, but, for the time being, he had an idea that he wanted to share with me.

He began, "What if I put you in charge of something very important that I need done every Wednesday afternoon after school?" In an instant, I already liked where he was going with this because detentions were served after school on Wednesdays until 5:00 p.m. If he wanted me working for him every Wednesday afternoon, it already meant that I would probably be exempt from detentions.

"Okay," I responded. "What is the 'something very important' you need done?"

"Well, our football games on Tuesday nights produce quite a bit of trash in the stands and under the bleachers. What I need is a few guys to get in there and clean that up, but I need it knocked out in 30 minutes or less so you won't miss the bus." Before I could scoff at the idea of working for free, he continued, "I'll give you five bucks apiece."

This was a great idea, and as much as I wanted to dislike Mr. Spencer, this discussion made quite a positive impression on me. Not wanting to immediately accept the offer, I asked, "And you'll let me pick the other guys myself?"

"Yep," he agreed. "Anyone you want as long as they ride one of the later buses. Just come straight to my office after school next Wednesday, and I'll walk you over to the stadium and let you in."

This was awesome. Not only was this an opportunity to make a few bucks, but it was also a great opportunity to make a few friends because surely the guys I picked would be grateful to me for including them.

After school the following Wednesday, my three new coworkers and I reported to the front office and were promptly escorted across the property to the football stadium, which was no larger than any other typical middle school football stadium. It had seats only on one side of the field, and it would be easy for the four of us to finish picking up all the trash before our bus came at 4:00 p.m. I reminded the guys that we would get five dollars regardless of how fast we cleaned up the trash, so it would be best to just hurry up and knock it out as quickly as possible.

After a solid 15 minutes of picking up the previous night's mess, we returned to Mr. Spencer's office to collect our pay. To top it off, he let us into the teacher's lounge to spend our money at the vending machines if we so desired.

And I definitely so desired.

It was great walking out of the school with a soft drink in one hand and a candy bar in the other. As I joined the rest of the kids from my neighborhood who were waiting for the bus, they all wanted to know where I had been and, more importantly, where I had gotten the Dr. Pepper and the Snickers bar. To answer them would have been anticlimactic and boring, so I just shrugged and smiled.

Mostly because of this new job, my eighth grade year was in the beginning a drastic improvement over my seventh grade year, and Mr. Spencer was definitely onto something when he decided to provide a space for me to prove my worth. Money and special privileges weren't my only benefits in working for Mr. Spencer after school that one day per week. A relationship began to form, and I stopped seeing him as the mean assistant principal who paddled kids when they got out of line. Slowly but surely, I unknowingly began to respect him and his authority. This new outlook finally dawned on me when one of my teachers sent me to the office one day for—surprise, surprise—refusing to do my work.

Mr. Kyle, my history teacher, was a volleyball coach who had no apparent interest in actually teaching history, which was fine with me because I had no desire to learn anything about history. Each day, class would begin with roll call before Mr. Kyle turned around and wrote his notes on the chalkboard. As students, our only assignment was to handwrite those notes on our own paper and turn it in at the end of the week. Each Friday, we handed in that week's notes before taking a simple multiple choice test.

While the other kids loved how easy Mr. Kyle's class was, I despised it because it was ridiculous to simply copy notes from a chalkboard. To me, that was not how school should work. There was nothing educational about turning in a few pages full of notes that came from someone else's brain. My problem wasn't with how little I learned. My problem was with how pointless it all was. My problem was with a teacher who wanted to make his life easier by making mine harder, and it was not okay with me to exert any amount of my own energy just to make his job easier. *As a matter of fact, I will not be copying your notes. If I fail the test on Friday, then maybe we can discuss your slave-driving ways, but if I pass your tests, then there is no reason for me to be required to copy your notes.* I wasn't a fan of *show your work* in math, so I sure as hell wasn't a fan of it in history.

The first time I had no notes to turn in on a Friday, Mr. Kyle threatened me with a trip to the office. In fairness to him, he didn't know me well and was totally unaware that this threat was never a successful one with me.

A few minutes later, I sat in Mr. Spencer's office trying to argue my point and justify why it was not necessary for me to copy notes every day since I was passing my tests on Friday. My case made no progress, and it was difficult even arguing with Mr. Spencer anyway because of who he had become to me on a personal level with all the special treatment away from class. Defeated, I returned to history class and complied.

After sitting in history class and monotonously scribbling the same boring drivel for days, I had finally had enough and decided to quit complying. However, I also didn't want to go back to Mr. Spencer's office and fight the same losing battle as before. Instead, I found my own way to comply while also having a little fun with it.

I learned how to write backwards.

Sitting in class and choking back my own laughter, I copied Mr. Kyle's notes verbatim, letter by letter, in a mirrored handwriting. It was only legible by looking at it in a mirror or by turning the paper over and holding it up to a light. The absurdity alone of this idea was enough to keep me entertained, but it was also fairly difficult learning to write in a totally new way.

Yes, I had found a way to turn the easiest grade into a difficult task, but I loved every second of it. Even better was the fact that Mr. Kyle didn't collect the notes until Friday when it was time to take the test, so by the time he realized what I had done, an entire week had passed.

Suffice it to say that he was incensed and refused to accept my work when it was given to him that Friday, and it was only made worse as I feigned ignorance, pretending to be totally unaware that I had done anything wrong. The whole class was soon aware of what I had done, and it was the first time I ever heard a teacher cuss in class. "What. In. The. Hell am I supposed to do with this?!"

As usual, my smart mouth only made it worse. "What do you normally do?"

At his wit's end, he yelled, "Get out! Go to the office right now!"

"I can't be in the hall without a pass," I politely responded, as if the rules suddenly mattered to me.

With his blood pressure showing in his eyes, he yelled, "I'll send a yellow slip with someone else, but I want you out of my class!"

So once again, I sat across from Mr. Spencer in his office. He just looked at me and smiled, but it was the kind of smile that preempted bad news. The yellow slip had not shown up yet, and he wouldn't let me tell my side of the story until he knew what the teacher had to say. He only knew that I had done something so bad that the teacher sent me without any paperwork. This ultimately worked to my favor because Mr. Spencer could only imagine the worst possible scenarios, none of which were anything close to the actual reason I was sent to the office.

Minutes later, Mr. Kyle showed up with an office referral, a bad attitude, and four pages of backwardly-written notes. He stormed into Mr. Spencer's office, slammed my work of art on the desk, and protested, "This student has no place in my class. He agreed to follow instructions but has instead made a complete mockery of my class!" My teacher showed Mr. Spencer each page individually, complaining that I had followed the rules only via some weird technicality and that it was an obvious attempt to not complete the assignment as it had been given.

"Thank you, Mr. Kyle," came the official reply from Mr. Spencer. "I'll keep Mr. Tumey for the remainder of the period today and let you know later how we resolve this."

With that, my history teacher fee-fi-fo-fummed his way out of the office and back to class. By that point in my life, my sense for detecting trouble was finely tuned, and it was obvious to me that Mr. Spencer was not the least bit perturbed. He said nothing as he watched Mr. Kyle vanish out of sight, at which point he removed his eyeglasses and slowly placed them on the desk before placing his palms directly to his face and holding them there for several seconds. Since it seemed unlikely that this was about to turn into a game of peekaboo, I waited quietly to see what kind of facial expression would show up when he removed his hands. My intuition told me that he was bemused and amused all at the same time, and when he grabbed the stack of backwards notes with both hands, it was clear that my intuition was right. He was smiling from ear to ear and appeared to be fighting back laughter.

Opening the dialogue, I proudly proclaimed, "Well at least it wasn't insubordination."

Ignoring my comment, he held up the small stack of paper and asked, "Care to explain this?"

"Yeah, those are my notes from history," I said, somehow maintaining a straight face. "We have to copy those word for word every day and then…"

"I know that," he interrupted. Attempting to prove a point, he handed me one of the pages and commanded, "Read this to me."

I was quite proud that I had the forethought to write on only one side of each page while leaving the backside blank. Without a mirror, it was only possible to read my writing by turning it over and holding it up to the light, which I was now able to demonstrate for Mr. Spencer.

Proving he was human, the assistant principal erupted in laughter and snatched the paper out of my hands. He put his glasses back on, still laughing, and held the paper up to the light to read it himself. "How on earth did you learn to write backwards and actually make it legible?" He allowed himself a few more laughs before continuing, "Your backwards handwriting looks better than my regular handwriting!" I shrugged, not really knowing what to do in this Twilight Zone where the disciplinary figure was now laughing at my silly behavior.

In a turn of events that completely baffled me, Mr. Spencer informed me that he would speak with my history teacher and try to convince him to accept my notes since they were graded based only on completion. The following Monday, I walked into history class unsure of how my teacher was going to treat me. After roll call, Mr. Kyle abruptly told me to step outside. Feeling like this was not a good time to press my luck, I stood and quietly did what I was told as the teacher followed me into the hall and shut the classroom door behind me. *Oh, crap. Nobody can see us out here. There won't be any witnesses if he kills me!*

"I'm only going to say this once, so you better listen," he scream-whispered at the bottom of his lungs within inches of my face so that nobody could hear him except for me. "My boss and I had a long discussion about you after school Friday, and he convinced me to not only accept that nonsense you turned in last week but also to allow you to continue doing that as long as you pass your tests on Friday." He paused and looked away before putting his finger directly into the center of my chest. "But you're on thin ice with me, Tumey, and the second you screw up again in my class, forget about it." Without even asking if I understood him, he turned and walked back into class.

Victory!

❧ ❧ ❧ ❧ ❧ ❧

That should have been a turning point for me, but it wasn't. Mine was the classic case of *give an inch and he'll take a mile.* Instead of appreciating the fact that Mr. Spencer had clearly blurred the lines, I felt like I had somehow defeated my history teacher. I wasn't content with a little flexibility. I wanted special treatment across the board.

History class went well for a while, but the grades in the rest of my classes continued to decline, causing me to fail on a larger scale than ever before. Even in my favorite classes, I chose to help others rather than focus on my own grades. As a whole, I felt like I was above the need to prove myself to my teachers. Their tests were a waste of my time because they were always dumbed down to the lowest common denominator, or so I felt. There was no personal reward in proving how well I knew the material, but there was a huge payoff in tutoring someone else and seeing their grades climb as a result of something I did. It was also awesome to see the look in a classmate's eyes when something suddenly made sense. Teachers often talk about the "aha" moment and how great it is to witness, and although I've never been a teacher by vocation, I have enjoyed many opportunities to witness that "aha" moment myself, and it is great...perhaps addictive. I always thought knowledge was wonderful to have, but even better to share.

By the time Christmas vacation had rolled around that year, my grades had completely tanked, as had my behavior. Football season was over for middle schools, so my Wednesday afternoon cleaning job at the football field was no longer available, and the thought of having any kind of friendship with an assistant principal started bothering me, too. I was much more comfortable choosing my behavior rather than allowing a school employee to influence me. I saw it as a weakness if I allowed anybody to trick me into behaving the way that they wanted me to behave. I never fully trusted anyone's intention if it involved changing who I was as a person. It was clear that Mr. Spencer had done more than a few things to try to reach me, but I was suspicious of his motives. At the end of the day, this was still the same guy who'd told me during our first meeting, "But if you get out of line, we will help you get back in line by any means necessary."

After Christmas break, my behavior had gotten to the point that I was going to the principal's office several times a week, which resulted in more phone calls to my dad, which resulted in more paddling at school, which resulted in more punishment when I got home.

My mother still lived forever away, and my dad was growing increasingly annoyed with the constant phone calls from the school. After all, he worked nights, so those daytime calls were the equivalent of calling in the middle of the night. Eventually, my dad and the principal came to the conclusion that I should just get paddled twice a day for the remainder of the school year regardless of whether or not my behavior warranted it on any given day. Perhaps they were employing the philosophy that an ounce of prevention is worth a pound of cure. Who knows? Every day after second period and again before sixth period, while most kids were stopping at their lockers to get books for the next class, I was stopping by the principal's office to get swats.

At the time, it was just a part of life for me. Even on the days when I behaved just fine, I would swing by the office twice a day to get paddled. Before long, the reality struck me that I could act however I wanted because the punishment would be the same. *I've gone days without messing up, and nothing changes, so what's the point in trying to do what they want if I'm getting punished either way? I'll just have all the fun I can think of and at least earn my swats.* As always, it was easiest for me to just develop the necessary coping strategies and simply survive to the end of the year.

In the early 1990s, it was still admirable—even biblical—to rule a child with a wooden paddle, so it never dawned on me that it was wrong for them to do that to me. The corporal punishment debate can remain in another conversation, but it was ignorant at best in my case because it was clearly ineffective and produced no positive results, but the thought never once crossed my mind that I was being treated unethically or abusively. It was normal.

Ultimately, no type of discipline ever "worked" for me as long as my mind was set on following my own will.

When eighth grade was over, the principal met with my parents to inform them that my academics were so lacking that I needed to repeat the eighth grade. Of course, everyone involved knew this was not actually the case and that my grades were a reflection of my unwillingness to do any work rather than an actual measure of my scholastic aptitude.

My parents lobbied to have the school pass me so that I could advance to high school. The principal admitted that my failure was just as much the school's fault as it was mine. The school had nothing to offer me. There was nowhere for me to fit in academically or otherwise, and where fear tactics usually are effective in forcing compliance, nothing worked with me.

Although I had failed literally every class that year, the school agreed to pass me, allowing me to advance to high school where I would have a second chance at a new school.

Theoretically.

PLEASE KEEP HIM

With the worst two years of my life officially behind me, it was time to enjoy yet another summer break. My summers were peaceful and without incident because summers don't involve progress reports, report cards, or anything else related to school. It was always such a relief to not worry about getting into any trouble during the summer, and it was also quite a treat to stay holed up in my room all day mastering whatever musical instrument I could get my hands on. Although I had started learning how to play guitar at an unusually early age, it was merely a pastime until my early teens, when it started becoming apparent that I might actually have some real talent. For me, it was more inviting to spend time alone in my bedroom all day without the threat of interacting with people, and being a recluse provided a way for me to dedicate an immense amount of time to honing my musical craft.

During the summer of 1993, pretty much every possible aspect of my life improved. My mother returned from Seattle and moved back into the house where we grew up. My dad's house was on the same street maybe 10 to 15 houses away, so going back and forth between my two homes was easier than ever. Also within walking distance was the high school, which meant I would no longer need to ride the bus to and from school every day as I had in middle school. This not only meant sleeping a few minutes later in the morning, but it also meant getting home after school as soon as possible each day to practice music, play video games, or anything else that seemed fun.

All of my cousins from the neighborhood were older and went to West Mesquite High School long before I did. At any given point throughout my entire childhood, someone in my family was playing football, baseball, or basketball for the Wranglers. When my first year of high school finally rolled around, my brother was a junior, and we were nothing alike. Clint followed the rules and did the work. He made friends with other students and his teachers actually liked him. Basically, he was the opposite of me.

Clint was an office worker. For an entire class period, he went to the office and helped however they needed. It was free labor for them and free credit for him. With a name like Tumey, one could safely assume that he and I were related, and the assistant principal at the high school, Mrs. Bivins, asked Clint during that first week of school if we were brothers. He tried to deny it at first, but she knew better and told my brother to be sure and let me know that she better not be seeing my face in her office anytime soon, which Clint gladly rubbed in my face after school that day.

If the elementary school warned the middle school about me, it only made sense that the middle school warned the high school about me, so it didn't surprise me when I learned that the assistant principal knew who I was before I knew who she was. It was slightly disappointing, but not the least bit unexpected.

That first year in high school would prove to be considerably different than any of my previous years as a student. High school teachers seemed to treat students less like children and more like young adults, which was nice. But teachers were also much quicker to kick me out of class for being a disruption instead of constantly trying to handle me on their own. My teachers at WMHS made few attempts to control or even thwart my behavior, which meant I probably spent more time in the principal's office than the principal himself. Furthermore, they didn't paddle me in high school as they had in middle school and elementary school, resorting instead to detention, in-school suspension, and suspension.

Mrs. Mote was my fifth period English teacher that year. She was one of the few teachers who actually tried—in vain, of course—to reason with me and get me to behave well in class. She was a rookie teacher in her first year, and the school administrators probably shouldn't have allowed me to stay in her class. I might have been a mild disruption as a child, but in high school my behavior was far too much for someone with no previous experience. It wasn't just unfair to her; it was unfair to any student in her class who was there to actually learn something.

Before long, Mrs. Mote started asking the office to *please keep him*. After I'd had enough with the recurring office visits, I decided to simply stop going. She didn't stop sending me, of course; I just didn't go. If she gave me an office referral and sent me out of class, I would exit her room and simply roam the halls or perhaps hide out in the restroom. Often, I would just leave the school altogether and go home, but there were several occasions when I chose to go to wood shop instead. This seemed completely logical to me because wood shop was my sixth period class, so *why not just go to shop during fifth period, too?*

The reaction of Mr. Bryant, the shop teacher, was unforgettable the first time I strolled into his class during the wrong period. He knew I was not supposed to be in his class until the following period, but he was unsure exactly how to proceed. For whatever reason, Mr. Bryant allowed me to stay in his class when this eventually happened again...and...again...and again. Throughout my first year in high school, whenever Mrs. Mote booted me from her class, I just went straight to wood shop instead. That happened at least a couple dozen times during my first year of high school.

English was not the only class that saw my performance fall to historically low levels. In fact, every class that year seemed to be a disaster for me. Failure had become second nature, and the shock of earning epically bad grades had long worn off. By the end of my first year of high school, my only passing grade was a 70, which was for one semester of physical education. In a class that demanded little more than changing clothes and playing softball, I made the absolute minimum passing grade only because the coach didn't want to fail me and risk having me in his class again the following year. The rest of my final grades that year ranged between 30 and 68.

Altogether, my first year in high school was a complete waste. But unlike middle school, high school actually required the accumulation of credits. Of the six possible graduation credits that year, I earned half of one.

Even if my grades had been fine, my attendance alone would have caused me to fail because I missed nearly a third of the year due to suspensions.

With only a few weeks left in the year, the stress of repeating the ninth grade was beginning to overwhelm me. I was in wood shop when I had the epiphany that my behavior was both the cause and effect of my troubles. School was always a miserable place for me, so I had developed a coping strategy to make it through each day without losing my mind, and that strategy resulted in an extra year of school. What I thought was the solution was actually the problem. A better idea would have been to do well enough to continue forward instead of failing and repeating. With a little luck and some hard work, maybe I could have skipped a grade somewhere along the line and graduated a year early instead of repeating a grade and graduating a year late.

Daydreaming about how miserable life was becoming, my thoughts drifted to Mr. Bryant, who was standing at the front of the class with his back to us as he wrote something irrelevant on the chalkboard. My memory flashed to Mr. Kyle, my eighth grade history teacher who had spent so much time with his back to us, and it bothered me. Staring at the back of Mr. Bryant's head in shop class, I wondered if I could get away with throwing something at him, but that idea immediately went away because even at my worst, I was not violent. It wasn't a problem at all for me to torment mentally or emotionally, but I never physically hurt anyone, and I was not about to start with Mr. Bryant.

Still, the fantasy would not leave my mind, and I started wondering how he might react if I threw something and missed. *What exactly would he do?* Curious beyond my control, I quietly stood and lifted my desk above my head. I don't know what it looked like, but it certainly felt like I was Donkey Kong preparing to hurl a barrel at an unsuspecting plumber.

It was surprising how light the desk felt in my hands. I hurled it toward the board just a few feet to the left of Mr. Bryant. The plan was to barely miss him, and that's exactly what happened. The desk smashed into the wall and onto the floor, holding together much more than I would have expected. It was a well-made desk, so it basically remained in one piece while a few tiny pieces broke and slid across the floor.

With the speed of a sedated sloth, Mr. Bryant slowly turned around with the most hilariously confused, wide-eyed glare imaginable. The other guys in class held in their laughter for the moment while Mr. Bryant stared right at me. Without moving, he spoke to me as one might speak to a librarian, "Uh, Mr. Tumey…is there a problem?"

"Nope," I answered, pleading not guilty.

He said, "Okay…well, is there a reason…I mean, your desk…What's this all about?"

Genuinely and thoroughly offended, I snapped back, "How the hell would I know?! Don't look at me!"

It bothered me that he was so quick to put the blame on me just because I happened to be the resident "bad kid" in class. It didn't matter to me that he was correct in assuming I was the culprit, but it definitely bothered me that I was always the first suspect when something bad happened.

His eyes jutted out in disbelief while the rest of his face frowned with disappointment, and then he politely suggested, "Okay…well…um…you're the only one in class without a desk."

Busted.

My impulsion and lack of planning trumped any reasonable defense. There was no point in even trying to argue. With the rest of the class in hysterics, I shrugged and went to the principal's office, where it was determined that my first year of high school was officially over, and after summer break, my second year would begin with two weeks of alternative school.

Mesquite Intervention Center might as well have been called the Federal Bureau of Prisons. To my knowledge, only the worst of the worst earned trips to alternative school, and it was somewhat intimidating to think of what it might be like. At the time, M.I.C. was just a house that had been gutted and repurposed into a large room with small cubicles lining the walls. Each work station faced a windowless wall, and dividers to the left and right prevented anyone from seeing anyone else. For good measure, it was also against the rules to turn around. If a student needed anything, he quietly raised his hand while maintaining eye contact with the wall in front of him. Failure to follow this rule would result in disciplinary action.

There was only one teacher at M.I.C., but he was only there as a guard. There were no lessons being taught, so it probably wasn't even accurate to refer to him as a teacher at all. Students completed assignments from a stack sent by their teachers, and those teachers were requested to send enough work to ensure the student would not run out of things to do. After a day or two, I found an appropriate pace to complete my work, and the days actually went by fairly quickly.

My time in alternative school was fairly forgettable except for one fine detail that was completely unrelated to school, trouble, or any other negative thing. Because it was on the other side of town, it was not within walking distance from where I lived. There was no bus for me to ride, and my parents were not available to pick me up at the end of the day, but Grandaddy—my maternal grandfather—was available and gladly picked me up every day.

One might expect a grandfather to lecture his troubled grandson at any given opportunity, and since he was my ride home every day for those two weeks, I had no choice but to listen to everything he said for the entire 10 minutes. Thankfully, he did no such thing. To the contrary, my grandfather picked me up with a smile on his face, and without exception we talked about every possible thing in the world except his awful grandson.

When I was an adult, 15 years later, this memory was still a lasting impression that I shared in a letter to my mother:

> *I'm sure I've mentioned this before, but one of my favorite memories of Grandaddy is from the time I was in high school and had to go to alternative school…Not once during those two weeks did he ever say anything to me about being in trouble, and he didn't give me a hard time about having to take time out of his day to drive all the way to downtown Mesquite to pick me up. Instead, every day…he was waiting for me, asking how my day was the moment I got in the car, as if I had been at the fair or on a field trip instead of alternative school. He made me feel special and important even though I was being a pain in the neck by getting into trouble.*

Through genetics or by example, my grandfather must have passed along this method of love to his daughter—my mother—because I would experience it again later in my life, and it would be exactly what I needed when I needed it the most.

After I had served my time in alternative school, I returned to my home campus at West Mesquite High School. It didn't even feel like the same school. All of my classmates from the previous year had advanced to their second-year classes, leaving me behind in classes that were filled with complete strangers who had always been a year behind me. As usual, my reputation had preceded me, so most of my new classmates were excited to see me in their classes because they knew there was a certain likelihood that fireworks could ensue on any given day with me in class. Teenagers can be sadistic little jerks who love to live vicariously through others, and I gladly obliged. However, something had happened in my personal life during the summer between my first and second ninth grade years. I had become quite involved in church and had started trying to turn my life around.

When my second year of high school started, it was a chance for me to prove myself, maybe even redeem myself. In a matter of weeks, that is exactly what I did. My grades shot up while my classroom disruptions disappeared. For once, it was fun to be me. After six weeks, my first report card proved that it was no myth. I was—drum roll, please—a good student! Better than just good, my grades were high enough to land me on the honor roll.

My dad took my report card to work, made copies, and passed them around. Surprise, surprise! Clay Tumey was not a failure after all.

False.

I had always believed that good grades were merely a measure of effort, and I respected people who were able to put forth effort because that was a struggle for me. However, when I finally realized how little effort I needed in order to make nearly perfect grades, I suddenly despised people who were proud of their barely-passing grades. At the time, I lacked understanding that everyone is made differently and that the same people I looked down on were probably skilled in areas that I had little skill. In my mind, it was just embarrassing that there were people who were proud to have studied for hours only to pass by the skin of their teeth. I felt that the only goal was to pass the next test, pass the next test, pass the next test.

What a waste.

Suddenly, I felt stupid for falling into the trap of proving how not-stupid I was. I decided that I had been right all those years by refusing to simply comply and conform. At first, I had been happy to have gotten such good grades on that report card, but then the praise and commendation suddenly felt condescending and offensive. And I did not like that.

School was still overwhelmingly boring, and my classes were still filled with people whom I assumed had no concept of learning. When my grades were horrible, I somewhat envied people who were able to put forth enough effort to earn passing grades, but once I started to make an effort and still found myself bored, I hated school on a whole new level.

Granted, it might have been nice actually having a little freedom in life, but it didn't take long for me to realize that my teachers were only more pleasant under these specific circumstances. Their attitudes toward me were completely conditional. My behavior directly affected how people treated me, and while this might seem perfectly acceptable to some, it was detestable to me. *What kind of freedom would force me to please others? What kind of freedom would force me to be normal? What kind of freedom is synonymous with compliance and conformation?*

Exactly!

Insubordination is true freedom and they don't want me to have that. It's literally against the rules to be free.

I soon hated everything about my new, easier life. I gave up trying to impress everyone, and I stopped worrying about making good grades. My involvement in church managed to stave off an immediate self-destruction because of the influence my peers and youth pastor had on me. Returning to church each Sunday was usually enough to at least keep me from completely reverting to the behavior that I had preferred throughout most of my childhood, but I never fully addressed my problems and mainly looked at church as a safe place to be loved despite the bad choices I made elsewhere. I looked forward to being around my church family each week, but I wasn't truly following the Jesus that I learned about there.

Fortunately, my behavior never did return to the epic desk-throwing proportions of previous years. But even after I completely gave up in all of my classes, I was still able to coast to a passing grade in a few of them, which only made me further assume school was a joke. I could see no one else's perspective but my own.

As a result, my second year in high school was still an overall failure. When the following school year began, I still didn't have enough credits to be considered a sophomore.

When I should have been a junior in high school, I was a third-year freshman.

⁂ ⁂ ⁂ ⁂ ⁂ ⁂

On July 4, 1995, I finally turned 16. My parents didn't pay for me to take driver's education as they had done for my brother prior to his 16th birthday. In fairness, my brother was a much better kid and gave my parents no trouble compared to me. His grades were consistent, and he actually put forth a decent amount of effort in school, so it was no surprise that my parents awarded him more privileges than they did with me.

Before my third year in high school, however, my mother promised to pay for my driver's education if I got all A's on my first report card. *Deal!* Aside from having to wait six weeks, there was absolutely nothing difficult about this challenge. My lowest grade was a 90 in history, which was a bit too close for comfort, but the rest of my grades ranged between 92 and 98.

For the first six weeks that year, I was inadvertently placed in a test preparation class that was mandatory for all sophomores, but since I was not technically a sophomore, they planned to remove me from the class. However, my teacher was able to work with the front office in allowing me to remain in class as a helper, and my grade was determined based on the average grades of all the students that I helped. This was creative, and I loved it, but my tutees did not do so well that first six weeks, so the 77 that I received for that class was actually the lowest grade on my report card.

Under the circumstances, I knew my mother would understand and not hold that grade against me, and I was right. Excited to share my report with her, my only concern was how soon I could be enrolled in driver's education, which my mother maintained would be when I got all A's for an entire semester. *What?! This was not the deal! It was only for the first six weeks, not the semester! This is so unfair!*

Infuriated, I immediately let my grades tank again. My highest grade of 98 was turned into a barely passing 72, but the most drastic change was my 93 in biology that was reduced to a failing 65. Likewise, my conduct grades sank accordingly. Ironically, my 77 increased to a 94 in the test preparation class, where my grade was determined by the people I tutored.

The only motivation for passing those classes was the unimaginable terror of being a fourth-year freshman the following year, so I certainly made sure to pass everything that year, but it was not without great effort to toe the line as much as possible. It became a habit of mine to calculate the minimum possible grade I could get on any given test and then figure out how many wrong answers I could afford and still get the minimum passing grade. If I needed a 75 and the test had 40 questions, I would only do the first 30 questions and ignore the remaining 10 questions. That gave me a great deal of pleasure for several reasons. First of all, there was no room for error as this method of test-taking demanded perfection, which is a challenge for anyone. Second, the level of egotism this displayed to my teachers was optimal. It was my *arrogant little bastard* way of showing them that their class was a joke and that it was beneath me. For a multitude of unhealthy reasons, that appealed to me.

I never made all A's again on any report card, and I wasn't enrolled in driver's education until the following summer. I turned 17 during the first week of that class while most of the other kids were still 15. Considering the fact that I was a third-year freshman, I had become accustomed to being the oldest kid in class.

I didn't even care anymore by that point.

⁂ ⁂ ⁂ ⁂ ⁂ ⁂

With the unbearable stress of school, the one thing I found solace in was my life as a musician. My music became my identity. People knew me as more than just a musician. I was an artist. Though I had grown up playing music, I never really wrote my own songs until my high school years. One year for Christmas, my dad gave me my first piece of recording equipment—a Fostex 4-Track—and I decided to give my best effort at taping my own music.

My first recordings were total garbage. The Casio keyboard in my bedroom was my only access to anything remotely resembling a drum kit, so I plugged it in and started recording beats. What started as an interest turned into a full-blown fascination, and before long I finally came up with something that was almost good. It was only music because I had no microphone to record vocals. Even if I did have a mic, I had never written lyrics, so there wasn't anything for me to sing anyway.

During the school year, my brother often had tons of friends at our house after school playing Mortal Kombat. One day when they were all in my brother's room playing, I was in the living room recording more of my music until one of the guys walked through on his way to the kitchen to get a snack. On his way back through, he noticed my Casio keyboard and asked what I was doing. I told him I was recording a song. He laughed and thought I was joking, so I played the song for him. That was the first time anyone ever heard one of my recordings. At first it was quite embarrassing because the quality was so bad, and I knew it. My confidence quickly grew when my brother's friend got excited and asked with a trace of disbelief, "Is that really you?" Yes, it was really me. He said it was pretty cool and continued back to my brother's room where the rest of the guys remained playing video games.

By myself again and soaking in the exchange that had just occurred, I sat there smiling for a few moments before the same guy came walking back down the hall and into the living room, except this time, he had one of the other guys with him. He wanted me to show off my recording again. Within a few minutes, nobody was playing Mortal Kombat because they were all in the living room listening to the music that I made with nothing more than a Casio keyboard and my new tape deck. Frankly, it was a pretty big moment for my teenage self.

That was the day that music became my identity. The experience made me want to write more songs, and with my first taste of approval, my only option was to practice as much as possible and become a star. A few weeks later, that same friend asked me if he could borrow my tape. Although I enjoyed the ego boost that came with his request, I was nowhere near ready to hand my music over to anyone. It was my only copy, and I did not want anything to happen to it. But since he was older and one of the cooler guys in school, I reluctantly let him take it for a day. Maybe he might listen to it in his car and forget about it, in which case I would just have to ask for it back. There was no foreseeable harm in that.

The next day, everyone was over playing Mortal Kombat when he handed me the tape. He proudly said to me, "I made a copy, so here's the original back." *You made a copy?!* I didn't know what to think. *I barely wanted to let you have this music for a day…much less forever!* Then I thought of how cool it was that he spent money to buy a blank tape so that he could listen to my stuff whenever he wanted. My mind was racing back and forth, and I couldn't decide whether or not to be mad. Before I could reply, he continued, "I let all the guys in the field house hear it after practice today. Everyone thought it was awesome!"

Now my mind was made up. I was definitely angry!

"Why did you do that? I was barely okay with you having it for a day, and not only did you make a copy of it without asking, but you let all those people hear it. I don't even know them!"

To say the least, he did not quite understand what made me so upset. He thought he was doing me a favor, and looking back, he probably was. Actually, it should have flattered and even encouraged me. I should have thanked him, but I got mad at him instead.

It didn't take too long for me to get over that little incident and go back to recording again. This time, I made sure no one would hear my music, much less take it and make copies of it. *No one will ever have unfinished material of mine ever again. There is just too much at risk.*

The better I got at recording, the more fun it was. The more fun it was, the more time I spent recording. The more time I spent recording, the better I got. This cycle repeated itself over several months until the day I finally realized my songs were missing lyrics, the part of the song that actually tells the story. As a child, I had written some pretty entertaining stories, and of course there was the poem in sixth grade that people got all hot and bothered about, so it only made sense to me that I could probably write song lyrics, too.

Having all the tools to make a tape, I could not have been more excited to let people hear it, and the first thing I did was give copies to the guy who had already shown that he'd gladly share it with others. He would show it to people who would otherwise never hear it. I spent too much time making music to bother myself with making friends anyway.

My reach was limited to my brother and a few neighborhood friends, but before long it seemed like everyone wanted a copy of my tape. With no intention of turning a profit, my answer to everyone was the same, "If you give me a blank tape, I'll make you a copy."

This went on for a few days until I got tired of doing it for free and finally decided to make a little money. I could buy a dozen blank tapes for $10. After paying my friend $2 in gas money for taking me to Best Buy to get the blanks, my overall cost was $1 per tape. At a price of $2 per tape, it was still cheap enough for people to buy but expensive enough for me to enjoy a little profit for once.

I could not believe that I was actually making money off of something that I had only stumbled upon just a few months earlier. Selling my music for actual money was the coolest feeling. What started out as a hobby in the privacy of my home turned into a feeling of appreciation and acceptance that I had never before experienced. My first tape barely made $100, but that meant over 100 people thought enough of me to spend their money on something that had originated in my mind.

Before the end of the school year, I recorded a second tape with new songs and sold it for $5 instead of $2. The price increase was partly because I thought it was worth it and partly because I wanted to make the extra money.

If school was unimportant before, it became especially irrelevant once the thought of being a professional entertainer entered my mind. When summer rolled around again, the thought of returning to high school for a fourth year was not appealing, but my parents made it clear that dropping out was not an option, so back I went.

At the beginning of my fourth year in high school, I was finally a sophomore. Those who began high school a year behind me were now a year ahead of me. Most of the people who had made a big deal about my tapes had either graduated or simply forgotten about me. As encouraging as it was to be someone special the year before, it was devastating to return to being nobody. When I was approached to write and record the basketball team's pre-game warmup music, I lied and said all of my equipment was stolen. That was easier than admitting that I could not accept the highs and lows of being an artist.

Twelve weeks into my fourth year at West Mesquite High School, I wondered if I would be old enough to buy alcohol by the time I finally graduated. That kind of thing makes for a funny punch line in a movie, but it was absolutely not a joke in my world.

I gave up.

I went to the guidance counselor's office and asked about the process of dropping out. Was there a particular form to complete *or do I just stop showing up to class?*

The answers were no and no. She did not want me to drop out, but she somehow knew the perfect way to tell me. "I'm not telling you what you should or shouldn't do," she said. "I'm not even telling you what you can or can't do. I'm just going to give you some information, and you can do with it as you please." She proceeded to tell me about the newest campus in our district that provided a more productive environment for students who were at-risk, students like me whose problems revolved around something other than academics. Each day was only four hours long, and homework was not allowed. Special permission was required—yet rarely granted—to even take a textbook home. Best of all, it was self-paced, which meant I didn't have to worry about any mindless bricks weighing me down. The only downside was the length of the waiting list for students wanting to transfer to the school. “If you quit today,” she explained, “you won’t be allowed to go there, so you would have to stay here at West until a spot opened up.”

Deal breaker.

The counselor was honest and believable, so it’s not that I thought the waiting list thing was a ploy, but the answer was still no…no, I would definitely not stay at West Mesquite any longer. The next day, she called me to her office with the news that somebody somewhere worked some magic, and if I was still interested, I could start at my new school the following Monday.

Game on.

❧ ❧ ❧ ❧ ❧ ❧

From an educational standpoint, Mesquite Academy was the best thing that ever happened to me. It provided an environment that allowed me to make actual progress, and it created a new world where success was not only expected but demanded. At The Academy, anything less than a B was a failing grade. Furthermore, there was a minimum requirement for earning credits each semester, and if a student failed to earn the minimum, he would receive a warning. If he failed to earn the minimum requirement a second time, the student was no longer allowed to attend The Academy at all.

Period.

On the surface, the rules at my new school seemed rigid and impossible. The doors opened at 7:50 a.m., but you were considered late if you did not have both feet in your homeroom class by 8:00 a.m. If you were even a few steps from class when the clock struck eight, you were not allowed to attend school that day. That’s right, not allowed to.

Time was much more valuable in a self-paced program like The Academy. Also, all studying would be done in class, but there was no classwork. There were only books, and you read them yourself as if visiting a library to do research on your own. There were four classes—math, science, history, English—and each class had a teacher who was available if needed, but they mostly administered tests and recorded grades.

With approximately 15 students in a class at any given time—each doing their own lesson—there wasn't the traditional setting of a teacher standing in front of the class teaching everyone at once. Students were instead given a syllabus specific to their courses and were responsible for studying at a reasonable pace for the next test on their syllabus. Each class period was two hours long, and there were only two periods per day. With a total of 10 periods per week, students had the liberty of choosing when to go to each class, but we were required to go to each of our four classes at least twice a week.

The Academy was structured in a way that promoted freedom and responsibility, but the greatest advantage for me was that no classmate could hold me back. I studied at my own pace and took tests at my own pace. As a result, I earned more graduation credits in my first two months at Mesquite Academy than the previous three years at WMHS.

Finally, school was not a dreadful experience and major progress was underway in my life. Not only was the structure of The Academy perfect for me, but the relationships between teachers and students were also positive and genuine. The principal, Keith Adams, was not some hard nosed disciplinarian who enjoyed the role of enforcer. Granted, he would definitely enforce any and all rules, but more importantly, Mr. Adams actually cared about each individual student that walked through the doors of his school. And for the kind of students enrolled at Mesquite Academy, compassion and consideration were of utmost importance.

In my adult years, I often make light of the fact that I was in the ninth grade for three years. It's an easy punchline that falls into the *funny because it's true* category. What isn't as well-known, however, is the fact that I went from sophomore to senior within months of transferring to Mesquite Academy. For more than 12 years, I had never adapted to normal school, and normal school had never adapted to me, but The Academy created a system that I needed.

I take no credit for how well Mesquite Academy served me. In actuality, I didn't really change anything about myself. I just showed up to The Academy and kept being the same kid I had always been. I wanted a certain amount of freedom and responsibility, and that's what they provided me. They demanded a certain level of performance and maturity, and I was happy to comply.

It was a perfect fit.

After three semesters at The Academy, I was within reach of obtaining the necessary credits to finish high school, and in May of 1998, I graduated and earned my high school diploma.

Finally.

DIAMOND RINGS AND GUITAR STRINGS

In April of 1997, I was nearing the end of my first semester at Mesquite Academy when the phone at my house rang. My dad answered the call and heard the familiar voice of Jim Graham on the other end of the line. Jim was a longtime friend of my dad's. He wasn't technically related to me, but he was one of those guys who felt more like an uncle than a family friend. He was active in our church's youth group and overall just a ton of fun, but he was a muscle bound athletic type who was built more like an NFL running back than a religious mentor. Jim could bench press nearly a quarter-ton and was the kind of guy you wanted on your side in a street fight, but he was just as silly as he was tough. He had a childlike sense of humor, and he was perfect for the youth group at my church. Jim Graham was just one of those guys that everybody liked.

Mr. Graham was also an established jeweler and successful business owner. Gold & Silver City—a small shop in northeast Dallas—was more than a jewelry store; Jim was also an expert in coins, flatware, fine china, crystal, and essentially anything that could turn a profit. After growing his business to an extent that he needed a bigger place, Jim bought a second store nearby and began to grow that location as well.

Northlake Jewelers, Jim's second store, was more aesthetically pleasing than the smaller Gold & Silver City and offered a better location with more appeal to walk-in customers. With too much business to operate the store on his own, Jim hired a store manager who would essentially function as a salesman while Jim focused on doing all of the in-house jewelry work himself. As a third-generation jeweler with decades of experience, his work was top notch.

He had too much work to do on his own, but other jewelers were too expensive to outsource work to and still earn a profit. Furthermore, Jim wanted to train his own apprentice who would eventually take over the store years down the road when he was ready to retire. He needed someone young enough to accept apprentice pay but talented enough to learn the craft in a reasonable amount of time. Most importantly, Jim needed someone who was trustworthy enough to welcome into his store, which maintained an inventory worth a quarter of a million dollars.

When my dad answered the phone, I heard only his end of the conversation. "Hey, Jim. How's it going?" Following typical buddy banter, my dad said, "Clay? Yeah he's here. Wanna talk to him?" Yes, Jim wanted to talk to me, but I couldn't imagine why. Maybe he had tickets to a baseball game or something. It was the middle of the week, so maybe he was just calling to remind me to bring a friend to church on Sunday.

Taking the call, I said, "What's up, Jim?"

"Not much," he answered. "Just wanted to give you a call and see if you're interested in working."

"Uh," I hesitated, trying to remember what it was the other kid in our youth group used to do for Jim as a summer job. "Yeah, I guess. Doing what?"

"Working here at the store," he said. "Can you come by tomorrow around noon and talk about it?"

I agreed out of reflex before really thinking about it. "Yes, sir, definitely." I grabbed a pen and wrote down the directions to his store before handing the phone back to my dad.

At 17, both of my ears were pierced, and my clothes were baggy. For this meeting though, I wanted to look like a respectable man, so the small hoops came out of my earlobes and I borrowed a collared shirt from my dad. Fortunately, his clothes fit me by then, so his closet doubled as my closet whenever necessary, and it was definitely necessary for this potential job interview at a jewelry store. Jim didn't give any sort of job description over the phone regarding the position he was trying to fill, so it was completely unclear to me what he might have had in mind. He was one of the few people in my life at the time that I trusted without question though, so I wasn't really worried about it. If he wanted me on his team, there was no way imaginable that this would be anything but a great opportunity for me.

The next day, it was raining heavily, so I left with plenty of time to spare so I wouldn't be late to my appointment with Jim. Always punctual and rarely nervous, I showed up a solid 10 minutes early, turned off the car, and enjoyed a deafening silence. For some reason, my left ear always rang when the ambient noise was not loud enough to drown it out. For no explainable reason, my nerves were actually getting the best of me, and it was uncomfortable. Jim—the same man who can be seen roughhousing with me in a picture from when I was probably four years old—was someone who suddenly intimidated me. *What if I say something stupid? What if I'm not good enough for this? What if he thinks I've done this before and changes his mind when he finds out I'm completely unqualified for whatever job he needs done?*

In my mind, I began rehearsing idle chitchat. *If he says hello, I'll say how are you? If he says how are you, I'll say fine and thanks. If other people are there, be sure to offer a polite greeting. Be sure to shake hands like you do at church, except make sure you don't say anything funny because you don't want to come off as a silly kid. Be sure to remain serious and manly. Now is not the time to be Clay the Class Clown. You're a man, so behave as a man would.*

When I entered the store, Jim came out of his office to greet me and introduce me to the salesman who was also named Jim. *Great. Jim and Jim. This is about to get real confusing.* The exchange of pleasantries went exactly as I'd hoped. I shook their hands and executed my best man-walk to Owner Jim's office where he went around to his side of the desk and waved his hand to an empty chair meant for me. *When grown men treated me as a man—with their handshakes and formal dialogues—I no longer felt like a common child, and it was one of the things I enjoyed about being in trouble...*except this was not a trip to the principal's office. This was real-life adult stuff, and it was awesome! Salesman Jim disappeared and left me alone with Owner Jim.

Sitting across the desk from Jim, I watched as he grabbed a pen that was resting on a yellow legal pad where he had scrawled a few bullet points with the penmanship of a blind man having a seizure. *Are those notes or an EKG?* My eyes were locked onto his notes, fixated at how incredibly illegible they were. *I've heard of calligraphy, but that looks more like catastrophe.* It took everything in me to keep from laughing at the punchlines racing through my mind. *Pay attention! He's talking to YOU!*

"Well," he began, "the first thing I was going to tell you was no earrings are allowed if you want to work for me, but I see that you already took care of that." Again, my pride swelled as my prescience prevailed. "So here's the deal," he continued, "I want to train you to be a jeweler. I think you have the talent to be a good one, and this is a great chance for you to learn a trade that can set you up for the rest of your life." He wasn't trying to convince me. He was simply laying down the facts, and I listened. Jewelers are a stingy bunch, and they don't want anyone else encroaching on their territory. They will take their entire workload to the grave before sharing their business, but Jim was opening the door and letting me in. This was even better than I first imagined after our brief phone call the previous day.

He explained what my hours would be—after school every day from 1:00 p.m. to 6:00 p.m. and 10:00 a.m. to 5:00 p.m. on Saturdays—as well as my pay rate. Also discussed was the increase in pay that I could expect as I became more self-sufficient in my craft. The more he spoke, the clearer it became that this was not an impulsive decision on his part. Jim Graham—successful businessman and excellent-at-everything guy—invested no small amount of time or energy in deciding how to grow his business. And as was unbelievably fortunate for me, I was the person he picked for the job. He later told me that he had not considered a second candidate. Had I not accepted his offer, there was no immediate alternative.

The following Monday, I drove to work instead of going home after school. My hours at school were 8:00 a.m. to noon, and I didn't have to be at work until 1:00 p.m. With an hour between school and my new job there was ample time to hit a drive-thru for lunch on the way to the jewelry store, and that soon became my daily routine.

Showing up to Northlake Jewelers on my first day, I was not the least bit anxious. By this point, it had sunk well into my ego that I was some sort of Chosen One, and my arrogance was only matched by my excitement. One could not have possibly known less about jewelry than I did when I walked into the store that day, but my mentor was about to change that. My first lesson that day, however, made a lasting impression that would ultimately stretch far beyond my life as a jeweler:

"Don't take shortcuts. You'll probably screw up more things than you fix at first, so just learn from your mistakes. But if you start taking shortcuts, you'll have to learn how to fix those, too, because they always come back to bite you in the ass. Always do the best work possible the first time around."

Epiphany.

Jim could have taught anyone how to be a jeweler, but his particular teaching style matched my learning style perfectly. He first demonstrated something while explaining what he was doing and then had me try it right away. His teaching was quick but thorough before he watched as I tried to replicate whatever he had just shown me. When I messed up, he flatly explained without emotion what I had done wrong and reminded me that mistakes are part of the learning process. He never belittled me for making the same mistake twice, but he also refused to let a recurring problem continue. Likewise, when things went well, he recognized my progress. Jim didn't offer useless encouragement for the sake of my self-esteem though, and I appreciated that. Consequently, there was an added weight to his words when he acknowledged a job well done. There was no fluff in his compliments, and as he began to express confidence in my craftsmanship, it provided me with a great sense of accomplishment.

For months, the majority of my days at work were spent in a small room that we called the shop. It was the size of a small bedroom and hid behind a giant two-way mirror so that the shop was not visible to customers but the showroom was still visible from the shop. Early on, Jim explained to me that most of his customers were elderly and would probably stop coming to him if they knew a kid was working on their precious jewelry. That made complete sense to me, so it didn't even bother me that I never received credit for the work I was doing.

Since life is never perfect, neither was my new job. Soon after I began working at the jewelry store, I started to experience friction with the second Jim, the salesman. Owner Jim was happy with my work, but Salesman Jim seemed more concerned with bossing me around. Looking back, it's easy to note that I was unbearably cocky by that point in my life, and my attitude didn't exactly hide behind a silent mouth. My respect for Owner Jim was enough to keep me in line with him most of the time.

Besides, he'd built his own business from the ground up and was now teaching me everything he knew. Only a complete moron would disrespect that.

On the other hand, Salesman Jim was little more than a talking head from my perspective. He could sell water to a drowning man, so his role at the jewelry store was relevant and necessary, but when no customers were in the store, he was almost always eating a noisy bag of chips or reciting movie lines with Owner Jim. Nearly two decades later, I can still quote the majority of Blazing Saddles although I've never actually seen the movie.

Things with Salesman Jim got worse before they got better. He constantly tried to talk music with me, which I also hated because *I am an artist and he is not even a musician.* To me, talking about music has always been painfully boring. I loved making it, and I loved listening to it, but I hated when anyone attempted to engage in a conversation about music with me. Salesman Jim was particularly fascinated with rock guitarists, and he claimed to have a friend who was a guitar legend. "Dude," as every sentence seemed to begin, "you gotta bring your guitar on Saturday. My friend Jimmy is gonna swing by, and I bet I could get him to show you a few things."

"Yeah," I replied, "that's what this store needs is another Jim."

"No, dummy. Jimmy!" He paused briefly and clarified, "As in, Jimmy Wallace."

"Never heard of him," I said.

With that, Salesman Jim fired back some condescending remark about how he thought I was a guitarist and *how do you play guitar in Dallas and not know who Jimmy Wallace is?* As it turned out, I knew exactly who Jimmy Wallace was. He banked at the place where my stepmom worked, and she had once given me his CD. This guy was a bona fide stud on guitar, and he was coming to the store on Saturday. *Heck yeah I'll bring my guitar.*

That Saturday, I made sure to take one of my guitars and a small amp to work with me. Around lunchtime, Mr. Wallace came in the front door and greeted Salesman Jim with a handshake and a big smile. Watching through the two-way mirror from the shop, I immediately recognized him and was stoked to meet him and possibly hear him play my guitar. I was a teenager about to meet a professional musician. It was a big deal.

After being introduced by Salesman Jim, I immediately told Mr. Wallace that my stepmother had given me his CD recently and it was awesome. He was an incredible guitar player so I explained that I played guitar, too. In fact, I could also play bass guitar and drums and some piano and even sing or rap if I really had to. My life story went on and I was eventually rambling about having sold hundreds of copies of my tapes at school. Recently, my first paying gig as a live musician was totally by accident, but I was regularly asked to fill in at least two or three times a month, and they were actually paying me to come play. Sure, it was only $20, but that was pretty good for a kid who taught himself everything he knows.

I went on for what probably seemed like hours without a breath. This was my one opportunity to impress a real pro, and I was not about to let him leave the store before learning how amazing I was. Finally, Mr. Wallace politely extended a hand to quiet me before offering a piercing bit of wisdom that soon became my mantra:

"If you have to tell them who you are, it's probably because you're not."

Seamlessly, he moved to where my guitar was and played a few notes that were unlike anything that had ever been played on my guitar. This guy was amazing, and all I could do was stand in awe of the way he made my guitar sing. Nothing I ever played sounded anything close to this, and oh by the way *if you have to tell them who you are, it's probably because you're not. What did that even mean? Is he saying that I am as amazing as I think I am but to just keep it a secret? He's never heard me play, so how does he know how good I am? What was his point?!*

Without saying much, he continued to give us a quick exhibition of excellence before standing up and handing the guitar back to me. "Let's hear you play," he politely offered, but there was no way I was about to follow his playing with mine. He was so good that I momentarily forgot I even knew how to play guitar at all. *No, thanks. I don't believe I'll be embarrassing myself today.* After all, he had a point. I had to tell him who I was… because I probably was not.

Putting the guitar back in my case, he asked me what band I played in, but the reality was that I had never played in a band. I had only recorded my own music by myself and occasionally played bass guitar at church. The recent paying gig I had mentioned was really nothing to brag about, and it was also at a church that was not growing and would soon probably stop paying for a live band anyway. The more honest my story became, the more unexceptional I felt, but he could tell that my ego was taking a beating as our conversation went on. He shifted to discussing the positives of being a musician regardless of pay or status, but I don't recall much of anything else from our conversation after that. He asked if I'd met any cool people through music, but I hadn't. I guess I didn't have nearly as much to brag about after all.

Mr. Wallace soon left the store and the day continued as usual for Jim and Jim, but I was still hung up on the thought of never again telling people how awesome I was because it meant that I probably was not. It was a paradox, and it baffled me as much as it bothered me. *How will anyone know how great I am if I never tell them? Why would I keep that to myself?!*

Reconsidering my worth as a musician, I was thankful to be a jeweler.

During my last year of high school, life was fantastic. School and work were both great. They were incredibly time consuming—about 60 hours per week combined—but that was fine with me because they were both extremely rewarding and enjoyable.

In September of 1997, my phone rang and a guy named Quincy asked to speak with me. He had gotten my name and number from a mutual friend, and he was looking for a bass player to play with him on Sunday nights at Pleasant Grove Christian Church in Dallas, Texas. Quincy handled himself professionally and made a good impression over the phone, so I agreed to meet him a few hours prior to the evening service the following Sunday. The music was simple to play, but I was interested to learn more about the opportunity.

The youth group at PGCC was small—perhaps a few dozen at best—but the atmosphere was welcoming and friendly. After the service, they invited me to hang out in the gym where a handful of guys played basketball while another group played table tennis. There was also the obligatory group of girls chitchatting as they slowly walked laps around the gym. Not knowing where to fit in, I just meandered about and waited for someone to approach me instead. Being "in the band" meant there was almost always someone wanting to talk to you, and that evening was certainly no exception.

I met a lot of people that evening, and they were all incredibly nice, but most of them were forgettable. One girl in particular stood out to me though. Her name was Candice, and she actually went to one of the high schools in my district. At 16, she was only two years younger than I was, but she carried herself like an adult, and her conversation was anything but adolescent. We discussed music, of course, and we liked a lot of the same bands.

With things going well at the jewelry store and Jim paying me generously, I was fortunate to enjoy things that most people my age could not afford. Whether it was a concert or a movie,

I never missed out on anything because of a lack of money, and my friends often came along on my dime because they rarely had an income of their own at that age. In fact, just days before meeting Candice, I had bought four concert tickets to see Third Day. I had no idea who I would invite to go with me, but I knew it wouldn't be a problem finding three people to join me.

After church that evening, I overheard Candice mention that she thought the Third Day concert would be really good. Although I had known her for only a few minutes at that point, I immediately invited her to go.

Over the next several months, Candice and I became very close. We spoke on the phone almost daily and often late into the night. Our conversations were not the typical flirty chats that occur between most teenage boys and girls. She was the sweetest girl I knew, but that alone was never enough for any girl to keep my attention at that age. For me, there had to be substance to a conversation, and Candice was a blast to talk to because she never bored me. She was a great listener, which suited me well because I loved to talk. She was also cute and had the kind of hair you see only in shampoo commercials, but we never dated.

She was my best friend.

⁂ ⁂ ⁂ ⁂ ⁂ ⁂

During the summer of 1999, I was still working at the jewelry store but no longer living at home with either of my parents. My brother and I were roommates in the house where we had grown up, except it was just the two of us since our parents both lived elsewhere by then. My job at the jewelry store was turning into a miserable, dreadful experience every day. Owner Jim had trained me well and I was doing most of the jewelry repairs for the store, which I absolutely loved. Occasionally, he allowed me to work on custom designs or even make my own jewelry. The job itself was not the problem at all, and it was becoming a passion of mine to mend broken pieces of jewelry that did not otherwise appear salvageable.

That was the real payoff for me, and I loved my job. The money was a blessing but the work was rewarding. Unfortunately, no matter how much I learned or how well I performed, I never seemed to earn the respect of Salesman Jim, which I suppose is only fair since he certainly hadn't earned mine. Technically, he was my boss, but I never acknowledged him as such, and he never made any decisions regarding the store anyway. It was pretty simple—show up to work, do the job, then go home.

As time went on, Owner Jim started to devote more of his weekends to being a father. He often skipped work altogether on Saturdays, but that was the perk of owning a business and hiring people who can run it for you, so it never bothered me when he failed to show up. The only thing that bothered me about his absence was how differently Salesman Jim treated me when the owner was not around. My breaking point finally came after getting in trouble several days in a row for something Salesman Jim had told me to do.

With business slow in the mornings, Salesman Jim wanted to get on the Internet and kill time because there was little else for him to do at that time of day. But he didn't know how to get online, so he asked for my help. For three consecutive days, Owner Jim walked into the store just as I was helping Salesman Jim get online. From Owner Jim's point of view, I was just playing on the computer instead of doing my work, and Salesman Jim didn't bother correcting the boss's error.

For me to be playing on the computer was completely unacceptable because of how much work I had, but the warnings were still mild and playful. On the fourth day, Salesman Jim once again asked for my help getting the computer turned on and connected to the Internet, but I was too busy and really didn't want to get in trouble anyway. He told me it would take only a few seconds and reminded me that he was my boss anyway. Not being in the mood for arguing, I walked out of the shop and into the office to get the computer working for him. Sure enough, Owner Jim came strolling in the front door and saw me *playing on the computer,* as he called it. Pissed and not wasting any time, he yelled as he walked, "If I come in here and see you on that damn computer again, you're fired!"

That alone was not enough to worry me because he was the type of man who would immediately retract statements once he realized he made a mistake. The mistake, in this case, was that it was Salesman Jim's fault, not mine. I was just following orders.

Without saying a word, I walked back to the shop. I didn't hesitate, but I wasn't in a hurry either. I was walking quickly enough to avoid getting yelled at but slowly enough to see if maybe Salesman Jim would speak up and defend me since he was the one getting me in trouble every day. It hadn't bothered me the other days when he didn't have anything to say, but now that my job was potentially at stake I thought he would surely speak up and explain to the owner that I was doing only as I was told.

Nope.

Nothing.

Not a single word.

My resentment for the lesser Jim finally peaked, and that was the end of the line for me. Without feeling like there was anything I could do to change the situation, I started thinking of how to quit. Up to that point, Owner Jim had practically given me every tool imaginable to succeed in life, including countless invaluable life lessons that were in no way even related to jewelry. Unfortunately, it was no longer possible for me to continue working in an environment where someone like Salesman Jim had the ability to put my job at risk without even taking responsibility for it. My dream job was now a nightmare.

It would be several months before I finally quit that job in the worst way possible. After spending an entire weekend thinking about how I dreaded returning to work that Monday, my immaturity led me to simply call the store and tell them that I wasn't coming into work that day...or ever again. Without the standard two week notice, without the decency of a face-to-face conversation, and without much of an explanation at all, I quit.

❧ ❧ ❧ ❧ ❧ ❧

Even with my troubles at work, my personal life was actually still getting better. After graduating high school and moving into full-time employment at the jewelry store, my freedom had grown as I was living essentially rent-free with my brother at our childhood home, and my only bill was my truck payment and insurance. The majority of my money was spent on music—guitars, amps, drums, concerts, CDs—and things were wonderful. Fortunately, I was never girl crazy, so it never bothered me too much that I had gone most of my life without a girlfriend. There were more important things to worry about than girls, but as my friendship with Candice continued to grow, it became appealing to think of spending my life with her. She was attractive, but that was not what caught my eye the most. For me, it just seemed like she would make a great mother, and even though I was barely out of high school, my dreams were to have a big family, and I couldn't imagine a better person to raise children with than Candice. To make it better, we had a couple years of solid friendship to build on, and it just seemed logical that we could grow old together. Her parents liked me, and there was no reason in my mind that it might not work.

After giving it some thought, I finally decided to mention that I was starting to have feelings for her. It was a weird conversation for me because in nearly two years since meeting her, I had never tried to make a move on her or even show that kind of interest. Fortunately for me and my ego, Candice ultimately expressed the same interest in me that I had for her, but she did not immediately jump onboard and commit to forever with me the first time it was brought up. Instead, she spent her own amount of time thinking it out for herself.

We were officially a couple in August of 1999, and on May 20, 2000, my best friend became my wife.

Having recently quit my job at the jewelry store before we got married, my contribution to the marriage was quite useless from a financial standpoint. Candice worked on commission at a popular children's shoe store and made good money, but her new husband contributed next to nothing in the earliest days. Her income and financial responsibility kept us above water the whole time.

In the spring of 2001, my dad called me and told me about a guy named Steve whom he met at a popular guitar shop in Dallas. My dad was always quick to let people know that his son was a musician, and Steve was interested in meeting me to discuss filling a spot in his band. My initial reaction was something along the lines of an eye roll. In my opinion, if this Steve fellow was so desperate that he was calling the sons of random strangers, then his band must be pretty awful. To make it worse, his band was just another praise and worship band, which meant they weren't even writing their own music. I was not at all interested in that. What caught my attention, however, was that the band was a full-time venture who got paid when they played. They were already booked for an entire summer by the time I spoke with them so *yes...yes, I think I will call Steve.*

Thanks to Jimmy Wallace, I had become well versed in the art of not telling people who I was because it probably meant that I wasn't. Instead, my phone call with Steve consisted mostly of pleasantries and general philosophies about music. We decided to meet at a rehearsal space where another band of mine practiced, and it was a pretty immediate connection with Steve and the rest of his band. Their personalities seemed to work with mine, and they were nice people. Before we played a single note together,

I already liked them, and they seemed to like me, too. It was obvious that I was a fit for their band, and it was pretty exciting for me to think of finally playing music for a living.

While it was not the dream I had envisioned as a child, playing in this new band was nothing to be ashamed of. It was easy to believe in Steve as a leader because he had quit a successful job selling houses to invest his time and money into the band. He had pieced things together himself and was responsible for making it all happen, working hard to get bookings much in the way he worked hard to sell homes. He was also a talented guitarist and was fun to be around. It seemed like the beginning of something great, and that summer was amazing.

At home, however, it was becoming more apparent to me that I was not fit to be a husband. Early on, I wondered what I'd been thinking when deciding to get married. I was only 20 years old, and I was so anxious to be an adult that I totally skipped the part of life that was supposed to be fun and adventurous. I was already working full-time before I even graduated high school, and there was never a time when I just went and explored the world or the people in it.

Candice was still the same amazing person she had always been, but marriage quickly felt more like a burden than a blessing. More than anything, I just wanted the freedom to do whatever I wanted whenever I wanted, and I wasn't man enough to realize that I was being a selfish child. Isolation and detachment, my adult versions of pouting, were my only resorts. When I wasn't gone somewhere playing music, I parked myself in front of the computer screen at home and burrowed as deeply into the Internet as time would allow.

It was obvious to me that my wife was unhappy just the same as I was, but it was a quiet misery. She never nagged me or threw it in my face that I was neglecting her and our marriage. We never fought or even raised our voices at each other, but there was no reason for me to expect that things would ever improve because I was too lost in my own narcissism to acknowledge that I was the problem.

As for the band that I was in, things had gone sour by the end of that first summer together. I was increasingly difficult to work with, and my attempt at getting one of the guys replaced backfired when they booted me instead. This became a bit of a trend for me over the next few years because no amount of talent could overcome how terrible I was as a bandmate. People just didn't like me once they got to know me.

After struggling to find my place in the music industry, I started looking for something else to do. As a teenager, I decided that I would pursue rock stardom until the age of 25 because as important as it was for me to succeed in music, it was more important to start a family and have as many children as possible. To me, age 25 seemed liked a reasonable deadline. Besides, if I wasn't a star by then, the likelihood of me becoming one wasn't worth risking my dreams of becoming a father.

At the age of 24 years old, there was little hope for me to have the kind of music career I'd dreamed of, and although it was a year shy of my self-imposed deadline, a new career opportunity came along, so I decided it was time to let go of one dream and pursue another.

⁂ ⁂ ⁂ ⁂ ⁂ ⁂

In December 2003, working at Solar Turbines seemed like a solution to many of my problems. It was a major corporation that was owned by Caterpillar, an even bigger corporation. The work was hands-on, and the fact that it was unfamiliar to me was an added bonus that was reminiscent of my first days at the jewelry store.

My mother and stepfather each had established careers with Solar, so it only made sense to me that I might be able to do the same. Having a stable job and forgetting about music also would give me a chance to work on my marriage, which was becoming more depressing by the day. The new job also allowed me to finance a brand new truck that I had wanted for so long.

The following spring, Candice and I decided to buy a new house in a new community just outside of Rockwall, Texas. The neighborhood was just out of reach for us financially, but it was a really nice house in a part of town that was exploding. Much of my family was moving to the area as well, and that only made it that much more appealing to us. We moved into our new house in September 2004.

With a new job, a new truck, and a new house, my life was starting to pan out just fine. At the age of 25, I thought I had it all.

It was good to be me.

POKER

Although I grew up in a family that loved to play poker, I never actually knew anything about the game. I didn't know the rules. I didn't know the hand rankings. I didn't even know the point of the game except that it involved taking other people's money. The only thing I knew was that my family sure enjoyed sitting around a poker table all night until one person had all the money.

Nobody in America works on my birthday because it's on Independence Day, so there's always a party of some sort somewhere. On my 26th birthday, we had a family get-together at my mother's house. All of the aunts, uncles, and cousins were there to swim and blow up fireworks. Later in the night, the poker game got started.

Not knowing how to play, I was just a spectator. And that was fine with me because my relatives were usually quite entertaining anyway. Even if I knew how to play, I didn't have any cash on me, so I couldn't ante up the $20 that everyone started with. But when one of my cousins gave me $20 and insisted I learn how to play, I had nothing to lose.

The rules of the game were pretty simple to learn. After all those years of thinking it was a complicated game, it soon became clear that it was pretty straightforward in terms of actual rules. What wasn't so simple was finding a way to avoid losing all of my money. I noticed that the same two or three people seemed to be winning all the money, so it only made sense that they were doing things differently than the rest, and that's what I wanted to figure out.

Although I ended up losing the $20 that my cousin gave me for poker that night, I still enjoyed the game quite a bit. I didn't expect to win my first time playing anyway, and since it wasn't my money to begin with, I couldn't at all classify that as a loss.

My first inclination about the game of poker was that it definitely wasn't a game of luck. There was obviously an element of chance to it, but at the end of the day, you can't win something on purpose unless you can lose it on purpose, and you can definitely lose on purpose in the game of poker. I hated that I couldn't solve the puzzle by simply playing with my family that first night or any of the subsequent poker nights we had in those first few months after I learned how to play.

Soon enough, I realized that the occasional weekend poker game with my family wouldn't be enough for me to dig and find the answers I was looking for, so I turned to the Internet. I started looking up anything I could find about the game of poker as well as poker professionals. It seemed highly unlikely to me that there were poker pros who simply got lucky for a living.

Over time, I started learning how much of the game was indeed a complete crapshoot. However, avoiding the crapshoot aspects and capitalizing on a few other key components of the game seemed to be where all the money was won. That, of course, fascinated me. When I started watching major poker events on TV, it seemed obvious that the people winning the majority of the money were definitely doing so on purpose, and I was convinced that it was anything but a crapshoot.

Having left my dreams of being a professional musician in my past, the idea of being a professional poker player seemed just as awesome. It's not that I wanted to get rich and be famous—although that was an obvious upside—but I loved the idea of having a career that I didn't dread. Even though I loved my job at Solar Turbines, it was still a job that I *had* to do instead of something I *got* to do. There was nothing spectacular or privileged about working for a major corporation that could replace me at the drop of a hat if I ever underperformed.

It would have been delusional for me to think I could be a poker pro without first losing a ton of money learning how to play the game. It's not that I *wanted* to lose money. It only seemed logical that most people do lose in the beginning, and I was definitely no exception.

I lost a lot, actually. But thanks to the Internet, I was able to learn at a much quicker pace than anyone who learned the game back in the old days. For me, it was about pattern recognition and knowing what was most likely to happen in any given hand. It wasn't about being psychic or lucky; it was about having a good memory and being able to connect the dots where most people couldn't.

As time went on, I was certain I could play poker for a living. It was a long shot to hit the big time, but America's poker boom was in full effect by then, so there were plenty of low stakes games to take advantage of. My goal the following year was to make the same amount of money playing as I was from my current job. It was a lofty goal, but not an impossible one to reach. If I could just find a way to manage my money properly, I was certain I could quit my job and play a game for a living.

Before long, I was playing online nearly every day after work from the time I got home until the time I eventually passed out. I was sleeping just a few hours each night, and some nights were completely sleepless altogether. Even in my days as a musician, I'd never functioned on as little sleep as when I started playing poker online, but no matter how tired I was the next day, I couldn't wait to get home and continue practicing the game that I so badly wanted to master.

For a while, I lost more money than I could have possibly counted. Thanks to credit cards, it was actually quite easy to get online and simply charge up a little bit more money. $50 here and $50 there didn't seem like a lot, and I ignored the statements showing that my balance was climbing into the thousands. To me, credit cards didn't reflect actual money anyway because it wasn't cash in my hands. Those figures were just numbers on a piece of paper, and I was completely disconnected from any sense of responsibility when it came to paying those balances.

Within a few months, my losses tapered as I began to learn a little bit more about the game of poker. I began to win at the smallest stakes available online, but that was beside the point. I was just happy to stop the bleeding. When I received my first payout from the popular online poker site where I had been steadily losing for so long, I felt like a millionaire. My first check was less than a thousand bucks, but it felt like so much more because they were actually paying me for a game that I had played in the comfort of my own home, and I was hooked.

With some of that money, I paid off a small bit of the credit cards that I had been using to fund those earliest deposits, but most of that first payout went to funding my first trip to a live casino just across the Louisiana border since we didn't have any casinos in Texas.

Admittedly, I probably had the wrong attitude when I walked into the Horseshoe Casino and paid $100 to play a game that I'd never played outside the safety of my family game or my computer. I was in way over my head and had absolutely no idea what I was doing. I thought the game itself would be no different than the micro stakes I had been playing online, but it was like I walked into another world at the Horseshoe. Those people actually knew how to play, and they took advantage of me in every way possible, and unfortunately for me, I wasn't even humble enough to realize it. I chalked it up to bad luck before walking back out to my truck and driving home.

After I got home, I went right back to losing at poker online again and racked up another few hundred bucks on a credit card that I would never pay off. It was free money to me, just like the $20 that my cousin gave me on my birthday that first night I ever played poker. It's not that I enjoyed losing, but the financial loss certainly didn't affect me mentally. I just wanted to learn how to win, and I would do so at any cost.

Following another month or so of winning at the small online stakes, I cashed out again. This time, it was just over $1200, which was far from the monthly amount I might need if I wanted to quit my day job, but it was enough to take back to the Horseshoe and give that another try. Instead of playing in a tournament though, I decided to play in a $2/$5 cash game. There was a distinct difference between tournaments and cash games. I enjoyed the tournaments more, but the cash game was easier for me to beat.

My second trip to Louisiana was considerably better than my first, and I was convinced that I had found my calling in life. I started talking about quitting my job to play poker, and was surprised to find how stupid everyone thought I was for thinking that was even possible. I had the support of Candice, but nobody else in my family had anything good to say to me about it. My friends weren't much help either, and I soon learned that I was going to be on my own if I wanted to find a way to make my dream work.

Regardless of how little support I got from my friends or family, Candice was actually on board with at least devising a plan for transitioning from my regular job to that of a small time poker pro. Put simply, I was going to continue working at Solar Turbines until I had saved up the equivalent of one year's salary. This would not only prove that I could actually win in the long run with poker, but it would also provide the necessary cushion for Candice to feel comfortable with my quitting my job.

Sadly, I didn't quite cope nearly as well as I'd expected when it came to maintaining a day job while playing poker at night. The stress of a failing marriage was starting to eat at me, and all I really wanted was to be left alone. I had finally found something I could do with my life that allowed me to live by my own rules, but it felt like nobody wanted me to do it. Worse, they didn't even think it was real.

❧ ❧ ❧ ❧ ❧ ❧

To me, the hardest part of being called an addict is that nobody believes you when you say you're not an addict. Instead, they insist that you're merely in denial, and there's no way to even prove them wrong. To have your entire mental state called into question is bad enough, but when there's no actual evidence to the contrary, it's quite difficult to endure.

Before long, I came to the illogical conclusion that my friends and family were only jealous of me. After all, I'd found a way to turn a game into a sustainable income. Some in my family had worked their whole lives to amass a respectable living, and I was on the verge of solving the puzzle that would allow me to sit at a table and play a game with strangers for the rest of my life. *They're just jealous* was the only explanation I could come up with for why they weren't willing to support what I was hoping to do.

And with that, the dark days began.

❧ ❧ ❧ ❧ ❧ ❧

After a couple of years at Solar Turbines, my options were beginning to look slim. My mother managed what seemed like half of the facility, and with company policies being in place to prevent nepotism, that ruled out any possibility of me going to work for anything that fell under her management. Worse, my stepdad was top dog over field repair, and that excluded me on a global level from ever going into any position in the field. As much as I loved my parents and respected who they were professionally, it felt like they were keeping me from ever doing anything big in the company. That was a stupid conclusion for me to come to at the time, but my life was slowly turning into a giant heap of stupidity, and that was only the tip of the iceberg.

What began a couple of years earlier as a great job opportunity with tons of potential seemed to dissipate into another job that I dreaded every morning. The more I hated my job, the more I was drawn to playing poker for a living. Or, perhaps, the more I was drawn to playing poker for a living, the more I hated my job. Who knows? Who cares? All I wanted was to be happy, and I'd have stopped at nothing to achieve that.

Toward the end of 2005, I began to realize I would never be happy in my marriage, and I wanted out. I loved Candice, and she meant the world to me as a person and as a friend, but I just hated the thought of being married. I felt like we'd gotten married way too young, and I regretted it. Those feelings had nothing to do with Candice as a person. I just wanted to be on my own and experience life without having to worry about how my choices might affect someone else. I started to resent key people in my life for allowing—and even encouraging—me to get married so young when I had no grasp of how to live a responsible life on my own, much less with another person. I was a terrible husband, and I knew it. More than that, however, I just wanted to rid myself of the burden of working through our problems. With my typical brand of selfishness, I just wanted to leave the situation and not deal with it at all because that seemed a lot easier than anything else. I fell deeper into my own hole and began isolating myself to levels that were extreme even for me.

There came a point when I would come home from work and go straight to the room where my desk was. I would stay on the computer without getting up for anything except to use the restroom or perhaps grab a quick snack. Candice would often join me in that room, but it didn't do any good. I was just as removed from our marriage as I was from life in general.

For the longest time, my family got together every weekend. The women hung out together in the kitchen chatting or perhaps playing canasta while the men stayed out in the garage drinking, smoking, and of course playing poker. But family nights soon became miserable for me, and my attitude was so terrible that it was ruining the fun for everyone. Eventually, they stopped inviting me altogether because my attitude had declined to the point that I would berate and degrade my own family and friends when things didn't go my way. I was a total jerk, and as much as my family still loved me, there was no way to enjoy a friendly game of anything if I was involved.

In retrospect, it's easy to see that I ruined an otherwise enjoyable family routine. I don't know how, but my family continued to love me in every way possible. Twice, I found out about an impromptu poker game and showed up uninvited because of how oblivious I was to the fact that they were actually trying to get something together without me. But instead of getting mad and telling me to leave, they just played it off as though nobody wanted to play poker that night and *Hey, Clay! Glad you showed up. How've you been?*

No matter what, my family still loved me.

My cousins were more like brothers, and my aunts and uncles were more like bonus parents. And that wasn't just my perception either. That was really how things were in my family for many years. If someone was having a tough time, everybody felt it. When it became clear to my family that I was self-destructing, they tried to intervene and do whatever they could to get me back on track. They didn't ridicule me or shame me into getting my act together. They just reminded me of how much they loved me. After all, we were all ultimately one unit anyway, so if I was hurting, then so were they.

Although I wasn't very approachable, there were more than a few occasions when someone from my family tried to reason with me. Invariably, each time an aunt, uncle, cousin, or parent pulled me aside to have a talk with me, they were quick to let me know that they weren't judging me or trying to tell me what I was doing wrong. They walked on egg shells with me, and most of those conversations began with *I know this might make you angry, but I love you too much to just sit back and say nothing.* Or, as one of my more vocal cousins put the same message much less eloquently, "If I didn't give a damn about you, I'd just sit back and watch you crash and burn because we all know that's exactly what's about to happen if you don't get your crap together real soon."

Ironically, it was more painful to watch my family struggling to find a way to reach me than it was to actually be the reason they were struggling in the first place. Since I felt like everyone completely misunderstood everything about me, I didn't feel like I was the cause of any problems. I just felt like it was everybody else's fault for being too dumb to understand.

I found myself hating them more and more every time I was around them because I felt like they weren't supporting me in any way. No matter how much they told me they loved me, I didn't believe it. I felt like they wanted me to conform to their idea of *successful*, and it made me angry. I got sick of hearing about how lucky I was to have such a great job, such a nice house, and such a perfect wife. I didn't want to hear about how good I had it. I just wanted someone to actually support and encourage me in the one thing I wanted to do in life.

Poker.

Again, everything came back to poker, and nobody wanted anything to do with me as long as that was my focus. It was me against them, and I was determined to prove everybody wrong.

❧ ❧ ❧ ❧ ❧ ❧

By the time I was able to win consistently at the game that everyone else thought was pure gambling, I had long given up any kind of hope that my family would understand anything I was doing in life. I began looking for reasons to never speak to them again. One by one, I validated my opinions of them based on something that was usually related to finances. Either they didn't have enough money and were jealous of the fact that I could earn a living playing a game, or they had too much money and didn't agree with the idea that someone could earn a living outside of anything besides decades of hard work.

I genuinely didn't understand why anyone found it so hard to believe that poker was a reasonable career choice. It was weird to me because the same people who had supported and encouraged me as a musician were now telling me that it was foolish and downright irresponsible to leave a steady job to pursue a dream. I never understood why they promoted chasing some dreams but not others. On the rare occasion that it didn't make me angry, I was just totally confused about the whole situation. Candice, on the other hand, was the only one who actually believed I could play the game and win, but I was even skeptical of her. *Maybe she's for real, or maybe she's just saying what she thinks a good wife should say.* There was no way to really know.

Ultimately, Candice was the one person who supported me, yet she was the one person whose opinion affected me the least. It's embarrassing to admit that now, but it was the truth back then. In a perfect world, I would have understood exactly how much Candice really wanted me to pursue my dream and succeed, but I was so lost in the illusion that my family wanted me to remain miserable in my day job that I was never able to appreciate just how amazing my wife was during the worst days of our lives. In actuality, the only real stipulations that she had were things that we mutually agreed on: I wouldn't run up credit cards without paying them off every month, and under no circumstances was it okay for me to pay interest on anything. To me, that sounded simple enough, but as I soon found out, my ability to maintain my finances separately was just terrible.

From the day we got married, Candice had always managed our finances, and she was great with money. I simply gave her my paycheck and all was well, not because she asked or demanded it that way but because I just trusted her to be the responsible one in the family. However, when I started trying to manage my own money from poker on the side, I was clueless. Soon, I began to break our agreement and was charging up credit cards left and right. I also wasn't paying the balances in full each month, which meant I was paying interest. Still, where most wives would have come unglued and turned it into a fight, Candice put her thoughts to paper in a note that she left me before leaving for work one morning:

> *I think you have a problem. I'm not sure exactly what it is, whether it's playing, spending, or something else. I need you to fix it though before I go crazy as well. I slowly feel less and less close to you, and that makes me so sad. I love you very much. I don't feel a lot back from you though. I want you to win as badly as you want to if only just to fix this mess. I know you're good enough, too. I want to get on with our lives. Please help me to get us past this hurdle.*
>
> *I love you,*
> *Candice*

Any sane person would have read those words and known that it was time to face the issue and perhaps accept the fact that I was not only ruining my life but my wife's life as well. But with sanity becoming just another blip in my rearview mirror, my immediate emotion after reading her note was anger. *Playing is not the problem. Spending is not the problem. Nothing else that* I'm *doing is the problem. All I need is for people to just leave me alone and stop hounding me about every little mistake I make!*

I decided Candice had an ulterior motive and was ultimately lying to me to try and trick me into going back to work. I thought she was no different than anyone else in my family.

When I felt like I was alone and nobody was on my side, I decided to lash out and cause whatever amount of pain possible, partly because I was angry and partly because I wanted to be sure they got the point that I didn't want them in my life anymore. *If they refuse to see things my way, then what good are they to me?*

Nobody understood me, but it seemed like they weren't even trying. All they wanted was for me to conform to the same boring life that they had, and I hated it. I didn't want to do the things they were doing, and I didn't want to live the way they were living. Sure, I wanted to be successful and have a lot of money, but I didn't want to hoard it and keep it to myself forever. *What's the point of having money if all you ever do is save it?*

Money was only a tiny piece of the puzzle, though. What bothered me even more than the financial matters was the fact that I just felt completely abandoned. Even with Candice overtly stating that she supported me and believed in me, I felt like I was on my own, and the only thing I could think to do to offset that feeling of abandonment was to dish it right back to an even greater degree. By that point, I didn't even know who *they* were anymore. Somehow, *they* had just become a pronoun that described anyone who wasn't me. It was quite literally anyone who didn't pat me on the back and say, *Heck yeah, Clay. Just keep doing exactly what you're doing! You're awesome!*

I began to hatch a plan that I thought might, in some way, get back at my family. My mother had a certificate of deposit at my bank. It was in her name and mine, which meant I could claim it as my own if I wanted to. The money definitely wasn't mine, but the bank didn't know that. It wasn't millions of dollars or anything, but it was enough to raise eyebrows if it suddenly turned up missing.

I was still hung up on the whole *abandonment* thing with my family, but if I was going to prove to anyone that I didn't need my family, stealing that money from my mother seemed like a great place to start. Besides, she clearly didn't need that money since it was in a just-in-case savings account essentially earning nothing and not doing a single bit of good for anyone else in the world. I couldn't make up my mind though. I didn't know if I wanted to steal the money out of spite or if I just wanted to take it and spread it among people who needed it more. Either way, it didn't matter. I was set on taking that money, and I would figure out the rest as I went.

That was years before smartphones and daily online banking alerts, so I knew it would be a few weeks before my mother realized the money was gone. What I didn't know was that banks won't just let you pop in on them unexpectedly and withdraw $26,000 as if that's no big deal. After being told I would need to make an appointment to withdraw the entire amount in cash, I shrugged it off and said it wasn't that important. There were no red flags with the banker who helped me with that transaction because, on paper, it was just as much my money as it was my mother's. The CD had matured that day, but I declined to roll the money into a new savings account of any sort. I explained to him that I only needed a few thousand dollars that day and *sure, just go ahead and put the rest in my checking account, thanks.*

Soon, it began to weigh on me that I might have done something incredibly illegal, and I was scared to get in trouble. At that point, I was no longer worried about putting the hurt on my mother or anyone else in my family. All I wanted to do was avoid trouble, so I decided to just play it off as fraud when asked why all that money was transferred from the CD to my personal checking account. But it wouldn't make sense for someone to steal my identity only to transfer money into my account, so I felt like I had to go through with the plan and withdraw the money little by little over the course of a couple of weeks.

So that's exactly what I did.

With each visit to the bank to withdraw more money that wasn't mine, I became more detached from the mother it belonged to. I tried to envision all the ways she might react after finding out I stole her money, and my imagination ran wild. *She'll probably hate me and demand that I pay her back immediately even if it means I have to sell everything I own. I bet she thinks I stole it to gamble with, which means I'll get to hear another lecture about how I'm a gambling addict.*

I began to react to the things I thought my mother might do or say. I was so far gone by that point that I was actually having arguments in my head, except I was speaking for both my mother and myself. It was insane, but at the conclusion of it all, I didn't regret stealing her money because of all the things I'd pretended she might say to me.

As for the cash itself, I used it as best as I could. I helped a friend in need, a family in need, a stranger in need…anyone I thought was worthy based on the simple fact that they were in need. I loved helping people whom I felt deserved it even if it was with money that wasn't mine. Several weeks went by before I heard anything from my mother or the bank about the money being gone, and I wondered if it had somehow slipped through the cracks.

Then Candice called.

Then my mom called.

Then the bank called.

I was at the Horseshoe in Louisiana, of course, so I was preoccupied and not the least bit concerned about whatever issue they seemed to be having. After all, I never handled the finances, so I shrugged off the idea that any money had been transferred or withdrawn. But by the time I returned home a few days later, everyone had a pretty good idea of what had happened. My fear of getting into trouble had returned, and I didn't know what to do. I wasn't sure if I'd actually broken any laws, so I felt like my best course of action was to just try to lie my way out of it.

Initially, I denied everything. I feigned ignorance and suggested that someone must have stolen my identity. I even went so far as to go down to my bank and fill out the necessary affidavits for the police report that would soon be filed. To everyone but me, it seemed like an obvious case of identity theft, but the banks had cameras so they would surely catch the person who did this.

From the surveillance footage, it was clear to anyone with half a brain that I was definitely the person responsible for taking the money, and the investigation came to an end immediately. Since my name was on the account, I hadn't committed a crime. Sure, I had lied on the affidavit, but the police didn't pursue anything with that. As far as they were concerned, case closed. The bank also didn't have any interest once they realized it was a family matter.

That evening, my mother and father—who had been divorced for over 15 years at that point—showed up at my house with Candice. I didn't know the bank had pulled pictures from the video, and I definitely didn't know that everyone knew beyond a shadow of a doubt that I had stolen all of that money. What I did know, however, was that it was definitely a bad thing any time my actual parents were in the same house at the same time. It usually meant someone had died, but I knew better. I could tell by the way they walked into my house and looked at me that it was over and that there was no more lying about what I had done.

I didn't even bother trying to explain anything. I just denied everything and put up the necessary walls to prevent any real dialogue with the people who loved me the most. It was a pitiful display of behavior on my part, and everyone reacted accordingly. Nobody said much, and it was a somber moment that was only made worse by the fact that nobody said anything other than how much they loved me and everything was going to be okay.

I couldn't deal with that.

I would have preferred being called a loser because at least I could have argued or fought with that. I didn't want anyone to love me right then, and I sure didn't want them to pretend like this was just some simple little thing that was wrong with me.

With the four of us sitting quietly in my living room, the familiar sound of silence returned. My dad had turned off the TV when they first got there, so all I could hear was the ringing in my ears, and I hated it. I didn't want to sit in silence, and I definitely didn't want to be in the same room with my mom and my dad and my wife—the three people who loved me more than the rest of the world combined.

I found a spot in the carpet to stare at because I didn't have the courage to face any of them. I didn't even know why I was so sad. *It's just money. Big deal! Who cares?* The air was too thick to breathe, and I wanted to leave the room. When I heard my mom sniffle, that was all the influence I needed to find a different place in the house to sit alone, so I went to the computer room and sat at my chair, looked at the screen, and ignored my dad as he followed me without saying anything. He hugged me where I sat and told me everything was going to be okay. I hated him for that because *no the hell it won't be okay. How can you say that?*

I ignored my dad's hug and stared at the blank computer screen in front of me. My mom was sobbing in the other room, and I just assumed Candice was doing the same. I really didn't know, and I really didn't care. I just wanted to be somewhere else.

Anywhere else.

I would have been perfectly okay dying right then and there if it meant never having to deal with those people again. What little bit of hope I might have ever had of getting them to understand anything about me absolutely vanished the second they saw those photos of me at the bank stealing from my own mother. But they weren't even concerned about the money, and all of my lies weren't the main problem either. All they cared about was finding out what was going on with me to cause such cruel behavior. I was sick, and they knew I needed help.

When I was a child, my dad did little more than spank me into submission when I did something bad. And my mother was on the complete opposite end of the spectrum; all she wanted to do was love me to death. Nobody had ever found out the motivations behind my behavior. They had never understood exactly what caused me to behave the way that I behaved.

That was a bad day, and I didn't want to have the kind of dialogue they were wanting. I just wanted them to leave. I wanted them out of my house, and I never wanted to see them again.

I missed a great opportunity in that moment to witness just how much my family truly loved me. At my lowest points, they weren't angry or upset with what I did. They just wanted to know how they could help. It wasn't about the money. It wasn't about the lies.

All that mattered to them was my well-being.

❧ ❧ ❧ ❧ ❧ ❧

At the time, the main thing I learned from that whole experience was how terrible bank surveillance was. It was fairly clear to anyone who knew me that the man in those photos was definitely Clay Tumey, but to a random observer, I really didn't think they would've been able to make the connection. Once I got past the initial embarrassment of being caught lying to my mom about taking her money, my mind gravitated toward this realization that bank cameras were actually quite bad.

If that's the best they have, I thought to myself, *then I can't imagine how in the world they would ever catch a bank robber.*

For kicks, I got online and searched bank robbery stats and found that roughly half of them were solved.

Only half!

So the obvious revelation there was that roughly half of them *weren't* solved, and that totally fascinated me. It boggled my mind that getting away with robbing a bank in America was merely a coin flip from a statistical standpoint. It didn't make sense, but it was right there on the screen in front of me. Furthermore, my nation averaged 20 bank robberies per day, which I reduced into another statistic; over 10 bank robberies per day went unsolved every day in America.

Some people got away, and some people didn't get away.

I wanted to know why.

BANK ROBBERY 101

Failure is more informative than success. Watch just a few minutes of any postgame sports program, and you will quickly see that most of the commentary revolves around the mistakes of the losing team. Talk to a chemist with newly singed eyebrows, and you will likely hear very little about what went well during the experiment that—quite literally—blew up in their face. With everything from sports to chemistry experiments, the path to success is usually paved with failure.

Typically, I favor trial and error, and failure is even comfortable territory for me because there really is no pure failure if the lessons learned are applied to future success. However, with something like bank robbery, you might not get a second chance if you fail miserably enough on your first try. For that reason, I was not interested in testing the waters with my own life. Imagine the terror of knowing how bad things could get during a bank robbery if even the smallest detail went differently than expected. So I decided to do as much research as possible and essentially allow other people to be my guinea pigs.

I wasn't quite sure what I ultimately wanted from the criminal behavior that I was considering, but I definitely planned to do everything in my power to avoid being caught. In the six months or so prior to my first robbery, I devoted a great amount of time to the research of statistics, reports, and basically anything else that I could find on the Internet that might give me insight into my crime of choice.

Early on, I learned that approximately half of them were eventually solved. At a glance, it appeared—at least in a mathematical sense—the chance of getting away with bank robbery was about the same chance as winning a coin flip. That stat was more enticing than it was intimidating.

Blessed—or perhaps cursed—with an infinite curiosity, I always wanted to know more. There was a reason why some crooks got away while others did not, and that reason is exactly what I wanted to discover. I found it most logical to work backwards with cases where people got caught in the act or shortly thereafter. I had no interest in looking into successful bank robberies because I didn't feel that there was anything to learn from them. Reports about successful bank robberies produced a mixture of theories and partial facts, so there seemed to be little benefit in analyzing those cases. So I wanted to look into the endless amount of robberies that were unsuccessful because those suspects were caught and their failures were revealed. As the old saying goes, *you can learn a lot from a dummy.*

⁂ ⁂ ⁂ ⁂ ⁂ ⁂

Sitting with the Internet at my fingertips, I typed "bank robbery" into a popular search engine and began my journey. I was amazed to see the number of results my search returned. Bank robbers were not just a figment of Hollywood. They were very real and very active. That year alone, there were nearly 7,000 bank robberies in America. With such a vast quantity of reports to pore over, it was heaven for the inquiring mind.

Without really knowing what to look for, the first search result seemed like the reasonable place to start. It was a news story about a young man in Missouri who had robbed a bank on the way to his high school prom. He was an otherwise good kid who had no previous behavioral problems, much less a criminal history. But with the high costs of renting a tuxedo and a limousine—not to mention the potential cost of underwhelming his date—he decided that robbing a bank would give him the kind of cash to make his prom memorable.

He was right.

When the limo showed up at his house, he informed the driver that he needed to stop by the bank to get some cash before they went to pick up the girlfriend. After a few moments inside his bank, he returned to the limo, and off they went.

After a long night of chauffeuring over-dressed high school students around town, Carl the Limo Driver was relaxing on his couch at home while watching the *previously recorded* broadcast of the local nightly news. Sitting on his couch at about two o'clock in the morning, just as he was about to take a bite of his extremely late dinner, Carl looked up at his television to see a story on the news involving a limousine. The TV was muted, so he didn't know what the story was about, but he thought the limousine being shown on screen sure looked an awful lot like his. For a moment, he was distracted from the actual news story because he was too busy gazing at the familiar limo. He nearly missed the caption across the bottom of the screen giving the name of the bank that had been robbed earlier that day. Turning up the volume on the television, Carl the Limo Driver learned that the robber had done a good job of hiding his face, and there were no helpful tips from witnesses inside the bank except to say that the well-dressed young man fled the scene in a black limousine—Carl's black limousine! Suffice it to say that Carl the Limo Driver definitely called the police and told them everything he knew, including the identity and address of the young man whom police had nicknamed the Prom Bandit.

When I finished laughing at the thought of someone robbing a bank in a tuxedo and getting away in a limo, I tried to piece together what had gone wrong for the kid. Granted, he was probably doomed from the beginning, but the way he was caught was still worth looking at. Even though he was caught the following day, there was something to be said about the fact that no witnesses could give a helpful description of him, but I focused on his rookie mistakes.

First of all, I thought, *don't rob a bank on the way to prom.* It's just a hilariously bad idea to rob a bank while wearing a tuxedo and hopping into a super-stretched getaway car. Even if you don't get a lot of money, you'll definitely end up on the evening news because that is the kind of entertaining story people will glom onto. The media is often not interested in helping anyone solve crime. They just want a good story. Therefore, in contemplating how to successfully rob a bank, the first thing I decided was that I needed to be boring, normal, and unmemorable. Even if I were to get $15,000 in a robbery—more than triple the national average in 2006—I imagined a news reporter somewhere saying, "Big deal. He stole money from a bank. There is nothing else about this story that will interest our viewers."

❧ ❧ ❧ ❧ ❧ ❧

When I was a student, I took every shortcut imaginable. I never did the big research projects in high school that were required to pass English class as a junior and again as a senior. Fortunately, my older brother kept his own research projects, and I simply rewrote them in my own handwriting and turned them in as mine. That was the only reason I passed those two English classes.

However, as an adult in my mid-20s, I was now compiling the biggest research project of my life. After hours of assimilating every last detail from the reports covering the Prom Bandit, I had compiled extensive—although mostly mental—notes of things to never do in a bank robbery. That young man's errors were permanently etched into my mind, and I appreciated him for having no plan and ultimately being such a wonderful example of how to fail. This was just one example though. I needed more.

Returning to the initial search results online, I found a story of a woman whose case simply fascinated me. Her robberies flew under the public radar for an extended time because she was discreet, calm, and polite. Nothing she did was flashy, and nobody in her personal life ever suspected that she was robbing banks. She eventually got away with over 20 robberies, but much like the Prom Bandit, her errors led to her capture.

Something to understand about federal authorities is that they work completely differently than local police. If a police officer sees you doing something you shouldn't be doing, he immediately moves into action. As children, most of us are taught to not be tattle tales, but police officers are professional tattle tales. They blast their sirens, flash their lights, and swirl their authority around you like a tornado if they even think you are doing something wrong. Your case will go before a grand jury, and they will decide whether or not there is sufficient evidence to move forward with a trial. Federal authorities, on the other hand, are much more subtle in their approach. They are ambush predators who lie in wait, watching your every move while waiting for the perfect opportunity to make theirs. If you are a suspect in a federal case, you will likely be under investigation for a year or longer before you even know about it. This is why federal cases have such an amazingly high conviction rate, somewhere in the 90% range.

The Soccer Mom Bandit caught the attention of federal authorities after they noticed a pattern in a number of local bank robberies. In the span of about nine months, over 20 banks had been robbed, and they were all carried out by a woman in her mid-30s. Oddly, they were each conducted at or near 3:30 p.m.

Authorities assumed that the suspect simply preferred waiting until the end of the business day. With most banks closing at 4:30 p.m., they reasoned that this particular robber might have thought bank tellers would have more cash in their drawers as the day came to an end.

Aside from a vague physical description, the only thing they knew about the woman was that she drove a minivan, hence her nickname. As it turns out, the Soccer Mom Bandit was indeed a mother, and there was definitely a reason she only robbed banks at or around 3:30 p.m. She was a full-time mother who also kept two neighborhood kids after school for extra money. She put a good deal of thought into the most effective way to get away with robbing banks, and she learned what was required to inconspicuously rob a bank and get away. In the unlikely event that she ever became a suspect, she had a wonderful alibi in being an after school caregiver to a house full of children. After all, who could rob a bank while baby sitting a bunch of kids?

The Soccer Mom Bandit failed to understand that nobody knows when they are a target of a federal investigation until it is nearly over. Law enforcement officials somehow learned her identity through means that were never made clear in any report, but because of the unlikelihood that this busy homemaker was a bank robber, authorities passed on directly contacting her and asking about any potential involvement in the series of obviously connected robberies. Instead, they just watched her. Every day around 3:00 p.m., one of a handful of agents parked at her children's school, blending into a sea of cars full of parents waiting to pick up their own children after school. For weeks, various agents followed the woman as she picked up the kids from school and took them home. Every day, like clockwork, she drove the same route from the school to her house. It was a boring task for the agents and it wasn't time consuming, but it was definitely worth it.

Their patience paid off on a day when she turned left instead of right and headed to the city instead of going home. The agent following her that day felt this could very likely be their break in the case, and he went to great lengths to avoid detection. He called his partner back at the office and alerted him of the potential for an event. When the second agent was in the vicinity of his partner and the woman, the two collaborated and took turns following the woman in case she was paying close attention to her rearview mirror as she pulled into the parking lot of a bank and parked. Her children were old enough to prefer waiting in the car while Mom went inside, so she walked alone into the bank.

Moments later, she exited the bank as calmly as she had entered. The heist occurred in less than two minutes, and with the agents being able to confirm via cell phone that the bank had just been robbed, the identity of the Soccer Mom Bandit was no longer a mystery. But the agents never got out of their vehicles. They simply matched her composure and casual driving style as they followed her home undetected.

Right turn signal. Complete stop. Right turn. Speed limit. Nothing out of the ordinary.

Still communicating by phone and planning their next move with local police, the agents took a rather interesting approach and allowed Mom to get all the way home so the kids could go inside and play without realizing that the nicely-dressed men at the front door were there to take their mother away for the rest of their childhood.

Though I was reading about a woman that I had never met and would never know, I couldn't help but feel an emotional pain for her and her children. I felt no disdain for the agents who were merely doing their job, but by the time I finished reading about the Soccer Mom Bandit, I was distraught. I had yet to become a father myself, but it was depressing to consider the possibility of having those same nicely-dressed men separate me from my mother when I was a child.

Perhaps a healthier person would have been affected differently by that sadness, but it ultimately had no impact on my plans. The risk of prison might intimidate most, but it only motivated me. I felt like the stakes had been raised, and that excited me.

Having a better understanding of the opposition, a few more things became clear. The errors in the first case were easy to avoid, but the case of the bank-robbing mother was far more complex. It bothered me that it was never revealed where the original tip came from that put the authorities on her trail to begin with. It was a variable that I could not address in my own preparation, and my imagination ran wild with possibilities.

Did her husband somehow find out and tell on her? Did a well-placed surveillance camera somehow capture her license plate? How did they receive a tip so accurate yet so vague that they could only stalk her?

Immediately, it was clear that her first mistake was executing bank robberies in such a small radius. Because of her role as a housewife, she didn't have the geographical range of freedom to rob banks in other states.

Then it hit me, a tiny sliver of an epiphany. As simple as it might seem, these first two cases had something in common. Geography played a key role in both investigations. Carl the Limo Driver would have never seen that news story if it were on another station in another town. With that conclusion, I decided that I should never rob a bank in a town where people might recognize me if I ended up on the evening news. Likewise, if I planned to do multiple banks, then they needed to be separated by enough distance that nobody would connect them as a series.

For the most part, bank robbers were caught because of some minor detail that they didn't think about in advance. After obsessing over those details for several months, I felt like I knew all the things to never do during a robbery. Once I felt like I knew all the pitfalls to avoid, I started thinking of a plan to implement during my own crimes.

Growing up, one of my relatives was a bank teller, and I'd overheard more than once that bank employees are instructed to comply with anyone attempting to rob a bank. With the exception of any demands that might injure or kill, a teller is taught to simply give up the money and allow the criminal to leave. This not only bodes well for the sake of safety, but it also reduces any chance that a traumatic event will take place with the customers who are unfortunate enough to be in the bank when it is robbed. As a general idea, the amount of money a bank loses during a robbery is miniscule compared to the potential nonmonetary damage a bank robber can cause.

After months of reading about modern bank robberies on the Internet, I also learned that many of them were note-only robberies. It took me a while to realize exactly what the term *note-only* even meant.

A note!

In other words, a thief could literally write demands on a piece of paper and simply hand it to the bank teller. With standard procedures being what they were, those tellers would actually comply and hand over the money. It seemed odd, but if banks truly taught their employees to do as they were told, then a threat of violence was simply irrelevant in order to rob the bank. One could simply rob a bank with a sticky note and never so much as mutter a single word.

Without using guns or bombs or missile-launching drones, the potential for extreme danger and excitement was diminished. My fantasies shifted to those of a stealthy nature, and those suited my personality much better anyway. I've never been one to really bulldoze my way through a situation, and I was much more comfortable thinking of ways to rob a bank without anyone but the teller knowing. The note-only approach was absolutely the method for me.

FIRST TIME FOR EVERYTHING

At home, things were getting worse. My marriage wasn't magically improving, and I was miserable with practically every facet of my life. I felt like my family hated me, and I didn't particularly want anything to do with them either. My job was monotonous, and it was only made worse by the possibility that I might bump into one of my parents because we all worked under the same roof. Granted, it was a big building, but it was certainly not uncommon for me to see either of them on a daily basis.

A week before Christmas in 2005, I had an especially long weekend. Things had gone well during my most recent trip to the Horseshoe, and I was ready to finally quit my day job to pursue life as a fulltime poker player. By then, it was completely useless to try to convince anyone that I wasn't ruining my life, so I didn't try. I dreaded returning to work the following Monday morning, so I spent the entire weekend trying to think of a last ditch effort to get my wife and parents on my side. In fairness, they were 100 percent on my side, but I couldn't see it. I was too busy self-destructing, so I was completely blind to the fact that they were simply trying to save me from myself. My distorted perspective led me to believe everyone was against me.

When my alarm clock sounded that Monday morning, I was already awake because I had never gone to sleep the previous night. Instead, I lay in bed all night with a dread so powerful that I could barely move. It wasn't mild anxiety or a *case of the Mondays*. It was complete, absolute terror. To this day, I cannot explain what I felt that morning, but I knew bad things would happen if I didn't just stay home. The thought of walking into work and blowing the whole place up was appealing to me. My co-workers were good people and completely undeserving of a massacre, so it wasn't that I had a personal vendetta against them as a whole or even individually. I'd just gotten to a place where my pain was so great that I felt like I could only feel better by making others hurt more than I was hurting. Fortunately, I mainly just wanted to sink farther into my bed instead of exerting the energy to actually get dressed, drive 45 minutes to work, and kill a few hundred people.

But I wasn't lazy. I was just unable to move.

Incapable of even calling into work for myself, Candice did so for me. She didn't ask many questions, and even after all I'd put her through to that point, she was still willing to do whatever necessary to help me. It wasn't clear to me if she was being indifferent or simply doing a great job of hiding her emotions. Either way, she didn't stay around long that morning after calling into my work to let them know that I would not be there that day.

I was in great standing with my boss, and I had plenty of sick days. It was a great job after all, and they just wanted me to get well soon. They didn't press for details about why I couldn't come in that day.

...or the next day.

...or the day after that.

Each day was worse than the last, and by the end of the week, I'd missed five days of work without even attempting to explain to anyone what was happening. I didn't talk to anyone, and nothing else existed outside my bedroom door as far as I was concerned. With the exception of a few seconds here and there to stumble into the kitchen or restroom, I didn't leave my bed for a week. By the time the weekend rolled around, I was so lost in my own dive that I found myself wondering exactly why I was so depressed in the first place.

It was a strange feeling noticing myself judging myself. I was losing my mind but well aware of it at the same time, and that just seemed to make all the sense in the world.

It wasn't immediately clear to anyone that I had no plans to ever return to work. My wife didn't have much to say on the matter, and my mother mainly just wanted me to get in touch with the human resources department so I could be put on medical leave and not risk losing my job.

I was saved the following week because the company was closed for the holidays. My employer shut down from Christmas Eve until the first workday of the New Year, so I had an extra week to work on my excuse before I returned to work, but since I had missed more than three days, they required a doctor's note clearing me to return.

Since I hadn't been sick in the kind of way that doctors write notes about, I really didn't know what to do. *I was going to kill everybody* is a great reason to miss work, but it's definitely not something you want to share with your employer. With my parents working in management for the same company where I was employed, they were well aware of my options. My mother helped me get in touch with the right person at the corporate office in San Diego so that I could find a therapist and hopefully get my head back on straight.

I think it's too easy to say that I had a chemical imbalance. I prefer to accept the fact that I just failed to manage myself or my decisions properly. Nevertheless, I went on medical leave from work and sought therapy.

My therapist was quite amiable and so easy to talk to. Everything about her office—which was inside of a beautiful home out in the country—was welcoming, and it was the perfect environment for me to get comfortable and share all of life's big dilemmas with a nice old lady who somehow felt more like a grandmother than a therapist.

During my initial visit, I gave detailed accounts of my childhood, adolescence, and early adulthood as she constructed my family tree on a giant poster board that was resting on an easel in the corner of her office. I found a certain freedom in paying her to listen to me because she was so pleasant and peaceful. Her office was actually just another room in her house, but it was a nice house. As a child, I might have even called it a mansion. *She must be one heck of a therapist.*

My favorite part about going to the therapist was the part where I spoke about myself the whole time. I wasn't particularly interested in anything she had to say because I felt like she was merely applying the broad strokes of education to my very specific and individual life, and that somehow insulted me. My ego was out of control because it was completely in control. *What class could she have possibly taken at any point in her life that might explain who I am?*

I benefited very little from those appointments, but that was definitely my fault. I only went because of my obligation rather than some distant hope that someone might magically figure me out. Besides, nothing was greater than my need to never be figured out in the first place. Whether ironic or idiotic, that was the truth. I found comfort in being the only one to really understand Clay Tumey.

I never did return to work, and I gave up on therapy shortly thereafter as well. I did odd things here and there for money, but I wasn't responsible with the little bit of money I did earn, and things were falling apart around me. I lived in my dream house and drove my dream truck, but my dreams weren't much of a reality.

Shortly after the New Year, Candice found out she was pregnant, but I was not ready to be a father. I was still a child myself. I'd always dreamed of life as a father because I was convinced that I would be the best dad a kid could ever hope for. But by that point, it was painfully clear to me that I had no business raising a child.

❧ ❧ ❧ ❧ ❧ ❧

I spent the first few months of 2006 ignoring everything that mattered by returning to the one thing that excited me. I still wanted to rob a bank, and after five months of preparing myself and studying, I was ready to find out if I had what it took to pull it off. I wasn't overly concerned with the details of the robbery itself because I'd spent more than enough time in front of my computer screen learning exactly what to never do while robbing a bank.

The decision to rob a bank that particular day was rather spontaneous, so it wasn't like I went to sleep thinking about it the night before. I didn't have any Wild West bank robbery dreams or anything like that either. I simply woke up that morning and decided *I guess today is the day.*

Getting ready to rob a bank was no different than any other errand I might have been running that day. I took a shower, brushed my teeth, and dressed no differently than if I had been an actual customer going to the bank. Nothing was out of the ordinary until I got in my truck and backed out of my driveway. That's when the weight of it all hit me. *I'm finally going to do this!*

On the way to the bank, my nerves were completely out of control. I had random outbursts of laughter when my brain would experience emotions without knowing how to properly release them. Nothing was funny but apparently it was hilarious.

I'd done my homework. I knew what to do. I knew what to avoid. *Give them the note, take the money, and get away before the cops show up.* Simple enough, right? Absolutely!

I found a parking spot that was out of view from the bank yet still within a reasonable walking distance. It was crucial that nobody from the bank would be able to watch and see what kind of vehicle I got into after the robbery. Just as crucial, however, was the need to be in my truck and gone by the time all the guns and handcuffs showed up.

Even after finding the perfect parking spot, I was still nervous. I turned off my truck's engine. I looked to the left and to the right and again to the left and back to the right. My head was on a swivel like a giant child belligerently answering "NO" and I was scared it might twist off altogether. *Okay I definitely need my head to rob a bank.* That was hilarious as well, so I started laughing again.

I was paranoid and convinced someone was watching me and knew my every thought.

I was beyond scared, and I almost liked it. But I also knew it wouldn't serve me well to have a racing heart rate if something went wrong during the robbery. If something happened and I needed to rely on the speed and precision of a perfectly operating brain, I needed the rest of my organs to be under control as well.

Sitting in my truck, I tried to remember all of the things that should have been second nature by that point. *It's not like I just woke up this morning and decided to go rob a bank. I've been thinking on this—no,* obsessing *over this—for longer than five months. This is ridiculous!*

Of all the things that I had planned for, my own anxiety was not one of them. And I didn't know how to control it. Feeling like I had no other option, I put the key back into the ignition, started my truck, and drove back home.

No robbery. No money. No thrill.

Nothing but disappointment.

I promised myself I would try again one day, but if I couldn't calm myself on a second try, I would take that as a hint and just give up the whole idea forever.

❧ ❧ ❧ ❧ ❧ ❧

The next day was just another day in April when I stopped by the bank to get some cash. Steering into the parking lot, I found a spot and pulled in. I've never been one to pass on a good opportunity to just sit and enjoy a quiet moment alone, so I turned off my truck and enjoyed a deafening silence. I've since learned that I suffer from tinnitus—the perception of a constant, high-pitched ringing in my left ear when no external sound is present—but in 2006, I was not aware of such a condition. I simply thought silence had its own sound.

Sitting in my truck, I looked around the bank parking lot and appreciated its normalcy. In the distance, I could see a five-way intersection, and I marveled that science allowed people to trust traffic signals. At a red light, one must simply sit and wait for the appropriate command. Much like well-trained dogs, motorists are happiest when properly trained.

As a child, I was drawn to anything that could be analyzed or fantasized. In that moment, I was lost in the daydream of those traffic lights at the five-way intersection in the distance remaining red. A child with a morbid curiosity might yearn for the chaos resulting from all of the traffic lights simultaneously turning green and causing everyone to crash into one another, but that was too plain for my imagination. There was nothing spectacular to me about a bunch of people dying, but *if the lights all remained red, what would happen? What would those people do? How long would they blindly submit to that kind of idiocy before realizing they were being held captive by a primary color? At what point would the well-trained dogs think for themselves?*

At some point, the Texas heat politely reminded me that I was daydreaming. There I was, sitting in a parked truck for several minutes with no air conditioner running. It was hot, and I needed to move forward with my day.

In my truck, I was parked facing the bank. I looked through the windshield and laughed at the ironic name of the bank I was about to walk into. I wondered if it was an invitation or a threat. *Do they really Chase people?* I grabbed my envelope and exited my truck before heading across the parking lot toward the bank.

Walking up the front steps of Chase Bank, I cringed at my own stupidity. *Do they really Chase people?* It was reminiscent of all the times I would find myself giggling while walking into the principal's office. At a time when most people might be scared out of their mind, I found something to laugh at.

As I approached the front door, a man walked out and paused to hold the door open for me. I said thanks and hesitated to see if anyone was chasing him. I laughed again—internally, of course—and continued into the bank lobby.

Walking into a place that I had visited several times in my life, nothing felt out of the ordinary. A relative of mine had worked at this particular location for most of my childhood, so the building itself was familiar, but I was in my mid-twenties by then and I didn't see any familiar faces. The receptionist at the front desk offered a pleasant greeting, which I returned with a smile and a nod without breaking stride toward the short line of people waiting to see the next available teller.

It was the middle of the afternoon, and business was slow. It wasn't long before a teller called for me. "Sir, I can help you over here."

I bet you can't, I thought to myself.

After a few brief steps, I was standing before a friendly, approachable lady asking how I was doing today. I was doing fine, in fact. How was she? She was great and thanks for asking. How could she help me today? I needed to make a withdrawal, of course.

Earlier, in my truck, while pondering the potential madness of malfunctioning traffic signals, I was also filling out my withdrawal slip. It was no ordinary withdrawal slip, though. It was a simple blank envelope with three, succinctly written instructions on the face of it:

1) Put all $50s and $100s in this envelope.
2) I won't hurt you.
3) Do NOT look at me.

After handing the envelope to the teller, I paid close attention to everything she did. I didn't stare for the sake of intimidation. I just want to maintain absolute focus. I was looking for any sign that things might go awry. I was well prepared for just about any plausible scenario that might present itself, but I will admit that I was a little on edge during the few seconds it took her to read my carefully scripted words on that envelope.

She seemed frozen in time for a moment. I felt like I was watching a woman who wasn't sure whether or not she was being pranked. Without moving, she looked up at me with the quick glance of a seasoned poker pro trying to get a read on an opponent who had just moved all of their chips to the center of the table. I offered a subtle nod to confirm that this was definitely not a bluff.

She moved as though underwater—not with fear, but with a fluid consistency that went for accuracy in place of urgency. The panic button adjacent to her cash drawer was out of plain view from where I stood, but sleight of hand was not her forte, so this teller's ability to hide her hand's slight movement to the right was anything but hidden. I knew she was pushing the button, but that didn't matter because I also knew the math involved. I'd be long gone by the time anyone important might show up.

As she returned the envelope to me, I gave another slight nod before turning to leave.

Walking back through the lobby on my way out, I passed the same nice lady at the receptionist desk and she thoughtlessly wished me a great day. I smiled and wished her the same as I kept walking.

Out the front door.

Down the front steps.

Across the parking lot.

Into my truck.

Gone.

THE SHIFT

Hyperbole is what I consider to be the first big word I ever learned. Without remembering a single thing about the context of the lesson or anything else about that day in second grade, I clearly remember Mrs. Duncan teaching us the proper pronunciation, spelling, and definition of the word *hyperbole.* But I didn't know what a *non sequitur* was until I was nearly 30 years old.

That first bank robbery was undeniably one of the craziest, most memorable things I've ever done. Everything went perfectly, just as I'd planned it. I stood in line like a regular person, did my business like a regular person, and walked out the front door like a regular person. Nobody but the teller knew the truth about my visit. I didn't even hyperventilate or lose control of my senses.

As I left the parking lot of the bank, I didn't do anything crazy. For the first time in probably forever, I actually obeyed all traffic laws, and I sure as heck didn't speed. The drive home was about 45 minutes, and I needed to execute it with perfection.

Almost immediately, I reached in the envelope to be sure I was only carrying cash rather than any sort of dye pack or tracking devices. I was convinced that my *$50s and $100s* idea would relieve me of any real concern about anything other than money going into the envelope. From everything I could find online, most, if not all, of the bait money was in packs of $20 bills. That could have been a complete myth, and it's not like I could verify it, but that seemed most logical, and I trusted my instinct.

Grabbing a handful of money from the envelope as I drove down the road, it was definitely only $50s and $100s, and it totaled just under $3,000. I let out the loudest celebratory exclamations you could imagine and continued the celebration with a series of fist pumps and high-fives with my steering wheel. The money itself was secondary, but it was proof that I had actually just robbed a bank. *Speaking of proof, I need to get rid of this envelope!*

I had chosen to use an envelope rather than a normal piece of paper because I wanted to be sure the teller didn't keep the note. In the unlikely event that there was a miscommunication of some sort—or even if the teller just wanted to try and be slick by keeping the note—I wanted a foolproof way to be sure and never leave any evidence behind. But in keeping that piece of evidence myself, I also needed to get rid of it immediately following my crime just to be safe. As I drove, I tore the envelope into tiny little pieces and threw consequent confetti out the window as I drove 65 miles per hour down the highway back home. It would take a miracle for anyone to piece those together, and I was free and clear of any evidence except for the cash itself.

Without being completely sure what to expect in terms of money, I was both relieved and horrified at the relatively small amount of money I'd stolen. On one hand, the amount alone wasn't enough to land me on the news. That was the upside. Dallas is a big market, and there are better things to talk about than a major corporate bank giving a few thousand bucks to a criminal. On the other hand, I was risking my freedom for the thrill alone since the amount of money I'd stolen wasn't exactly going to win any bragging contests any time soon.

My drive home was without incident, and I was happy to see that there was no *Breaking News* on the TV. Sitting in my house, I was alone again with my thoughts, and I couldn't have been more pleased with the day's events. No matter how bad life got, I at least had this one thing that I could hold onto and keep to myself forever. And if I wanted to duplicate the rush, there were countless banks in the world just waiting to provide me with the same experience again and again.

And that's exactly what happened.

Again and again.

⁂ ⁂ ⁂ ⁂ ⁂ ⁂

In my normal life—the one where I was married and had a child on the way—things just weren't improving. I wasn't connecting with the responsibility of being a father, and I mainly wanted Candice to disappear and raise the baby on her own. It seemed clear to me that she was more than ready to raise a child, and it felt wrong knowing that I was only going to mess everything up. I had told her more than a few times that I didn't want to be together, but she held out hope for us. I would pop in and out for a few days or even weeks, but when I left, there was really no way for her to know when I might come back, if ever. Returning from one of my random trips to nowhere, I found this note on my computer screen:

> *I think you leaving when I asked you not to was very inconsiderate of the way I feel. It really hurt my feelings. I get that you didn't understand my reasoning but that doesn't matter. It doesn't matter if you think my reasons are stupid or invalid. You should have respected them anyway. It made me feel very unimportant to you. I'm writing all this because it's bothering me. If I tell you in person,*

you'll say I'm being ridiculous instead of just trying to understand where I'm coming from.

You really let me down. I know you didn't think it was a big deal but I did. I tried to tell you that and you left anyway. Going and doing what you wanted to do was more important than the way I felt. That means we have some major problems in our relationship. I'm scared of that. I don't want our lives to be like this. Please, please help me change it.

I want to make it very clear how upset this made me so there is no confusion in the future. Please talk to me about this. I don't understand why you had to go so badly that it was worth all this.

I love you,
Your sad wife

Our situation at home was tense, but Candice always made it clear that she wanted to work things out together. The fact that we were having a baby together definitely seemed to make the situation sadder.

There was a point where I was considering not even being there when the baby was born. I was completely disconnected, and I just didn't feel like that was something I wanted to experience. Thankfully, Candice spoke to my greater sense and all but begged me to be there when our son, Jett, was finally born in October 2006.

Candice was right when she told me that I would regret it if I missed the birth of our child. Maybe that's a normal thing for most people to know, but I certainly didn't believe she knew what she was talking about. It was just one of those things that I didn't have the energy to fight. But seeing my son come into the world was a life-changing experience that I'll never forget.

He was enormous—10 pounds, 7 ounces—and my typical male brain obviously took credit for that. Never mind the fact that he'd grown for nine months inside my wife, I somehow decided that my manliness caused him to be so big. True to form, I was bringing my pride straight into fatherhood.

Something changed when I became a dad. I don't know what it was, and I'm not sure why it happened, but no matter how useless I felt as a person by that point, I was totally drawn to my son's needs. As any father knows, a newborn baby needs his mother much differently than he needs his father, but I was convinced that my role as a father was crucial from the second Jett was born.

I wish I could say that was enough to snap me out of my crazy thinking, but it wasn't. With my new title of Daddy also came the pressure of showing the world that I could take care of Jett and Candice, but I simply couldn't. I wasn't working, and the money I was making playing poker felt contaminated because of how much everyone despised what I was doing. It felt so dirty knowing that people considered me *just a gambling addict,* but the worst part was not being able to prove them wrong. Nothing I did or said mattered to anyone. Unless I was working at a normal job, it wasn't acceptable.

A couple weeks after Jett was born, I left again. I went to Oklahoma to stay with a friend and to play at a local casino where the poker regulars were said to be even worse than the ones at the Horseshoe in Louisiana. After a few days, I came back home and tried to be a dad, but I was terrible. I didn't know what to do, and I didn't feel like my son wanted anything to do with me. In the short time that I was gone, it seemed like Candice and Jett had bonded for years. I felt like a total stranger in my own home with the person who knew me best and the tiny human we had made together.

Misery.

I went back to Oklahoma soon after and stayed a few days longer. For the first month or so of Jett's life, I would randomly disappear and randomly show back up. Sometimes I left a note; sometimes I didn't.

❧ ❧ ❧ ❧ ❧ ❧

In the months before Jett was born, my mother gave me perfect advice, and I ignored it. She told me, "Son, you have to understand something—and I'm telling you this from a mother's point of view here so listen and listen close—but when that little baby gets here, Candice is not going to waste her time with you. You're either in or you're out. She's gonna do whatever she needs to do to make sure her baby is taken care of."

Since the day we had started dating, Candice had treated me the way most men only dream of. I never once doubted that I was everything she'd ever wanted, even though I knew I probably wasn't. The list of people whom I ever believed truly loved me unconditionally was short, but Candice was on that list. I didn't think my mother knew what she was talking about when she suggested that Candice wouldn't be wasting her time with me once Jett was born.

After vanishing to Oklahoma yet again, I returned home and found our house completely empty. There was no furniture, no food, and definitely no wife or baby. My mother was right. Not too long after Jett was born, Candice packed all her things and moved in with her dad. I wasn't much help once the baby came, and Candice wasn't wasting any time getting herself to a safe and stable place to raise our child. And it wasn't just that Candice got a wild hair and left on her own. It was my own family who'd made it possible. It was a bit of a jolt returning home to an empty house, but it was more shocking that my family was able to gut my house in a single day without me knowing anything about it until everything was said and done.

My newly empty home was the perfect metaphor showing just how severe things had gotten, so I decided to quit playing poker, find a normal job, and stabilize my life a little. Things were getting darker by the day. The depression I'd experienced 10 months earlier when I'd suddenly stopped going to work was nothing compared to the despair I felt as I sat alone in my empty home. For the longest time, all I had wanted was to be left alone, but now that I was finally alone, it wasn't anything that I had expected.

I did not want to be by myself because as long as other people were around, I could simply point the finger at everyone else and blame them for my problems. But if I was truly on my own, there would be no one else to point the finger at when I finally hit rock bottom.

After wasting so much energy ruining so many relationships for the sole purpose of being free, it was the exact opposite of free. I was completely trapped in a world of pain that I had created, and I hated it.

❧ ❧ ❧ ❧ ❧ ❧

November 13, 2006

I am all alone in this house. If I didn't have my computer here with me, I would have done it already, but my time has been spent listening to an extensive catalogue of my own music. Procrastination has finally paid off as I postpone suicide for just one more song. Music was always an outlet for me, a way to express myself when no other means existed. In many ways, my music gave me life for so many years. How apropos it seems that my music now extends my life one song at a time.

Journaling was something I had refused to do as a student because I thought it was weird that a teacher wanted to know what I was thinking or how I was feeling. It was none of their business, and I wasn't about to reveal my innermost feelings for the sake of a passing grade. However, when I found myself alone in that empty house with nothing but a few walls and my computer, journaling was the perfect escape. I wasn't writing for the sake of anyone else, and I never expected to share those thoughts with anyone else. I was just keeping myself company.

> *I will admit that the huge majority of things happening lately are the direct results of my choices, but it is not an option for me anymore to hang around and continue to watch life pass me by. Candice has made it abundantly clear that she will do whatever she can to make our marriage work, but I don't believe her. She would be more accurate in saying, "I will do whatever I can without being forced to risk any of my precious money."*
>
> *It doesn't hurt my feelings, but it shows me that she doesn't really feel the way she says she does about me. She just doesn't realize that. Things would be so much better if she would have chosen me over money several years ago, but that has never happened, and it never will. Faced with the option of losing me forever or maybe losing money, she chose the money. That tells me everything I need to know about our relationship.*

It wasn't true that Candice chose her *precious money* over me, but I didn't care about the truth. I only wanted to believe things that supported my belief that the world was indeed against me.

About three weeks ago, I finally decided that I was going to go to Oklahoma to get a job and normalize myself a little. Staying in Texas was no longer much of an option because things simply were not going well. Leaving on a Thursday morning, I decided to stop at my dad's to hang out and tell them goodbye.

When I got home a few days later, I was surprised to see that Candice was moving all our stuff into storage, and she was going to stay with her dad until she went back to work (approximately six weeks or so). My mom apparently hired movers and had them move everything into storage except for our bedroom furniture. My brother got that. Of course, nobody thought I should know that, so I didn't find out until a week or so later. …oh well. I didn't really care about any of the furniture or anything. I had already told Candice she could have everything in the house, so whatever she decided to do with it was her choice to make. However, I thought it was kind of sad that she and my mother both lied to me about it. I guess it's contagious.

In fact, nobody had lied to me about anything. It was my own fault for randomly vanishing and being so out of touch with my family that I didn't realize they were moving forward with or without me.

At that point, I thought my life had sunk to a new low. I felt like I had nowhere to go. I figured I would just go to my dad's and stay there until things got better. In a lot of ways, I feel like they (my dad and

> *stepmom) are the only ones who really care to try and help me anymore, so when I needed a place to stay for the night, I thought I could count on them.*
>
> *I was wrong.*

At the time, I had a four-year-old brother and a seven-year-old sister who lived with my dad and stepmother. My dad didn't want me crashing on his couch for a night because he didn't want to have to explain to my little brother and sister why *Clay and Candice aren't together anymore.*

> *My dad said I should go stay at my house even though it was empty except for a mattress that was left behind when everything got moved. I didn't even have sheets or anything else that you take for granted on a daily basis. I had a blanket in my truck along with all my clothes. I didn't even have a towel to dry off with or a pillow to sleep on.*

I only had one choice. I returned home and slept on a bare mattress. I promised myself I would never again ask my dad for help of any kind. If it was too much to allow me to sleep on his couch for a night or two, then there wasn't much point in relying on him for anything else. For nearly a week, I stayed alone in that empty house and did nothing.

> *Tonight will be my fifth night sleeping here, and I think I'm finally getting used to it. I hate being alone, and I hate having nothing to do. I have no food. I have no money. I don't have enough gas to drive around looking for a job. I have nothing except a few bottles of water and this computer to update my life's all-time low. This is it.*

> *I don't think there's a single person who believes in me anymore. I feel completely abandoned, and I feel like nobody really cares if I eat or not. Candice brought Jett to see me last week, and I asked if she would stop at Taco Bueno on the way, and she told me no, so I guess that's even too much to ask anymore. I'll never ask her for anything ever again no matter how big or small it is. If two or three bucks is too much to ask, that pretty much tells me where I stand.*

The list of *people I'll never ask for help again* was growing quickly, and it didn't take much for me to decide that someone wasn't worth talking to again either. In simple terms, I was ridding myself of anyone who had nothing to offer me. One by one, it seemed that everyone proved that they weren't willing to offer any help until I was willing to give in and live by their rules, but I was still determined to live by my own.

> *I'm not going to write down what I feel like my realistic options are because some of them aren't legal, and I don't ever want anything I write to come back and haunt me in the end. I've done plenty to break the law up to this point, and I've avoided any trouble, so I think that's what I'll just keep doing. The end result can only be good. I can't explain that, so I'm not even going to try.*
>
> *My main goal in life is to be able to be a good dad to my son, and I can't go about that in the traditional way that most people are able to do, but this is the only thing I know how to do. If nobody in my family ever talks to me again, that's okay. If I never see some of them again, that's okay,*

too. If the only person who ever cares for me again is Jett, then my mission has been accomplished. Everything (and everyone) else is merely a bonus, and I will consider such as luxury.

❧ ❧ ❧ ❧ ❧ ❧

By then, the small amount of food I had was gone, and I was hungrier than I ever thought possible. Although I'd sworn to myself to never ask my dad for anything again, hunger pangs can change even the most determined mind. Predictably, things did not go as planned.

It's about 4:30 p.m. right now, and I just got back from my dad's house. I went over there because I was hungry, and I knew I could at least make a sandwich there. I'd been up since 7:00 a.m., and I hadn't had anything to eat. I ended up leaving my dad's without eating. I was hungry the whole time, but shortly after I got there, he started talking to me about everything that's been going on, and I was going to wait until that conversation was finished before I ate. Once we were done talking, I wanted to get some food and get on the Internet for a little bit, but he said he didn't want me to use his computer. I have no idea what he's thinking, but I'm not going to sit around and be treated like a child whose daddy won't let him on the computer.

I didn't eat that day, and the next day was no different until I was pleasantly surprised with an unexpected visit from the one person I didn't want to see any time soon.

11/14/06

I'm still alone, but at least I have food now. I ended up just lying in bed last night and listening to the radio. Around 8:00 p.m., I heard a truck drive by. I looked out the window, and it had already passed, but I could still see the brake lights reflecting off the house across the street. I could tell that the truck was pulling into my driveway. Since our house is for sale, this normally wouldn't seem weird, but it was much too late for someone to be coming to look at the house. I got a little freaked out because I didn't know what was going on, and all I have here is a golf club. My brother has all my guns, so it was a little unnerving thinking I had an unexpected visitor and no way to defend myself.

I was walking around the house in the dark trying to figure out who was parked in my driveway, but I couldn't see the truck. About that time, they started backing out, and I could see it was my dad's van, so I went outside to see what they wanted. He and my stepmom were bringing me some groceries. They brought me cereal, milk, sandwich stuff, and plenty of other things to keep me fed for at least a couple of weeks or so. I'll just have to stretch it out to make it last.

Today is the day I'm going to finally make something happen.

I was too thankful to be embarrassed. I was just a few steps shy of being a beggar on the street, yet I was lucky enough to have groceries show up to my front door. I had literally nothing to eat in my house, and I wasn't sure I could have lasted another day without eating.

There still wasn't enough gas in my truck to drive around trying to find a job, but I at least had enough to drive to the one job that I knew would pay cash on the spot: American National Bank in Rockwall, Texas.

> *11/15/06*
>
> *"Today is the day I'm going to finally make something happen."*
>
> *I wrote that yesterday just before getting in the shower and getting ready to leave. I had planned to leave at 2:45 p.m., and while I was getting ready, I heard a baby cry. I could tell it was Jett, but I didn't know if I was hearing things or if Candice was actually here at the house. I went into the living room, and I saw that she was here with a handful of cleaning supplies. My cousin is coming down from Tennessee with her family and they're staying here next week, and I guess Candice wanted to clean everything for them.*

Even though it was a bit awkward, I enjoyed visiting with Jett while Candice cleaned. He was barely two months old, so he didn't do much, but that didn't matter to me. I just enjoyed being in the same room with him. My plans to go to the bank that afternoon were thwarted because my son was there to see me, and that was just fine with me.

The following day, however, there would be no such visit to interrupt me.

It's 12:15 p.m. right now, so I still have a little bit of time to burn, so I'm just listening to the radio and eating a little bit before I leave.

I've got nothing to lose this time. There are only two different things that can come out of this, and they're both good, so I'm excited about that.

I was cryptic in my journaling on the off chance that someone was able to read what I'd written, but the *two different things* were simple. I was either going to get away with another bank robbery and have money to float me a few weeks while looking for a job, or I was going to get caught and go to jail. I was content with either scenario, so it felt like a win/win situation.

However, another unique set of circumstances prevented me from going to the bank that day.

11/16/06 - 2:15 a.m.

It's becoming comical how absolutely nothing is going right anymore. I can't help but laugh at things lately. When I went to leave earlier (Wednesday afternoon), I turned the key to start my truck, and all I heard was a click. My battery had completely died, and I couldn't start my truck. I don't have a phone here, and even though my brother lives on the next street over, I didn't really think he would really want to have me coming over to use his phone. I decided I would just walk a mile or two up to the gas station and use the pay phone to call my dad to come jump my truck off. I got about halfway there and realized I didn't have any money to use the payphone anyway, so I had to walk back home. While I was walking home, I decided I would go to my brother's house and use his phone after all. When I got to his street, two cops drove by and stopped at his house. I had a pretty good feeling that it wouldn't be a good time for me to pop in to use the phone real quick, so I went ahead and walked home, and by then, my neighbor was home, and I used their phone to call my dad. He was about to leave to go to church, so he wasn't able to immediately come over. Instead, he waited until after church. By then, it was too late to go anywhere to look for a job or anything like that, so I guess I'll have to wait another day.

This is getting old!

❧ ❧ ❧ ❧ ❧ ❧

In the year that I'd been robbing banks, I never once did so out of necessity. I rarely kept the money for myself, and I enjoyed the feeling of giving to those in need with money I'd stolen from the banks.

But in November 2006, I was definitely stealing out of necessity. It wasn't as much about the money as it was about needing to be rescued somehow. I was convinced that I was headed to an early grave if something didn't change soon, but I didn't want my son to grow up without a father. No matter how much of a loser I was, I fully believed that I could change things for the better if I just had the right opportunity.

I chose to rob a bank just a few miles away from my house. It was easily the riskiest job of all the ones I'd done because of the bank's proximity to my house. Additionally, Rockwall was not exactly a high-crime area for things like bank robbery, so the likelihood of showing up on the news was also increased. For every reason imaginable, it was very likely that I would get caught. And quite frankly, that was completely okay with me. Under those circumstances, it only made sense that I follow through with my plan and enjoy the benefits, whatever they might be.

The day I originally planned to do it was when Candice showed up to clean the house. It's hard to rob a bank while watching a newborn baby, so that day wasn't an option. I couldn't do it the following day either when my truck wouldn't start. I'm not superstitious, but I started to believe that these things were an omen that I would definitely get caught if I decided to follow through with my next robbery.

In the back of my mind, I knew that was for the best.

ROCKWALL

Exactly one week before Thanksgiving in 2006, I parked my pickup truck in a spot just in front of The Black-eyed Pea in Rockwall, Texas. It was a few minutes before 3:00 p.m.—too late for lunch, too early for dinner—but I had no plans to stop and eat. Instead, this particular location offered the perfect cover for me. Directly behind it was the American National Bank of Texas.

This particular Black-eyed Pea was in a strip mall, so it was connected to several other stores. The bank itself was actually its own freestanding building behind the restaurant but easily accessible by the sidewalk connecting the two buildings. One faced north; the other faced west.

Sitting in my truck, I went through a familiar routine. I turned off the engine of my pickup and sat alone with nothing but the radio playing. Talk radio was usually my preference, but with the top of the hour approaching, commercials were the only thing playing on the radio. Commercials are sufficient white noise for the mind-numbing process of preparing to rob a bank, I guess. I didn't really notice, nor did I care.

By that point, I was no longer a rookie. I was an experienced criminal. Fortunately, my arrogance never fully ran the show when it came time to rob a bank, so I still was very aware of what to do and what to avoid. Using an envelope in place of a note was my preference for all the obvious reasons, but I wondered if it might create some sort of pattern that investigators might pick up on. There would be no fingerprints, no DNA, no handwriting analysis or any other sort of magical CSI tricks to track down the identity of the *presumed armed and dangerous* suspect. But the pattern of using an envelope was definitely there for anyone who looked.

Sitting in my parked pickup just in front of The Black-eyed Pea, my perfect handwriting went onto the envelope in those same three short lines of instruction as I reminded myself that there was nothing to be nervous about.

Taking the keys out of the ignition and opening the door of my pickup, I grabbed the small envelope and slid it in my pocket as I stepped out and began walking toward The Black-eyed Pea. After approaching the building, I turned right on the sidewalk for a few steps before the sidewalk turned back to the left as I walked past the restaurant and toward the bank, crossing a few small shops in the process. I wondered if any of those shops might have surveillance cameras, but it was more of a curiosity than a concern. Without a criminal record at the time, there was little reason to worry about my face being recorded and possibly given to the police as evidence later. After all, there would be only about a dozen cameras in the bank just waiting to do the same, and that didn't bother me either. All I cared about was getting in and out as quietly as possible, returning to my truck, and avoiding detection by anyone who saw it all. Unless someone chased me from the bank—incredibly unlikely, by the way—it was impossible to see my getaway vehicle.

Entering the bank, I felt nothing. Fear—neither healthy nor unhealthy—was nonexistent. My body and mind were not providing any feedback. The bank itself was also familiar to me. I lived just a few minutes away and I'd been to this bank before on considerably more legal terms. I wasn't familiar with the people in the bank, but I knew the general layout, so it was not an uncomfortable scene for me.

Predictably, the nice lady at the front desk greeted me with a smile and a sweet southern pleasantry. My manners remained intact, so I replied accordingly as I walked past her desk to the short labyrinth roped off just before the teller windows. There was only one person in line, but I continued through the entire maze like a rat before stopping where the little sign directed me to do so and waiting for the next available teller.

The next available teller happened to be the one working the commercial window. "Sir, I can help you over here," she said. This was something I had never considered though. Never did a scenario occur in my mental practice or my actual experience that involved a commercial teller window—the place where actual businesses do their thing instead of lowly personal account holders. There really wasn't anything to be worried about, but the unexpectedness of it all was enough to force a polite *no thanks, I can wait* from my mouth.

As soon as I declined her invitation, I immediately regretted it and wondered if every soul in the bank immediately knew I was there to break the law. Of all possible responses to her invitation, *no thanks, I can wait* was probably the worst. Who in their right mind would prefer to stand in line one moment longer than they had to? I'd immediately concluded that the commercial teller would have more money and would therefore hand over that larger sum of money, and that larger sum of money would be enough money to land my stupid face on the news for all to see and to *please help police identify this man.*

Disaster.

The previous night, it seemed likely that I would get caught during my next robbery, and now this seemed to be the first step in that direction. When thinking about it the night before, it hadn't bothered me. But now that I was in the heat of the moment, it suddenly seemed worthy of a little distress.

Predictably, the commercial teller simply smiled and insisted that she'd be happy to help me. It was every intention of mine to grab my back pocket and pretend that *Oops, I forgot something in my car. I'll be right back.*

No, I wouldn't be right back, but that seemed like the safest way to exit instead of turning and sprinting in a panic over a failed attempt that hadn't even happened yet. Only a fraction of a second had passed since she had offered to help me, but it felt long enough that I could nearly see the hands on the wall clock moving in the distance. Without knowing how to disengage my body's autopilot function, I proceeded to the counter and handed her the envelope with those three magical lines printed neatly on the face of the envelope:

1) Put all $50s and $100s in this envelope.
2) I won't hurt you.
3) Do NOT look at me.

❧ ❧ ❧ ❧ ❧ ❧

Bank tellers have their own routine during a robbery, a routine I was completely familiar with after witnessing it firsthand throughout 2006. They always had some mixture of terror and confusion, and they each moved slowly and precisely. They followed instructions perfectly before pushing that useless panic button.

My attention wandered because there was nothing interesting about this process anymore. Instead of studying her to make sure she didn't do anything crazy, my eyes drifted to the tiny piece of bank property giving the name of this particular teller. It was an uncommon spelling of an already uncommon name. I only knew this because I had a cousin with the same name. My mind stopped wandering aimlessly and settled on the thought of how my cousin might have handled this situation if she were in the teller's position. I wondered if she would have been scared, and I wondered how enraged I might be in finding out someone had robbed her. Surely the teller in front of me had family members who would soon be finding out about my crime, and they would all hate me and have the worst things to say about me. They would judge my entire life from this one event, and they would expect me to serve the maximum prison sentence allowed by law, which would probably still not be enough to them. In an instant, I had just made enemies with an entire family that I would never meet.

Bummer.

Jaqueline interrupted my thoughts when she returned my envelope full of $50's and $100's. My shrug said *sorry* and my mouth might have done the same. I don't really recall. The whole *bank robber* thing was losing its appeal to me, and I just wanted to leave. I didn't know remorse was in my emotional toolbox, but there I was wishing I could go back in time and make a different choice earlier that day.

It was too late to worry about that though. I was already holding an envelope full of money that didn't belong to me, and that wasn't exactly the best time to consider emotions. I turned and walked toward the front door at a pace that any regular paying customer would maintain. Unexpectedly, the bank lobby greeter lady addressed me by name on my way out as she wished me a great day. "Have a nice day, Todd."

I had no idea who Todd was, but being the well-mannered southerner that I am, I simply nodded and wished her a good day, too. I'm sure she saw my smile, but I doubt she heard my chuckle.

Poor Todd was going to have to answer for this one, but that was none of my concern.

❧ ❧ ❧ ❧ ❧ ❧

After exiting the front door of the bank, I turned right and walked down the sidewalk adjacent to the front of the building. It was filled with windows, and I wondered if anyone inside the bank was watching me. It didn't matter one way or another if they could see me because there would be plenty of video footage of everything that just happened. Besides, I was walking toward the back of The Black-eyed Pea, which conveniently obscured the vehicle I would be getting into shortly. Nobody who could see me getting into my truck would know what I just did, and nobody who knew what I just did would be able to see me getting into my truck.

It's amazing what a little forethought and preparation can do.

❧ ❧ ❧ ❧ ❧ ❧

As planned, I made it back to my truck without having broken into a complete sprint. No cops were in sight, and the helicopter overhead was not of the law enforcement variety. It was just another beautiful day in Rockwall, Texas. The remote starter on my truck served no real purpose, but it made me feel cooler knowing that my Batmobile was running and ready to flee as soon as I unlocked the door and climbed in.

The money stayed in the envelope as I drove away, but the envelope was noticeably thicker than usual. I drove to a gas station to get a Coke and some gas. While filling up my truck, I took the cash out of the envelope and put it in the console of my truck. I folded the envelope and tore it. I folded it again and tore it again. I did this as many times as it would allow before I tossed it into the trash can just next to the gas pump. It wasn't as safe as throwing evidence confetti out the window at 65 miles per hour, but it was good enough. If someone found my envelope in that trash can and somehow traced it back to me, then they deserved to catch me.

Unlike any other bank robbery, the Rockwall bank left me doubting whether or not this was something I wanted to continue. There was nothing fun about it, and I hated that the teller's face was engrained in my mind long after I left the bank. I wondered how the robbery might have affected her. Some tellers were more collected than others, but she seemed a little rattled by the whole thing, and that bothered me. My intent was never to hurt or even scare any individuals. I was robbing Big Business, not Jaqueline.

Ultimately, I just didn't know how it impacted her or anyone else, and that bothered me. I'd never before felt bad about robbing banks because I felt like the tellers understood what I was doing. I felt like they knew they weren't in any danger and that nothing I did was a threat to their personal wellbeing. I thought some might actually understand or perhaps have some level of empathy for me. Instead, I was the one feeling sorry for them. They didn't ask to be a part of my drama, but I was the reason they were present at the scene of a crime.

Stealing money from banks was easy, and I enjoyed the game as long as I felt like it was me against an establishment. But when I thought about the actual person who was on the receiving end of my demands, it stopped being fun. The things that excited me in previous robberies were overshadowed in the Rockwall robbery because of that human connection. It was no longer just a big, wealthy bank that I was robbing. It was an actual human being named Jaqueline, and she had been victimized by some guy.

I didn't want to be *that guy* anymore.

When I got home, I walked through the front door and paused. My house was all but completely abandoned. I'm not much for personifying inanimate objects, but the house seemed to understand that it was no longer anybody's home. The walls were just as blank as the floors, and the entire place was lifeless.

My house embodied everything that I had become: full of potential yet completely void of anything worthwhile.

❧ ❧ ❧ ❧ ❧ ❧

When I finally counted the money from the Rockwall bank, it was just over $7,000. That could have lasted me a few months, but money had never been my motivation, and I wasn't about to let that change. After previous robberies, I'd found worthy recipients to share the money with. In addition to the thrill of getting away with what I was doing, it was also quite addictive being able to randomly help the needy. From close friends to popular local charities, I enjoyed stealing money from the bad guys and giving it to people who could do something better with it. I'm smart enough to know the math involved, and I realize that I wasn't truly stealing from the bad guys, but that's how it felt, so that's how I justified it.

I really didn't need $7,000 for myself because I wasn't paying any bills or anything else by then anyway. I was living in a vacated house and driving a truck that I'd stopped making payments on as well. All I really needed was a little money to get me by for the short term because I'd stopped playing poker and still had no job prospects. My basic needs were food and gas money.

After a couple of weeks of failing to find respectable work, I had no choice but to go back to Oklahoma. No matter what anyone said, exploiting the ignorance of the masses is simply a lucrative venture, and that's all poker was for me by that point. It wasn't fun, and I didn't particularly enjoy it.

The end of my rope was fast approaching, and I had no real plan. A night never passed that I didn't fall asleep wondering about my son and feeling sad for him because of the trash that he had for a father. No matter how awesome his mother was, I knew she couldn't be two people, and it was just depressing to even consider how that might affect my baby boy as he grew up.

But with each morning, I ignored reality just a little while longer and hoped that something would eventually change on its own. I didn't want to believe that I had the power to fix anything because that was just another thing to fail.

The descent continued.

THAT'S ALL I GOT

I don't like Starbucks.

Granted, I don't *dislike* Starbucks either. I just don't drink coffee. I've also never had my clothes dry-cleaned, so it would be perfectly normal to wonder why, on an otherwise normal day in December, I parked at a commercial building that was half Starbucks and half Stephen's Cleaners. But the building was sandwiched nicely between two other buildings. One of them was Chick-fil-A, a place I frequented with far more regularity than I would ever admit on the record without some sort of endorsement deal.

The Starbucks building shared a parking lot with Chick-fil-A except for the fact that they were divided by a small grass median—the kind of small grass median that is easily driven over in a 4x4 pickup should the need ever arise. The parking spots on the Chick-fil-A side of the shared parking lot were slanted but still pointing directly toward the Starbucks building.

As I walked across the parking lot—away from Chick-fil-A and toward the Starbucks building—I went over the short mental checklist to be sure I had everything covered per my usual routine. The envelope in my hand had the same neatly printed instructions on it that I had always used, and the key to my truck was in my other hand.

After my first few robberies, I wondered if some banks might ever try to trap me between their sets of double doors. It seemed unlikely, but it wasn't impossible. I had decided a small ball-peen hammer might prove to be useful. I didn't plan to ever use it as a weapon, but I'm sure I would have been comfortable using it to fend off any potential superheroes. But that wasn't the point. It simply served as a Plan B if I ever found myself trapped inside a building with glass doors. A building, for example, where a robbery had just occurred.

Still walking and approaching the Starbucks building, I turned slightly to the left and walked past the front of the building. At this point, my destination was in sight and only a few dozen steps away across another very small parking lot. The total distance from my truck in the slanted Chick-fil-A parking spot to the Chase bank I was about to walk into was shorter than the length of a football field.

My previous robbery flashed through my mind and I recalled the teller's face as I offered a pathetic *sorry* before turning to leave. In the last few steps before walking into this next bank, bits and pieces of a lifetime's worth of memories came and went at a rate far greater than I was comfortable with. It was like reliving most of my life right then and there. I remembered all of the times I had gotten in trouble as a student and how comfortable I had been sitting in the principal's office. Or in detention. Or wherever the punishment would be doled out that day. While walking, I was wondering at exactly what point *apathetic* turned into *criminal.* Something definitely went wrong during my development as a child.

What made me this way? Was it gradual or overnight? Why didn't anyone stop it? Did they try and fail, or did they fail to even try? Was it my fault entirely? Do rules actually even exist? Does the world disappear behind me when I'm not looking? Will they lock the doors? Will a small ball-peen hammer really break this glass if they lock the doors? Shouldn't I be afraid of what I'm about to do?

No, of course not, I interrupted myself. *They have procedures to follow, and you know those procedures. Fear of the unknown doesn't exist where knowledge is present.*

Yes. Knowledge. I knew everything I needed to know, and nothing but a complete freak coincidence would prevent me from doing exactly what I came to do. There was no reason to worry myself with the chances of being caught. *Just walk in and do what you've always done.*

❧ ❧ ❧ ❧ ❧ ❧

Inside, the bank was employed mostly by women who would probably follow the rules instead of trying to be a hero. Then I saw something—a really big dude who definitely fit the description of a hero who you might find on the evening news talkin' 'bout what he done did and how he ain't no hero for it. He was in a nice suit and worked one of the teller windows, and I contemplated whether or not I would go through with my plans if he called me up before one of the other tellers. It seemed like an easy decision to make though. This was not about forcing my will on any person who crossed my path. This was not about brute force or aggression. This was about exploiting the system and solving the puzzle.

"Sir, I can help you over here," a female voice called to me from my left. She wore the standard banker smile while waving me over to her window. I met hers with a smile of my own and apologized for daydreaming. She laughed and politely asked what she could do for me today.

I gave her the envelope.

As expected, she immediately looked up at me. That's the one thing that all tellers had in common after reading that note. I guess none of them were raised to know it's not polite to stare. In fairness, no other teller had actually stared at me, but by comparison this teller was definitely staring at me. It didn't feel like the passive, inquisitive *is this real* type of gaze that I had seen many times before. Those never bothered me because I thought they were reflexive, involuntary, and harmless. To those nonverbal queries, I simply nodded confirmation. This teller, however, seemed to be sizing me up. My instinct was to stay still and just maintain eye contact with her without reacting. There was no telling what she was thinking, but I was certain I could read her mind. She was thinking of a way to be the hero.

After a few seconds, she let out an exaggerated sigh accompanied by a subtle roll of her eyes before slowly reaching into her drawer and grabbing a few $50s and even fewer $100s. She put the money into the envelope, but she seemed to be proving a point with how slow her every move was. I wanted to squirt some oil into her joints in hopes that perhaps her bones had seized up and restricted her movement.

Congratulations to me. I just robbed a sloth.

I could tell by her movements that she hadn't fully complied with my demands. I had plainly stated to hand over ALL $50s and $100s, not just some of them. She clearly wasn't the least bit scared of me or the situation, but I didn't know which pissed me off more—the fact that she completely short-changed me or the fact that she didn't even bother pressing her panic button.

Without bothering to even reach for the envelope, my head tilted with irritation as I calmly said, "You can do better than that." With her palms face up at shoulder height, her entire body shrugged as she feigned ignorance. "That's all I got," she lied.

Finally, someone had outsmarted me, and worst of all she did it on a whim. She knew that I was not going to shoot her or attack her or even press the issue. The fact that she was breaking protocol was completely irrelevant to me at this point.

I was powerless.

Regardless of what might happen to her after her employer learned of her insubordination, nothing changed the fact that she had beaten me at my own game by somehow knowing that there was no real danger in front of her. Resigning myself to defeat, I grabbed the envelope and turned to leave.

"Lock the doors!"

Huh?

"LOCK THE DOORS!"

Not good.

This maniac was now screaming at the top of her lungs, and every last person in the building definitely heard her. With my back now to the tellers, all I could think about in that split second was the really big dude who definitely fit the description of a hero who you might find on the evening news talkin' 'bout what he done did and how he ain't no hero for it. But I simultaneously recalled a recent news story where a manager at a Chase bank in another state had lost his job for successfully stopping a bank robbery much similar to the one I'd just committed. The manager wasn't fired for being a hero. He was fired for not following the rules.

With the teller's shrills still echoing throughout the bank lobby, I was at ease and not the least bit concerned about potentially being tackled from behind. Instead, my imagination went to work and tried to solve in a split second what was now the most incredibly time-sensitive puzzle of my life.

Only a second earlier, I had turned and taken just a single step toward the front door with my left foot before the teller started screaming her plea for someone to lock the door. Without breaking stride, I needed to know exactly what my plan was before my right foot hit the ground.

To me, it seemed obvious that breaking into a full sprint would be a bad idea. Men who are seen running away from screaming women are almost always guilty of something. There were far too many people in the bank for me to avoid, and challenging the collective whole to a foot race was out of the question for me. It also seemed foolish to merely stop and pretend to be a statue in the middle of the bank lobby where it was somewhat likely—dare I say predictable—that the police would soon come and disallow me to maintain my statuesque pose for very long. The only remaining option seemed to be the simplest one of all.

As my right foot landed in an innocently normal second step, my left soon followed with another…then my right…then my left…*one step at a time. Just get to the front doors as quickly as possible without rushing and without being noticed…*

One step at a time while the maniacal lady behind you screams unintelligible nonsense at the top of her lungs…

Let her attract every last set of eyeballs in the building and you'll be invisible…

Walk.

Don't run.

Just walk.

❧ ❧ ❧ ❧ ❧ ❧

Like many bank buildings, this one had two sets of doors to exit through. The first was unlocked, of course. It was unlikely that anyone could really understand that she was saying, "Lock the doors!" The louder she screamed, the less you could understand what she was saying. Reaching for the second set of doors, I wondered if this would be the time that I might finally find out if the hidden ball-peen hammer strapped to my right leg just below my knee would be enough to break through a locked glass door. Thinking on my feet, I reminded myself to be sure to not touch the glass with my fingers if I did have to smash my way out.

In stride and now at the final set of doors, I leaned forward and attempted to push through with my shoulder.

It opened.

Like waking up from a nightmare only to realize there was nothing to be afraid of, I finally exhaled and remembered to breathe again. *Nothing to worry about here...*

...except for the man walking toward me from the parking lot at a pace that suggested he had business to handle. I wondered if I was that business before almost immediately laughing at my own stupidity when I realized he was heading toward the bank, not me.

My manners are fine. Normally, I would happily pause and hold the door open for a stranger who was walking into any building I was exiting, but I did nothing of the sort that time. Not only did I let the door close behind me as I left the bank, but I also told the kind gentleman that the bank was *kind of busy* and that he *probably should use the drive-thru* instead. Besides, it was late in the day and the lobby would soon close anyway.

With a smile and a shrug, he replied, "Oh, thanks. I'll just be a second though."

When he reached for the door—the same door that I had just passed through no more than five seconds sooner—it was locked.

The man was irate. He'd just seen me walk out of those same doors, yet they were somehow already locked. It wasn't fair, and he wanted them to let him in...right now!

What came next was a colorful mixture of vulgar language and spit as the kind gentleman turned into the best decoy I could ever hope for. He jerked the door handles in vain and even tried a few kicks himself. But he was no Chuck Norris, and the doors remained both closed and locked. To say he was merely upset is an understatement. He was throwing a complete temper tantrum for all to see. Who could blame him though? Sure, it was late in the day, but it was at least a half hour before closing time. But nothing he did or said would influence them to open the door.

He was the perfect decoy for me, and his anger must have erased my face from his mind. He couldn't tell the police a single thing about me except that I'd tried to warn him about how busy the bank was. No, he didn't see which way I went. And no, he didn't see what I was driving.

Perhaps my sense of humor is dark, but I simply could not fully contain my laughter as I walked across the parking lot toward the Starbucks building.

Then around it…

One step at a time.

Now out of sight to anyone in the bank, I was within range of my truck. I pressed the button on my keychain to start it. The rumble of my truck starting was unmistakable, and it always made something happen inside my dumb man-brain every single time I heard it start.

Every. Single. Time.

Any positive thoughts I might have had were soon interrupted when I saw a police car parked perpendicularly behind my truck. Worse, the lights atop the roof of that police car were flashing. The car itself was vacant, but an officer was a short distance away and sprinting back to his car.

My brain was no longer working and it felt like my heart would soon go on strike as well. Somehow, my feet continued with their stupid *one step at a time* routine. I wanted to stop walking, but I had no control. Sure, I was in my body, but I was only along for the ride.

I had no plan. My feet were on autopilot. I'd experienced that before and didn't know how to disengage them either. My eyes fully expected to witness a very bad end to my days as a crook.

Don't bring a knife to a gunfight.

But I didn't even have a knife. More like *don't bring an envelope to a gunfight.*

I was certainly about to die. I assumed the police officer was running back to his car for cover and, under the threat of a suspect on foot approaching him, unleashing a torrent of bullets into me. I wondered if I were hallucinating, but I wasn't. This was my new reality.

Much to the dismay of my perfectly fine good luck streak, this officer just happened to be in the right place at the right time. He was conducting a routine traffic stop just a couple hundred feet away from a bank that had just been robbed, according to the squawking radio attached to his shoulder. He was indeed the first responding officer to the crime scene I had just created.

Even as I watched the officer run back to his vehicle to crouch behind his open driver's side door to assume the shooter's position, my feet were still moving *one step at a time.*

This must be what it feels like to be one of those stupid bugs that flies into a bug zapper. You know it's there, and you know it's going to kill you, but you can't do anything but enjoy the ride.

When the officer reached his vehicle, he jumped in and slammed his car into gear in one fluid motion and flew his patrol car across the parking lot to the bank. I shook my head and laughed again as I opened the door to my truck and climbed in. Had the officer left his car where it was and ran to the bank on foot instead, my truck would have been blocked in, and I'd have had to find a more creative way to leave the scene. Instead, I slowly backed out of my parking spot and safely drove away.

Not that anyone was in the truck with me, but for my own sake, I needed to say out loud exactly what was going through my mind.

"I'm done."

Taking a deep breath and allowing my head to fall back into my headrest, I exhaled and agreed with myself.

"I am so done with this."

❧ ❧ ❧ ❧ ❧ ❧

I was sure nobody outside the bank saw me except for the kind gentleman who was soon arrested for assaulting those locked bank doors. I wasn't exactly concerned about his ability to identify me, and the police bulletin later confirmed that I had appeared 4 to 6 inches shorter and 50 pounds lighter than reality. I especially wasn't concerned that he saw what I was driving because of where my truck was parked. And since everybody inside the bank was locked in, I was absolutely certain that none of them saw me get into my truck.

Getting back into my truck was like returning to the base in a game of hide-and-seek. The base meant security and no concern of being caught. I turned on the radio and tuned to a favorite talk show of mine and drove away as though I had just enjoyed a simple meal at a wonderful restaurant. I wasn't interested in the envelope with the not-nearly-enough money in it.

That's all I got.

I had no interest in seeing how much money the teller had robbed me of, so I kept it in my pocket as I drove across the street to Chili's.

After paying for my food in cash, of course, I returned to my truck and drove down the street and into the parking lot of a major hotel chain that had free Internet and, most importantly, a giant collection of trash dumpsters behind it. I shredded the envelope and spread its remains equally among various trash receptacles before circling back to the front of the hotel.

I didn't go inside. Their free Internet was all I wanted, and it was wirelessly accessible to me as I parked in their parking lot. Still in the safety of my truck—my home base—I turned on my laptop and began searching news stories about local bank robberies. News travels at two speeds—lightning fast or not at all. And apparently there was nothing newsworthy about what I had just done.

Mission accomplished.

It was always a habit of mine to rush to the nearest news source to be sure there wasn't a helicopter eyeballing me from above. In hindsight, it probably would have been easier to roll down my window and check the sky myself, but that always felt too revealing, not to mention extremely boring.

The coast was clear, and as always, I had nothing to worry about.

But my nerves were still a little rattled. That whole thing with the lady screaming *Lock the doors!* was a little too close for comfort. I was probably just a few steps from being locked inside that bank and finding out if that little ball-peen hammer strapped to my leg would have worked after all. And even if it had worked, what would the kind gentleman have thought as he walked toward the bank and saw me busting out of those glass doors like some kind of weird baby dinosaur breaking out of a giant glass-building egg? Given the temper he displayed when he was denied access to the bank himself, it was safe to assume he might have just as easily been the crazy type who definitely fit the description of a hero you see on the evening news who *just don' give a dayum because he done watched one too many episodes of COPS and knowed good and well how to take down a no good for nuthin sumbitch like that.*

For the first time, I felt a sense of relief after a robbery instead of a sense of accomplishment.

In a year of robbing banks, I had experienced a wide range of emotions—from fear to sheer exhilaration and pretty much everything in between—but those emotions all had one thing in common. They were extreme and exciting. Relief, however, is neither extreme nor exciting. It is bland and boring.

To feel relief is to acknowledge the gift of mercy, and mercy was nothing my pride was willing to consider. With a full tank of gas, the rest of my afternoon was spent aimlessly pacing the streets of Dallas.

Throughout 2006, my life had revolved around this grandiose notion that I was actually pulling off some great feat, but in my truck that afternoon, it became painfully clear that I simply wasn't accomplishing anything at all.

Nothing was fun that day. Nothing was fulfilling. Nothing was right.

Nothing mattered.

If a bank gives a few thousand dollars to some random guy with a note, it doesn't matter. It's considered an acceptable loss, and it's barely worth the bank's time to even attempt recovering that money. They simply tell the police and continue on with their day.

Nobody cares.

It was impossible to ignore the suffocating reality that my life was again pointless. There was no significance—good or bad—in anything I was doing. But it was too late to consider a new path again. *I'm too old for this crap!*

That lack of purpose was overwhelming and embarrassing. After a year and a half of planning and perpetrating the criminal equivalent of taking candy from a baby, I was back at square one.

A very empty and lonely square one.

⁂ ⁂ ⁂ ⁂ ⁂ ⁂

I felt sorry for my son who was two months old and completely unaware of how worthless his daddy was. It was a minor consolation that his mother was everything that a man wants for his children, but nothing can completely fill the void of an absent father. For once in my life, I had the actual opportunity to be something that nobody else in the world could be: my son's father.

Yet there I was trying to live out some type of Hollywood fantasy *just to see if I could.*

Not totally sure what my next step would be, I found myself taking solace in the fact that I had kept such great care of my little secret. Even from the very beginning, I knew one of my keys to success would be simply not telling another soul. Because souls have guilty consciences. And guilty consciences call the police. And police arrest criminals. Then criminals go to jail.

I also found myself appreciative of the fact that nobody could share in my embarrassment. I'd never been one to make goals, so it made total sense that none of my planning ever involved an end game. Consequently, it wasn't even clear to me whether I had failed or succeeded. Either way, humiliation had overcome me.

By now, I was so sick of returning to square one. My method of living was clearly not serving me well, but for someone whose pride rested comfortably in the center of his own imagination, I had to finally accept the fact that I could not solve my own puzzle. There was nothing special about me. I wasn't otherworldly genius. I was just a pitiful waste of mass. I couldn't even manage a functional existence.

In the coming year, I would make more than a few major decisions that would affect the overall course of my life forever, and they all hinged on the one decision I was finally ready to make.

I was done. I was so done.

With everything.

THE ROAD TO FREEDOM

It's hard to even imagine a world where a Sunday drive isn't an option. Some of my greatest memories involve driving. With a large enough gas tank and a long enough road, I could drive forever.

In Dallas, traffic has its own personality, and the collective mood of motorists can shift without warning. A source of stress for most, it provides an oddly comfortable space for me to kick around ideas inside my head. The chaos of rush hour traffic is enough to prevent my mind from wandering too far because for some strange reason, distractions help me focus.

I wanted to figure things out. Specifically, I wanted to figure myself out. What was my purpose? Did I even have one, or was I supposed to merely float through life trying to find a way to not be bored?

In the final few weeks of 2006, I was driving myself crazy. Nothing made sense, and there were too many options to consider. But something had to be done. Weeks had passed since deciding that I would never rob a bank again. That was one of my easier choices, of course, yet I wasn't fully sure how to proceed to the next stage of my life. I wanted to call my wife and go be with her and my son, but I also didn't want to be married anymore. Never mind the fact that I absolutely had no clue how to be a dad.

Trying to devise a plan as I drove aimlessly throughout Dallas, it was becoming obvious that there was only one path to healing. With each passing hour, it was more and more apparent that my best option involved complete transparency.

To everyone.

About everything.

⁂ ⁂ ⁂ ⁂ ⁂ ⁂

In all likelihood, my crimes would have remained unsolved. Given the manner in which I had committed them, there was no realistic possibility for anyone to connect me to any of those robberies. With the exception of some random coincidence, the only way I could have gotten caught was to call the police myself and tell them who I was and what I had done.

There seemed to be a million reasons why prison was the next logical step for me. First and foremost, being convicted for my crimes was the only way I could ensure that my past wouldn't creep up on me a decade later when my son would be approaching his teenage years. It's not that I wanted to go to prison while my son was an infant. I simply didn't want to risk being gone while he was a teenager. Getting caught was incredibly unlikely, of course, but it wasn't impossible, so I had to at least consider it.

Furthermore, I could feel that something had shifted in me, and I wanted a safe place to work on myself without the weight of responsibilities holding me down. Selfish as it sounds, that was my reality. More than ever, I simply needed a time out. I needed prison.

⁂ ⁂ ⁂ ⁂ ⁂ ⁂

The choice itself required little thought. To most, the idea of a criminal handing himself to the police seems absurd, but it was actually one of those decisions that seemed to make itself.

As with each of my robberies, I wanted to have a plan of attack. I didn't want to go blindly into a world that was completely foreign to me. I didn't want to just give myself up to law enforcement without having any idea what their process might involve. And I sure as hell didn't want to go to prison without the slightest idea of what that might be like.

It was weird trying to plan for such a bizarre thing. Would I simply call the police and tell them to come get me? Would they even know who I was? Perhaps I could simply stroll into the nearest police department and give myself up that way. But then what? I knew so little about the legal process that I wasn't even sure if they would arrest me on the spot for confessing to robbery or if they would first need to confirm my story. And after the arrest, would they let me go home until a trial, or would I go straight to jail and just sit around until it was my turn to see a judge? What exactly were they going to do with me? I had never been in actual legal trouble before, so I had zero experience to draw from. I needed answers.

Hollywood does a great job of telling partial stories. Sure, those stories are entertaining and pack a lot of information into a small time frame—in just a couple of hours, you can learn about flux capacitors and time travel, or you experience the mystery behind a kid who sees dead people—but it's impossible for Hollywood to tell the whole story in two hours. Something always ends up on the cutting room floor. Perhaps this is why I hate movies. They manipulate your emotions and induce reactions rather than actually telling a complete story and allowing the reactions to come naturally.

In movies about bank robbery, Hollywood completely fails at telling the whole story. Among the countless films I had ever seen about bank robbers, not a single one of them detailed the process of being arrested and going to prison. Robberies either end in massive shoot-outs or action-packed getaways or suspiciously ambiguous scenes where the screen fades to black as a team of bandits disperses and disappears into oblivion. Hollywood doesn't tell you what happens when a lone robber gets away with his crime but later decides to turn himself in, and that is exactly what I needed to know that day while driving down a busy freeway in downtown Dallas on a beautiful afternoon with just a few days left in 2006. I just wanted to know what to expect.

☙ ☙ ☙ ☙ ☙ ☙

Contrary to what I always wanted people to think about me, most of my decisions are driven by fear. As a child, fear manifested itself in many ways. In school, I was afraid to give my best effort in class because I was scared of someone else knowing more than I knew or scoring higher than I scored. Even in sports, I half-assed it because *try harder* seemed infinitely more tolerable than *practice more*. One implies I'm in control and the other implies I'm not good enough. To this day, I've never actually sprinted at full-speed for fear of learning how fast I'm not. I'd rather be called lazy than slow. Yes, it seemed illogical that I was both confident and plagued by fear, but such was the contradiction in me.

In the same instant that I was considering fessing up to my crimes, fear once again influenced my thoughts. The fear of being a peaceful white guy in prison suddenly struck me. As someone who had always *thought* his way through life, I wondered if I were physically able to handle prison—a place where I assumed *thinking* was at the bottom of everyone's to-do list.

Hollywood told me that prison was a place where people either rape you or try to sell you cigarettes. Being a fan of neither, I wondered exactly how I would survive. Just as quickly as I had decided to go to prison, I soon replaced that idea with the plan of simply carrying on with my life and skipping the penitentiary altogether.

Then, I remembered my mother. Or, to be more accurate, I remembered the absence of my mother. When I was 12, she had relocated to Seattle from Dallas while my brother and I stayed with our dad in Texas. I remembered how it felt having a parent completely removed from my life except for phone calls and regular visits. During that time, it was always great to see my mom and spend time with her, but having her in town as a visitor wasn't the same. The time itself was similar, but it was a completely different feel altogether, and I hated it.

As a parent myself nearly 15 years later, I wondered what it might feel like if police somehow solved my crimes years later and tracked me down. I wasn't sure if there was some sort of grace period after which police could no longer charge me with those crimes. And even if there was a grace period, surely it would be *several years?...a decade?...several decades?* I had only heard the term "statute of limitations" on television, but I didn't know what it really meant. If detectives solved my crimes with just a few days left before the statute of limitations expired, then what? I would still go to prison; that's what! And what if I couldn't carry my own weight in prison? What if I somehow got shanked in a prison yard fight over a pack of cigarettes? *I don't even smoke!*

Even if I survive prison, what kind of damage would it do to my son if I was suddenly removed from his life when he was 12? Yes, he would still have regular visits with me and even phone calls, but I knew from firsthand experience that nothing can replace the daily presence of a parent.

Quickly, the scenarios in my head were spinning out of control, and none of them were good. It was the only time I ever caught a glimpse of what remorse felt like. *What on earth have I done? Why on earth have I done it? This was a bad idea!*

I called Larry, my best friend, and asked if he and his family felt like having company that night. I didn't know what to do, but I knew I needed to at least be in the same house with people who cared whether I lived or died. Although I wasn't clinically suicidal, the bridge pillars flying by me at highway speeds were at least starting to look like options. I didn't want to actually die. I just wanted my current life to end.

I wanted to get somewhere safe—emotionally and otherwise—and figure things out.

Frankly, I don't even recall what excuse I gave Larry for wanting to visit. Maybe I offered to bring over dinner. Maybe he was making sketty—his lifelong term for spaghetti—and invited me to join. Maybe I completely fabricated some harmless reason for needing somewhere to stay that night. I really have no idea, but as true friends usually do, Larry and his wife welcomed me into their home for a day…then a week…then a few weeks.

I didn't do anything productive the entire time I stayed with Larry and his family. I slept on the couch, woke up on the couch, and remained on the couch for days on end. They were already a family of five plus two dogs and a cat, so it wasn't like they were lonely and needed my company. But there I remained, day after day, becoming a permanent couch potato and watching Maury Povich and wondering why the lie detector was such a drama queen.

Larry's house was just a few short miles from the house where my newborn son, Jett, and his mother, Candice, were now staying with family in a nearby neighborhood. Despite living minutes away, I rarely saw Jett or Candice during my time with Larry and his family. There was nothing for me to offer them at that point. She was my wife, and he was my son, but I was neither a husband nor a father. Sure, my title remained, but the embarrassing reality was that I was of no real value to anyone by then. I managed a few visits here and there, but they were always depressing and awkward.

Sheer misery for everyone.

During one of those visits, Candice let me know that a detective had left a message for me to call him. My brother had also told me of similar messages that were left on his voicemail. The messages weren't identical, but someone was definitely looking for me. The messages never stated reasons for the calls or visits either. The person leaving the message was a detective simply requesting me to contact him at my earliest convenience either by phone or in person.

It wasn't immediately obvious why he was trying to find me, but I quickly narrowed to three possibilities. First, it could have been about traffic tickets that had turned to warrants, which was of little concern to me. Another option was, of course, the bank stuff. But I felt that was highly unlikely because I didn't think that was something a detective would merely call someone on the phone to chat about. The third possibility seemed to be the most likely. *They must be looking for my truck*, since I hadn't paid on it in several months, and *the bank must want it back*. It seemed like a pretty slick trick to get me to drive to the police department—a place one would normally expect to be safe and trustworthy—just so they could repossess my truck. Surely they didn't think I was so stupid to fall for such a trick. *No thanks, Mr. Unnamed Detective of Unsaid Police Department. I don't think I'll be stopping by to have my truck repossessed.*

Just for kicks, I decided to call the number one day and talk with the detective. He wouldn't answer questions over the phone but was quite polite about it, of course. He promised it was no big deal or anything to worry about. He even told me it wasn't urgent and to simply give him a call next time I was in town. I clarified that I no longer lived at my house and that it might be several months, if ever, until I was in town again. With his friendly Texas accent, he reiterated, "Just come on by next time you're in the area."

It annoyed me that he wouldn't give me the slightest glimpse into why he was looking for me, but it also gave me confidence that it definitely wasn't a legal matter. I was positive that it was a trick to repossess my truck, so I called the lender and confirmed that they were indeed attempting to recover my truck. Strangely, they even gave me the phone number to the repo man himself, so I gave him a call.

The man who answered sounded exactly like the kind of redneck you might see in a reality show about the repo business. After a few short phone calls, we came to terms and agreed to meet. He paid me a small handful of hundred dollar bills for the peaceful recovery of the pickup truck that was no longer mine. After that transaction, I officially had no means of transportation. Aside from a small amount of clothes and a Rubbermaid tub full of personal items, my life had been effectively reduced to a backpack.

Without a truck payment, rent, or any other immediate financial obligations, I thought it only made sense to share some of the repo money with Candice. After all, she was the one taking care of my son.

The next morning, I planned to go to Oklahoma to visit friends and play poker at one of the Indian casinos where everybody was friendly and happy to lose their money one tiny dollar at a time. It wasn't a problem that I had no vehicle because the casino had a free shuttle to and from Dallas. I wanted to get back to Oklahoma so that I could plan my next step.

Before leaving Texas for the last time, I went to see Candice and the baby. They were within walking distance for a somewhat healthy man in his late 20s, so it was not a problem to throw some clothes into a backpack and walk to the house where they were staying. A winter storm was coming through that night, but it hadn't hit yet, so I wasn't the least bit uncomfortable walking less than an hour in flip-flops, track pants, and a thin windbreaker. In fact, it was kind of pleasant. Besides, I still had a pocket full of hundred dollar bills from the repo man, and I still wanted to give some of it to Candice.

When I arrived, Candice's family was out of town, which was a relief to me. I loved her family, but it was just better to see as few people as possible. I didn't want to fake my way through the shame of being a deadbeat dad who just popped in and out of the lives of his wife and son.

As always, the visit was melancholic. There was nothing happy about holding the baby I was failing to support in any way, and no matter how much Candice smiled or told me how much Jett had grown since the last time I saw him, it was simply miserable knowing that I was not living up to my role as father, and there was nothing anyone could do to fix that.

After a few hours, the bad weather started rolling in and the night was drawing to a close. The baby was asleep, but Candice stayed up talking with me in the living room. Earlier at Larry's house, I had told him that I wouldn't be coming back and that I would probably stay with Candice before catching the bus to Oklahoma the following morning. What I didn't expect was Candice telling me that I had to leave and couldn't stay overnight. Her family was out of town, and she didn't feel comfortable with me spending the night in their house.

By that point, the nightly news was over and she was ready to go to sleep herself, which meant I needed to leave. The cold front arrived during our visit, and the temperature had dipped into the teens. Since Candice wasn't about to wake up the baby to take me anywhere, I was on my own with nothing but flip-flops, track pants, and a thin windbreaker to walk to...wherever it was I was about to go.

A small part of me was angry that Candice wasn't concerned about where I might go or how I might get there. But the rest of me was proud of her. I never doubted that she would do just fine raising Jett on her own, but kicking me out of the house into sub-freezing temperatures with nowhere to go also proved that she was no longer trying to solve my problems. No matter how angry I wanted to be, I was mainly just reassured that she really had what it took to make the tough decisions regarding me.

However, as I left the house and started down the street, the freezing air quickly changed my attitude. Every last thought in my mind was replaced with anger. *How could she do this? To me?!*

In my backpack, I had the spare key to her car. She didn't know that, of course, but I had always kept it with me. Just in case.

The car was parked in the garage, but I knew how to open a garage without making much noise regardless of whether or not it was locked. I wouldn't *steal* her car. I would just *borrow* it to drive somewhere warm for the night and then return it in the morning in time for her to go to work. She would hate me for it, of course, but that didn't matter to me because I was literally freezing and needed to think of something fast. It was nearly midnight and the temperature was approaching single digits.

As I got to the end of the street, I turned and walked back up the alley. I walked at a pace that gave away the fact that I was both cold and about to do something wrong. I fumbled through my backpack to make sure I still had the key to her car.

I did.

When I got to the house where her car was parked safely inside the garage, I walked up the driveway, to the garage door, and stopped. I wondered exactly how quiet I could be. Candice was not exactly a light sleeper, so I wasn't worried about waking her up. I also wasn't concerned about any sound the car might make because I could simply put it in neutral and roll it down the street before starting it.

I felt nothing about the fact that I was about to steal her car because I needed it more than she did.

But what if there's an emergency? What if she needs the car and it's not there? What if she's still awake and sees me taking the car and calls the police?

I couldn't do it. There were too many risks. For once, I just didn't have the audacity to do the wrong thing. I turned around and walked away from the garage door, back down the alley, to the end of the street, and to nowhere in particular.

I didn't have a cell phone, so I couldn't call my only friend, and I didn't feel comfortable suddenly returning to his house unannounced after midnight. It felt almost obvious that he and his family were happy to have me off the couch and out of their house for once, so I searched my mind for any viable option and decided on going to the only local business that was open all day every day and might not notice me simply sitting there not spending any money. I decided to walk to the nearest hospital and sit in the emergency room all night until I could think of something better.

Earlier in the night, when the weather was nicer, a short stroll in my old man lounging attire was relaxing, but in the middle of the night in unbearable cold, it was quite miserable. Flip-flops aren't exactly the best footwear for walking across town with a backpack thrown over your shoulder.

Nearly six miles and two hours later, I finally walked through the automatic doors of a quiet hospital in Mesquite, Texas. I wasn't ill, and I didn't need medical care, but I couldn't think of a better place to sit among strangers in the middle of the night without drawing any attention to myself. Thankfully, nobody said anything to me as I walked in. There was a television just above a row of chairs. My eyes were on the TV but my mind went elsewhere. Still standing, my backpack felt like a pile of bricks, so I dropped it into a chair and collapsed backward into a chair myself.

The nearest clock showed approximately three o'clock. I tried to get comfortable, but if you've ever sat in the waiting area of an emergency room, you know how impossible it is to achieve any level of actual comfort. Besides, I was too hungry to fall asleep, so I just sat there and watched the looping news feed on TV until sunrise.

❧ ❧ ❧ ❧ ❧ ❧

My mother went to work early enough that I didn't feel bad calling her house at 7:00 a.m. I needed a ride to the bus stop where the casino's shuttle would pick me up for the trip north to Oklahoma, and my mom was pretty much the only person left for me to call at that point. She asked a few harmless questions, and I answered them, but I didn't really want to get into the full story. I was in need, and that was the bottom line. My mother was the one person in the world who would be there for me no matter what. Because of the winter storm that blew in overnight, the roads weren't entirely safe to drive on, but she was there within a couple of hours to take me wherever I needed to go.

When she showed up, I was hungry past the point of a minor stomachache. I felt famished to the point of complete depression. My mother fixed that, too, taking me to get breakfast so that I could eat on the way to the bus stop. I couldn't remember the last time I had seen my mother before that, but it had been several weeks, if not months. By then, I had done everything I could to hide from the people who cared about me the most, and I did my best to convince myself that they didn't care about me at all. I felt completely alone in life, and I took offense to anyone saying otherwise.

At the bus stop, I hugged my mom and told her I loved her. She loved me back, of course. Less than two hours later, I showed up in Oklahoma with nothing more than a backpack full of dirty clothes and a pocket full of legitimate cash from the redneck repo guy. I had no job, but the $1/$2 No Limit game at the casino seemed like a fine place to start. It was hard to ignore that my family back in Texas all thought I was a gambling addict, and the thought of them knowing the amount of time I was about to be spending at the poker tables made me cringe. I kicked around the possibility that gambling might indeed be a problem for me, but reality set back in and told me that poker was not a gamble in the way that my family thought it was. Yes, poker definitely included risk, and yes, certain aspects of the game were out of my control. But it only *involved* gambling, and I was not addicted.

Even if I were addicted to poker, I was also addicted to eating, and poker seemed to be my best opportunity to make any sort of income without having to rely on a steady work schedule. As a poker player, I could come and go as I pleased, and nobody could tell me what to do. I was definitely addicted to that.

It was impossible to ignore what I was leaving behind in Texas, but I felt it was for the best. While I cared about my wife and my son, I knew they would be fine and well taken care of, even if it meant relying on family to help watch the baby while Candice worked. As much as I was running from my problems, I also felt like I was the problem, and I was convinced that it was better for everyone involved if I was nowhere to be found. I decided I would stay in Oklahoma until it was clear what exactly my next steps would be. For the next few weeks, I lived at the casino and played poker on a daily basis to cover my basic living expenses.

As much as I had dreamed of playing poker for a living, I was still miserable and empty. But it had nothing to do with the game itself or the people I chatted and laughed with all day.

No matter how much I wanted to pretend like Texas didn't exist and that my life was now in Oklahoma, it just wasn't happening. The few friends I made were poker dealers who probably only liked me based on my tipping habits. The more time I spent in Oklahoma away from my family, the more I was forced to accept my life as it was—lonely and pointless. But it was my own fault. Everything that had happened to that point was based on a chain reaction of decisions that I had made. The reality of responsibility was starting to set in.

Eventually, I began to get sick. Not physically, but emotionally…perhaps mentally. More and more every day, things just got deeper and darker, and I tried to imagine a scenario in which I served a valid purpose in life. I started to believe that I was worth more dead than alive, but I was too full of myself to seriously contemplate taking my own life. Besides, I was actually quite afraid of dying.

The more time went by, the more my decision was clear that I should indeed give up my life and start over from scratch.

⁂ ⁂ ⁂ ⁂ ⁂ ⁂

Fully dressed and sprawled out on top of a completely made-up bed in my hotel room at the casino where I had been pretending to be the happiest guy in the world, it was time to get serious about life.

I went back to the decision I had made weeks earlier and knew it was time to call it quits and go to a controlled environment where I could start the process of working myself over from the inside out. I was over the fear of losing my freedom, and I was no longer worried about being the quiet white guy who might die in a prison fight over cigarettes. Those fears soon seemed insignificant compared to how bad life would be if I ran from manhood forever. The *pain of staying the same* had become greater than *the pain of changing*, and I was just sick of hurting.

The hotel room where these revelations were becoming clear to me felt more like a prison than anything I imagined actual incarceration might be like. Over the next several years, I would learn terminology to put into context exactly what I was going through, but in that moment, I had no idea that I was in a *prison of my own making*, as Susan Olesek would later say.

Sitting up in the bed, I looked at my reflection in the mirror across the room, and without any emotion I told myself, "You're going to jail, buddy."

After a brief pause, I laughed at the absurdity of the statement itself along with the comfort I found in both saying and hearing it. Just for kicks, I repeated the same line while impersonating any notable person who came to mind. In my best Chuck Norris voice, *You're going to jail, buddy.* And then my Clint Eastwood impression, *Are ya ready for jail, punk?* That one made me laugh even harder. But I completely lost it when Edith Bunker appeared in my mirror to whine, *Ohhh, Archie. You can't go to jail!*

I had the presence of mind to know that I was just having a little fun. I didn't *actually* see these people in my mirror, and I definitely didn't hear them. The body often releases fear in the form of laughter, and that's really all I was doing, I think.

It felt so good to laugh.

The air in the room changed. My lungs appreciated the fresh breath as my brain sent happy signals throughout my body. My smile even came out of retirement. I was destined for prison, and I couldn't have been more content.

With a clear mind, I could finally begin to theorize, test, and plan the next few months. First and foremost, I planned without regard for what anyone else might suggest. This was not for lack of concern or respect for the wisdom of others. I just felt that my plan would only work if I was the one making all of the decisions for myself instead of others injecting their own ideas. Besides, anyone I might talk to about this would likely tell me I was crazy.

It was weird to think about the conversation I would eventually have with police. I knew enough about law enforcement to know that it was probably much safer to have that first conversation over the phone and out of the physical reach of any overeager cop looking for a criminal to rough up.

As for jail itself, I wasn't sure how to prepare myself for that. My best idea was to find a way to replicate incarceration on my own until I was ready to try the real thing. It would be a sort of dry run, and I could still back out or at least postpone it indefinitely if I didn't like what I was experiencing in my own mock trials.

A dress rehearsal, if you will.

Before jail, I thought being incarcerated meant staying in a cell with concrete walls and steel bars similar to the infamous orange square on the popular board game Monopoly. I thought all meals were eaten in that cell, and it was only logical to think that each cell must have a toilet, a bed, and maybe a desk for writing letters to various pen pals across the country.

In my mind, a jail cell slightly resembled a small hotel room minus the carpet, telephone, and cable television. Therefore, I determined that I could simply lock myself in a hotel room and order my meals to simulate prison. This was crucial to my process because I didn't want to just jump headfirst into my new life without any prior experience.

Without much preparation, I decided to just give it a try. In the hotel room that had been my home for several weeks, I unplugged the phone, turned off the TV, closed the drapes, and sat on the bed doing absolutely nothing.

Just like jail, I thought.

An eternity passed before I finally ordered lunch a few hours later around noon. I've never been one to hate being alone, but I was so happy to see the delivery person who brought my food—partially because I was hungry but mostly because I was just happy to see another human. After paying for my food and closing the door, I returned to the bed and ate my lunch in a matter of minutes before returning to Hotel Jail.

Time flies when you're having fun, but it comes to a screeching halt when you're not. No matter how much I tried to pretend that being alone in a room with nothing to do didn't bother me, the sheer loneliness of it all began to affect me. Hours passed, but they felt like days. I counted the dots on the ceiling and pretended to see constellations. As usual, the Big Dipper was the easiest to find, and so was Orion's Belt. I even saw a few shooting stars, which seemed unlikely in a sky made of plaster.

Occasionally, my mind returned to reality, especially when I got hungry and needed food.

What felt like forever was actually only a day. After breakfast the following morning, I'd had enough and came out of the hotel room to get some fresh air. In my makeshift, self-enforced jail cell, I didn't even last two full days.

I gave it another shot and barely lasted a few days before needing to come out again. Never in my life had it ever been a problem to stay holed up in a room by myself for days on end, but when I tried to emulate jail, I suddenly felt trapped and hated every bit of it.

I continued building my tolerance, staying in the room until I just couldn't take it anymore.

Fortunately, things had gone well at the poker tables in those first several weeks in Oklahoma. I had won enough to maintain the outrageous daily rates for the hotel room I stayed in every night, and I had plenty of money for food. I had also made friends with the right casino workers, and they started comping my rooms and meals. I guess playing 16 or more hours of poker every day has its ridiculous perks.

I stopped playing and continued the Hotel Jail experiment as money allowed. When I had enjoyed a few good days in the poker room, I would disappear to the hotel room to see how long I could last.

Eventually, it worked.

Multiple attempts and several weeks later—and without knowing exactly when it happened—I was suddenly okay with sitting in a room and doing nothing all day. I kept myself entertained with little paper footballs that I thumped through imaginary goal posts. I hesitated at the idea of drawing uprights on the wall but then realized nobody in jail would think twice about vandalizing a small piece of the wall if it meant having a friend for the day. And that's exactly what I did.

Soon, I became an expert. If ever there was a professional *Paper Football League*, I would most certainly be the champion.

In due time, Hotel Jail grew on me. There were even days when I actually preferred being locked in that room all day rather than coming out to be around anyone. I still enjoyed having my food brought to me, but after a quick *thank you* and *have a nice day*, I returned to my world void of any human interaction.

Without any responsibilities, those four walls provided a great place to just sit and think.

It was easy to laugh at myself when I noticed that I was perhaps slipping in and out of sanity. As most comedies go, it was funny because it was true. I had plenty of time to reflect on my life as a low grade criminal and how that might affect my chance of finding a job when I got out. Long *before* my actual incarceration, I was already wondering about life *after* prison.

My fantasies grew larger and wilder, and before long I found myself wondering about my life as a book or perhaps even a movie. I wondered which famous actor might portray me. I also wondered how much I would hate them for how horribly they played my role. I knew I would refuse to do any interviews after the movie came out because it would be so completely inaccurate and...and...*a bastardization of my life!* I would despise everything right down to the very title. *Urban Castaway? Who the hell makes a movie that was nothing but 90 minutes of a guy sitting alone in a hotel room for weeks on end?*

Wow.

It was time for another break.

❧ ❧ ❧ ❧ ❧ ❧

For the most part, when I was outside of the hotel room I was just meandering through the casino, hanging out with the people who had created such an escape for me for so many months. I had stopped playing poker for the most part because I had enough money to cover myself until I actually went to the police.

Nobody at the casino knew I would soon be disappearing for several years, so it felt a little odd smiling and pretending that nothing was out of the ordinary. At the end of the day, however, I was totally at peace with ending this part of my life and moving on to the next.

Hotel Jail provided a wonderful point of reference, and it showed me that no amount of incarceration could restrict me from my thoughts. I was happy to spend unusual amounts of time sorting through those thoughts in search of an answer.

Each stretch became easier than the previous one. I eventually used hotel stationery for writing instead of paper footballs. I thanked the delivery people for my food and shut the door promptly instead of holding onto any hint of conversation they might offer. Sleep came easily, and the days became routine. I had spent months preparing myself in whatever way possible by staying in that hotel room and pretending it was jail.

I wondered how much time I would serve in prison, but no matter how hard I tried, I couldn't find anything online that gave me any reasonable indication of what to expect. Because of my complete lack of experience in the penal system, I wasn't even certain that I would get a prison sentence rather than something like probation since I had no previous criminal history.

At the same time, probation seemed like a waste to me because part of the allure of prison was the notion that I could go to a place where I could focus on the biggest problem in my life.

Me.

⁂ ⁂ ⁂ ⁂ ⁂ ⁂

When people are sick, they go to the hospital to be cared for by doctors, and they don't leave until they are well enough to reenter the regular, healthy world. In my best assumptions, it seemed like prison could be just that—a place of healing. Everything would be provided for me—meals, safety, protection from life—and I would save all of my energy for figuring out how to stop being the person I didn't want to be anymore.

As one might imagine, I was still a little apprehensive about making that first call to police. Coincidentally, my seventh wedding anniversary was just a couple of days away, and I somehow felt weird about turning myself in and spending my first couple of days in jail on my anniversary. Granted, a lot had changed in the seven years since Candice and I had gotten married, and we certainly weren't celebrating anything together that year, but I decided to wait until the day after my anniversary.

⁂ ⁂ ⁂ ⁂ ⁂ ⁂

On Monday, May 21st, 2007, I called Candice at work and told her we needed to talk. I explained that I would be going away for a while. This "away" was much different than all the times I had previously run from my problems. This wasn't going to be like the countless times that I had left her a note at home saying that I might or might not ever come home. This wasn't going to be like the times that I promised one thing and did another. I told her about the bank stuff and that I was returning to Texas to turn myself in. I didn't have much more information for her, but I promised to be in touch as soon as possible.

It was a relief to finally tell her what I'd been doing. I didn't go into all the details with her, but it was the first step in opening up the lines of real communication again, and I felt like that could only lead to good things.

As awful as I had been as a husband, Candice was still my friend when we spoke on the phone that day. For the most part, she simply listened to me as I fumbled for the right words to admit that I had indeed committed some fairly serious crimes and would now be facing the consequences. She didn't have any snarky comments, and she definitely didn't make me feel like the trash that I was. Just like all the times we had spoken on the phone a decade earlier as teenagers, she simply listened to me.

Most women in her shoes would have ripped me a new one, but one of the many wonderful qualities about Candice is her heart. There was no reason to kick me while I was down, so I wasn't surprised when she didn't have any nasty remarks for me. Aside from simply confirming that she had indeed had certain suspicions, she didn't really react to anything I told her. And it wasn't that she was giving me the silent treatment or anything like that. I was the one doing all the talking, so she was simply listening.

There were plenty of times during the dark days that I was thankful for Candice, and that phone call was one of those times. Even if our marriage didn't work out, at least I knew I could count on her to be there for me when I really needed it. I wished I'd never stopped believing that in the first place.

After we said goodbye, I called information and asked for the non-emergency number for the Allen Police Department. The person who answered the phone likely thought my call was a prank. It's not every day that someone calls the police with information about a crime and then follows with, "Well, it was me." The person on the other end of the line gave some quick instructions including the police department's address and the phone number to call when I got to Texas.

By that point, it had been several months since I'd had my own transportation, so I rode a bus from Oklahoma back to Allen, Texas. I wanted to be alone on that bus ride, but it was full of old people who had made their daily trip to the slot machines.

There was a nice old man sitting next to me on that bus ride who spoke to me about life in the way that random old men usually do. He rambled on in the chatty way that says little more than *I'm uncomfortable with awkward silence.* Still, I had no choice but to listen, and what he said was somehow applicable. I wondered for a long time after that if he were real or if I had imagined him. God knows I could have used a friend in that moment—imaginary or otherwise.

My new friend talked about how happy he was to be old and that it used to make him sad when he thought about turning 70. All the men in his life had died long before that age, and he simply didn't want to die young. I mostly stared out the window at the passing earth below me and wondered if he had any idea how much I enjoyed his white noise chatter. He asked me how old I was and I told him that my 28th birthday was just a couple months away on the Fourth of July. He laughed and said, "A freedom baby, are ya?"

Yeah, sure. A freedom baby.

Everyone always has something cute to say about my birthday, and it always annoys me. Somehow, all I could muster at this old man's comment was a subtle chuckle. It actually didn't feel so bad. He seemed familiar, and it was difficult to dislike him, so I quit trying.

He spoke with the charismatic, comforting tone of a man who had already fulfilled most of his dreams and knew just the right words to help you fulfill your own. He wasn't condescending when he smiled at me and said, "I remember being 28." He hesitated briefly before continuing with a smile that turned into a soft laugh. "I thought I had it all figured out," he said. I liked him talking to me, but I had no reply, so I simply sat and waited for more. He paused again before continuing. "I hope you don't think you have it all figured out."

"No, sir," I mumbled, not realizing he hadn't actually asked me anything.

He abruptly changed the subject and asked if I had any children. I told him about Jett and how he was the largest baby I had ever seen—10 pounds, 7 ounces, and 22 inches long at birth. He was two months old and currently at home with his mom. *Are you and his mother married?* I explained that the previous day was actually our anniversary but that we were also separated at the time. He insisted that I find a way to fix it. Somehow, I didn't want to strangle this old man every time he injected his opinions into my life. It didn't even annoy me. It just felt like I was talking to my Grandaddy. I simply sat and listened, thankful that he was there.

Almost predictably, he got off at the first stop the bus made, so our conversation was over after a brief 30 minutes. Before exiting, he shook my hand and told me to hang in there with whatever was bothering me. *Interesting,* I thought, *I don't recall saying anything was bothering me.* I thanked him and watched him exit the bus a little sooner than I had wanted.

As the bus returned to the interstate and headed a little farther south, I was finally alone with my thoughts. I wondered if the police would be waiting for me when it was my turn to exit the bus. I couldn't remember how much I told them about where I was going or how I was getting there, but it seemed to make perfect sense that they would somehow know.

Nevertheless, there were no police waiting for me as I walked off the bus. With nothing but a small duffle bag in tow, I strolled across a large parking lot to a hotel and called the police department to let them know where I was. They promised to be there shortly.

To me, *shortly* meant something like 5 to 10 minutes, so when 20 minutes passed with no sign of police, I thought they might have gone to the wrong place. Going back into the hotel lobby, I called them again and made sure they knew my location.

Yes, they knew my location. *We're on our way, so don't leave.*

Going back outside, I sat on the curb by the hotel swimming pool. All I had was my standard black shirt and track pants with flip-flops as well as that duffle bag on the ground next to me. After several more minutes, I finally saw an unmarked car pulling into the parking lot. As I stood to walk toward the car, I heard the unmistakable voice of authority shouting from somewhere that I couldn't immediately identify. I was completely caught off guard and a bit disoriented. I could hear commands, but they seemed to be coming from another dimension.

I wasn't sure exactly what was going on, but I sure as hell paid attention. In an instant, I was surrounded by officers, but only one of them spoke. His instructions were loud and clear.

I will admit that I was a little scared in the moments leading up to actually being handcuffed. As you might expect, having a team of trained marksmen surrounding you with guns drawn has a way of creating a certain level of fear. I can laugh about it now, but never before and never since have I listened to or followed instructions with such precision. An entire childhood's worth of teachers would have been extremely proud. I did *exactly* as I was told.

The whole thing rattled me a bit because I was expecting a single car to come get me, and when I saw the unmarked car, I just assumed that was my ride.

The officers did their job, and I did mine. They were robotic and precise, and so the hell was I. Once handcuffed, I was quite relieved—mainly because that's when they all finally put away their guns. What came next simply shocked me. The arresting officer, who had been strictly business to this point, changed gears and asked me a question in a completely disarming tone that was just as much curious as it was confused. "Why are you doing this?"

Almost immediately, I heard myself answering, "It's that time."

It felt so natural and accurate to summarize my reasoning for so many things into those three words. He didn't have much to say after that and politely ushered me to a squad car and put me in the back seat. I kept expecting a rush of anxiety about going to jail, prison, or whatever else lay ahead of me. I kept expecting to have some level of regret. I kept expecting a "what have I done" moment, but it never came.

What did come, however, was a short ride to the police station where a detective welcomed me into his office, removed the handcuffs, and began to ask every question in the book.

A lot of those questions were about dates, times, and similar details. After recording basic information, he started asking more complicated questions about my motives for doing what I had done as well as my motives for turning myself in.

My answers were vague and unclear, I'm sure. There were a lot of things I didn't totally understand myself. What I did tell him was that I was largely unsure of how I ultimately came to the conclusion that robbing banks was something I would do. I told him I was totally okay with him speaking with any of my family or friends who were willing to talk to him, but they would all give him different stories about me. My family might tell him I was a gambling addict looking for money to feed an addiction. My close friends might say I was a clean and sober guy who simply enjoyed a solid adrenaline rush. Others would swear that there was no way I was capable of doing any of the things I claimed to have done because I was *a godly man, a good Christian boy.*

They would all be wrong, of course, but it was quite difficult to explain why.

❧ ❧ ❧ ❧ ❧ ❧

After speaking with the detective, I was taken to a jail cell where I sat on a metal bed and wondered if I had completely lost my sanity or if I was instead on the path to finding it. The emptiness of the cell seemed appropriate. With the exception of the clothes I wore and the Styrofoam cup of water in my hand, I now had nothing in life, and that seemed to be for the best.

Eventually, I lay down on the metal bed and looked up at the bunk above me. Scratched into the paint were the kinds of things you see in a restroom stall at a truck stop in the middle of hell. I wondered why anyone would waste their time vandalizing such an isolated place.

Without trying, my entire body relaxed and I was dead to the world. It was the best sleep I'd had in months, if not years.

When I woke up the next morning, my stress was replaced with relief. In the most unlikely of places, my life was finally my own. It was an interesting paradox because the police had technically taken me into custody, but in doing so they actually gave me something that I didn't even know I needed.

For the first time in my life, I experienced freedom.

And that was the start of something new.

JAIL

Jail was everything I expected. There was a bed surrounded by four walls. Attached to one wall was a stainless steel toilet-sink combination. The meals were brought to my cell, and they were horrible. The guards had no desire to interact socially, and I was more like a dog at the pound than a human being. I remained in my cell alone with nothing but my Styrofoam cup. And my thoughts.

What an interesting experience.

My second morning in jail, an officer woke me up early and told me he was taking me to the county jail. This was a surprise as I knew nothing of how the legal system actually worked. I would soon arrive at Collin County Detention Center in McKinney, Texas. It was enormous and looked more like a university than a jail.

The intake process was thorough and lengthy. They took a new mugshot and got new fingerprints. I found this odd since it had only been about 36 hours since my arrest, and the first jail was also quite thorough when they took me into custody. It didn't take long for me to realize that each jail essentially disregards every other institution's work. They each have their own intake process as if taking suspects directly off the street.

The waiting area at the second jail was huge. It was more like a waiting area at a hospital than a jail. There were about five rows of connected chairs facing a television that was mounted on the wall. The floor was carpeted, and there were three phones for collect calls only. There were approximately 35 other men waiting for the next phase of being taken into custody—whatever that was.

It was ice cold in that waiting area, but it was against the rules to put my arms inside my shirt. In fairness, the rules didn't matter to me because I wasn't totally sure what to expect and therefore would not be putting myself in a position that might leave me vulnerable to attack. It was only my second day in jail, and I was convinced that everyone around me was well aware of that fact. My periphery expanded, and the slightest movement caught my attention. I was certain someone would want to fight me before the day was over.

After a few hours, lunch was delivered to those of us in the waiting area. The kitchen staff was comprised completely of inmates in red jumpsuits, and they passed out trays that looked like Meals on Wheels leftover from the previous year's holiday season. The quantity was small, and the quality was a few grades below edible. I ate the two pieces of white bread and trashed everything else. I quickly drank the eight ounces of water given to me in another Styrofoam cup, but they didn't allow me to keep that cup, so it went in the trash as well.

Returning to the rows of chairs in front of the television, I wondered exactly why Maury Povich was so popular. Sure, he's a nice enough guy, but I never found that type of program particularly interesting. I'm not a fan of paternity test lotteries, and I rarely believe polygraph results. My fellow inmates enjoyed the show thoroughly though. They were completely enthralled and even made bets with each other about who was the father or whether or not the lie detector test determined *that* was a lie.

As for me, I found more joy in watching the inmates around me. Some of them were sleeping off their few-too-many drinks from the previous night, while one group didn't seem bothered at all by the fact that they were in jail because that Maury fellow sure is entertaining. Others glanced around wondering if they'd be going home any time soon.

Later in the day, dinner was delivered by the same red jumpsuited inmates with their rolling cabinets filled with trays of food that was even worse than the previous meal. This time, there were no slices of white bread. Instead, all I ate was the small piece of cornbread before trashing the rest of the whatever-that-was food. On any other day, I might have noticed that I was hungry, but the butterflies in my stomach sufficed while I waited to be taken to an actual cell somewhere in the facility.

An hour or two after dinner, a detention officer (as they preferred to be called) came and yelled a long list of last names to those of us in the waiting area. After arriving nearly 12 hours earlier, I was finally going to a cell. At least that's what I thought was happening. Those of us who were lucky enough to have our names called were ushered over to a room filled with shower stalls. We were each given a towel, a small bar of soap, and a green jumpsuit to change into. We were told to bathe from head to toe and to be done in less than three minutes. Afterward, we would each go to a window where we would hand over our street clothes in exchange for another green jumpsuit and a rolled up mat. Either the jail taught yoga, or my new sleeping arrangements were going to be much worse than I had anticipated.

The last stop in the intake process before receiving my housing assignment was to sit in a room and watch an orientation video about the jail and all of its rules and processes. It was about 45 minutes long, and I'm pretty sure I was the only one who was actually paying attention. Most of the rules were pretty simple—*Don't fight. Do as you're told. Tell us if you fear for your life and we will place you in protective custody where the bogeyman can't get you.* But other rules seemed a bit ridiculous. For example, the exchange of food was strictly prohibited and punishable. The purpose of this rule was supposedly to prevent the weaker inmates from being bullied and having their food taken from them, but instead the rule actually meant that I was about to starve to death because there was no way I could survive on two pieces of white bread at lunch and a piece of cornbread at dinner every day. I was either going to have to eat food I didn't like or learn to enjoy hunger pangs.

Once the orientation video was over, the detention officer came and got each of us individually and took us to our new homes. Mine was a cell with an old white man who was already asleep for the night. I tried to be as quiet as I could because it felt very imposing walking into an 8x6 foot room where someone was sleeping. Silence was impossible because I had to unroll my mat and place it on the top bunk. He rolled over and grumbled some nonsense before sitting up in his bed and shuffling his feet around. From the sound of it, he was putting on house shoes of some sort. After a minute or two, I was comfortable in bed and facing a concrete wall just inches from my face. After sitting in the waiting area for more than half the day, I was happy to be on anything soft and horizontal. As I drifted to sleep, I heard the sound of the old man below me shuffling across the floor. I could tell he was walking toward the other end of the tiny cell, so I just lay still and kept to myself. The last thing I wanted at that point was pillow talk with someone I'd never met before.

After a few brief seconds, his feet stopped shuffling and what followed was a sound that reminded me how far off I was when I tried guessing what jail might be like. The old man below me was at the foot of my bed but facing the opposite direction where the wall-mounted toilet was. If I stretched, my foot would have kicked his head, but he was simply standing at the toilet.

Yep.

Urinating.
Inches from where I was trying to go to sleep.
Welcome to jail.

❧ ❧ ❧ ❧ ❧ ❧

My third day in jail was another learning experience. Unlike the previous two mornings, I did not have the option of whether or not I got out of bed. At 6:00 a.m., there was a man banging on my cell door demanding to see the wristband I had received during the intake process. Apparently it was "count time" and I was late to the party.

After being counted—to make sure we hadn't escaped, I guessed—breakfast was served in the dayroom, and I finally got a better view of my new home. It was nothing like I had imagined. The floors were carpeted, and it felt more like a library than a jail. This dayroom was large enough to fit 12 round tables at four seats per table. Breakfast was delivered by the same red jumpsuited inmates who soon began to remind me of Santa and his reindeer. As for the food, it was awful and borderline inedible. Again. This time, I had two tiny biscuits that were about the size of my big toe. Appropriately enough, their texture and taste were also probably something like my big toe as well. The food alone gave me second thoughts about my decision to turn myself in. And since it was against the rules to trade food, I could not give away anything else on my tray in exchange for more toe biscuits from other inmates. The butterflies were long gone and I needed real food in my stomach soon.

Grumbling at the dayroom breakfast table, my whiney thoughts were interrupted by the same yelling detention officer who had woken me up earlier that morning when I was sleeping through count time. Collin County Detention Center was a direct supervision facility, which means a detention officer was present inside the housing unit at all times to directly supervise and interact with the inmates. Every male inmate at CCDC was first assigned to the pod where this officer was now screaming basic instructions at us as though we were the Gomer Piles-of-shit to his Sargent Carter. For the most part, he simply reiterated instructions and guidelines that were already laid out in the aforementioned orientation video, but his delivery was considerably more irritating.

It didn't take long for me to hate him for how he spoke to the other inmates and me. I soon wondered what kind of person he was when he wasn't in uniform. *Does he have grandchildren? Do they know how horrible their grandfather is? Does he brag to the outside world about how tough he is for detaining violent criminals? Has he ever had to use that panic button strapped to his shoulder at all times?*

It was only my third day in jail. I had already found someone to hate, and I did not like that.

It was an early struggle to find purpose since I hadn't exactly known for myself just what the hell I was coming to jail for in the first place. Sure, I knew the actual crime and the relative details, but I wasn't totally sure what I expected jail to do for me. Would it be a place to heal, or would it just be a place to safely reside while the storm blew over?

Clearly, the storm itself was me, so it simply wasn't possible to sit and wait for it to pass. I knew that much, but it was a hard concept to grasp. Knowing little about jail and even less about myself, it wasn't immediately obvious what I should be doing while in custody, but I still felt like everything would somehow work out.

After breakfast—and after Officer Yeller's speech—I returned to my cell and climbed back into bed. I wasn't sleepy, but when you put two grown men into a small jail cell, their options are quite limited as to where they can go and what they can do. Nobody had given me pen and paper yet, so I couldn't sit and write. I definitely wasn't about to sit and chat with the strange old man in the bunk below me, so I got comfortable in my bunk and practiced my favorite pastime: daydreaming.

Soon, I heard a voice come over an intercom speaker that I hadn't even realized was in my cell. It was Officer Yeller in a non-yelling voice, "The dayroom is now open." Before I could totally figure out what he had said, I began to hear the loud clicks of automatic door locks releasing throughout the pod. Apparently we weren't confined to our cells all day after all. As the other inmates poured out of their cells, I simply stood at the window of my door and watched. A few of them gathered at different tables to play various card games, dominoes, and chess. Others went outside through a door just behind the pod officer's desk that I had not previously realized was even there. That door led to a large patio that was closed in with brick walls and a chain-link roof that would prevent anyone from escaping in the event that they could magically scale a 20-foot flat brick wall. There was also a basketball goal, but contact between inmates was not allowed, so the game of basketball itself was against the rules. Essentially, two things were allowed: walking in circles and sitting down.

Without knowing any inmates just yet, it seemed smarter to me to simply stay inside my cell and get a feel for this jail and, more importantly, the other inmates. Looking through that small window, I simply observed the other inmates from the safety of my cell while getting an idea of how everyone behaved in the dayroom. It didn't take long to realize that life in the day room was quite boring. The patio—or "rec yard" as they called it—was equally monotonous.

Jail was far more peaceful than one might expect. I kept expecting to see bad attitudes and perhaps even a few fist fights. The movies led me to believe that people in jail fight at the drop of a hat, but my experience felt more like church camp—a room full of people who were struggling to make any sort of awkward social connection. Nobody really *wanted* to be there, so they at least had that in common. As for me, there was nothing awkward about my social connections because I was not attempting to make any. I was completely content to stand there and examine everyone else's behavior.

Later in the morning, just before lunch, a man walked into the pod dressed neither as an inmate nor a detention officer. He wore some sort of identification on a lanyard around his neck and pushed two giant carts that were not unlike the carts that the red jumpsuited meal guys pushed around, except it was not late enough in the morning to be serving lunch just yet. I watched him closely because I was bored and had little else to do. As he was walking in, the pod officer yelled at everyone, "Rack it up!" I vaguely recalled this phrase from the orientation video, but even without the slightest bit of context, it was obvious that this order simply meant all inmates should return to their cells immediately.

Watching the guy in street clothes open up his carts, I could see that he was basically a portable convenience store. He had everything from snacks to personal hygiene and pretty much anything else you might like to buy in jail. Again referencing my memory of the orientation video, I deduced that this man was the Commissary Guy, but I had no idea how people were supposed to buy anything from him since part of the intake process is having any and all possessions—including money—processed as well.

One by one, inmates were allowed out of their cells to purchase commissary. I wondered again how purchases were made since nobody had cash in jail. As I watched, inmates handed a piece of paper that I presumed to be an order of some sort. Commissary Guy would then turn and fill bags with everything from ramen noodle soups to candy. The old man who shared the cell with me must have known that I was a little confused about the whole process, and he informed me that whatever money I had at the time of my arrest would be in my inmate trust fund.

I wasn't completely sure how much cash I had when I was arrested. The money from the bank stuff was long gone. Besides, I expected police to seize any cash in my possession because of the nature of my crime. Nevertheless, when it was my turn to come out of my cell and buy something from the Commissary Guy, that's exactly what I did. He informed me that I had enough money to *make store* as he called it. I didn't want to *make store* though. I just wanted to purchase pen and paper so I could finally start putting my thoughts to paper. After purchasing a writing tablet and a flaccid violence-proof pen, I returned to my cell, happy to finally be able to sit at the metal desk and write.

May 24, 2007

I have been staring at this paper for nearly ten minutes now, and I still don't know what to say. I have wanted to talk to you since the second I hung up the phone with you three days ago, and now all I can think to say is, "I have nothing to say."

My first letter was to Candice, the one person who I wanted to talk to the most…who probably wanted to hear from me the least. I knew I could just unload my thoughts to her on paper and feel good afterward, but my mind went completely blank, and I couldn't think of anything to write. All I really wanted was to sit and chat with her about nothing at all. A decade earlier, we were teenagers, and I could always just call her and chat about anything and everything for hours on end. Writing a letter in jail proved to be much more difficult than idle chat, but I rambled on.

This pen is really quite difficult to write with. It's only four inches long, and it's flexible…similar to a semi-wet noodle. Actually, it's just like the ink part of a normal pen. I guess they just remove that part and sell it to us. That's right…I said sell. I had to buy this piece of crap as well as the paper I am using.

Even as I wrote, I knew that I wasn't making any sense, but I couldn't help but recall something an English teacher once told me in high school. He said, "When you can't think of anything to write, just start writing anyway. Eventually, the nonsense will get out of the way and you'll come up with something worthwhile to write. When that happens, just keep writing. Whatever you do, just keep writing."

While I had failed that particular English class in high school a decade earlier, that particular lesson stuck with me at a time when I least expected it. There I sat in jail using a technique that I had learned as a failing student. My letter to Candice continued.

Time sure does go by slowly here. It seems like a week ago that I got here, but in reality, I'm only a couple days into this mess. I'm starting to have second thoughts about my decision to turn myself in, but there's no turning back now. I tried to call my mom last night, but she didn't accept the call. I can only call collect from here unless I'm granted special permission for a free phone call. I don't know why she wouldn't accept my call, so I'm not going to bother with calling her again…

I'm not exactly sure how visitation works here, but I'm pretty sure you can just call up here a day in advance or something and come see me. When I was booked in, they asked me to make a list of people who are allowed to visit me. I only gave them your name. I don't want anyone else coming up here. If you do come visit me, I would rather you not bring Jett the first time or two. I hope that makes sense without me having to explain it. I don't know that I can handle only seeing him through the glass without touching his hand or picking him up.

My writing was interrupted when the pod officer called for me and told me to pack my stuff. With no warning or explanation, they were moving me to another pod. The following day, I picked up where I had left off in my letter to Candice:

Last night they moved me to a more permanent cell. I really like it here. I share a room with a kid named Adam. He's only 19, but he's really cool, and I like his attitude. I feel like I got really lucky to not have to be locked up with some whacked out jerk. He's in here for robbery, too, except he did armed robbery, and he's looking at some pretty serious time...10-20 years. I'm pretty sure I will only be here for a short time, but I still have no real clue how long that'll be. I don't like thinking about it in case I'm wrong.

I knew that I would only be in the county jail for a short time before the feds came and got me, but in jail, it's nearly impossible to get reliable answers from anyone other than your attorney, and I didn't even have an attorney yet. In fact, I didn't really have much of anything. After the excitement of those first few days had passed, I was just another inmate waiting for just another court date. It wasn't long before my new home began to wear me down:

May 25, 2007

I wish I could more accurately describe this place other than saying how I feel so far. The cold temperature in the holding room where people wait to be booked in is unbearable. I have no idea why they make it so cold, but it's one of the more miserable and helpless feelings I've ever had. I was there for over 12 hours, and I never slept there…

For the most part, everything I wrote turned to complaining because negativity is the default energy in jail. My first week felt like a seesaw between positive and negative at times, but I had a moment of clarity on my fifth night:

I've always been prone to mocking people who are put in jail and suddenly have a better view of how they should live their lives. It always seems like people find all the answers in jail, but… this is different. I decided that my only real shot at fixing things…would have to be preceded by getting myself straight with the law and, more importantly, with God. I can only be honest by saying that I still don't really understand a LOT of things about God, but I don't know where to find the answers either. It's a very helpless feeling. As for legal matters, that's a piece of cake that will just take time…but it'll work out. At least I'm searching for the answers without concerning myself with what others may think.

After my first full week in jail, I reflected on the first day I had come in:

It's been a week now since I turned myself in. I still find myself daydreaming about the entire day really. Everything was so strange, as if it were a scene from a movie. For a while now, I've lived something only Hollywood could conjure up. It just seems so fake sometimes.

Fake was the one word that described how I had felt for so long. Most everything I had done was a direct contradiction to something else I had said or done, and very little of my life before being arrested made any sense whatsoever. During my earliest days in jail, however, it became clear that I was far more confused about myself than I had ever imagined possible. If knowledge was power, I was powerless in my own life.

I have so many emotions going on in me at the moment that I'm confused about how to ultimately feel, but I am content from just generally knowing that I have taken the first few steps toward being the man I'm supposed to be.

I just feel good.

TAKE TWO OF THESE

May 31, 2007

I feel so bland at the moment. I've only felt like this a few times in the last 10 days, and it really shows how much I've turned to food in the past when I'm down and out. There's nothing here to snack on. There's no late-night meal I can turn to or anything like that. These are the kinds of emotions that are very confusing to me. While I want so badly to be able to go to the nearest fast food drive-thru, the back of my mind is just the opposite and glad to be here because it knows the end result will be a more healthy body and mind.

I still have small disagreements in my head about a few things. One example is how I immediately want to compare myself to every person I've ever known who is either in jail or just got out of jail. The last thing I want is to be another person who thinks and says all the right things while being in jail only to go right back to their old ways the second they are released.

I guess it's different in my case since the change in myself was the cause instead of the result. This all makes perfect sense in my head, but it could just as easily be coming off as gibberish to anyone else. It's so easy for me to forget that this is only my second week of confinement.

I suppose this is the day I've been dreading all week...the day when I'm not overwhelmed with excitement or saying how this day was better than the last. Then again, I'm not even in a bad mood or even sad. I'm simply void of any emotion. If this is all I could ever complain about, my life should be a walk in the park on a sunny day for the rest of my life! The realization of what I'm even saying here is enough to put in me a good mood, but if I were in a good mood, that means I would have just wasted a lot of time writing all this other stuff, and of course that would put me in a bad mood. Maybe I'll just stay bland after all.

My cell consists of a concrete floor, four walls that are each solid white bricks, a stainless steel toilet protruding from one wall with a matching sink that is no larger than a mixing bowl, a mirror that isn't much larger than a handheld mirror, a metal door with a small window in it, a metal bunk bed that has someone in it right now, and a metal desk, which is where I sit as I write this. If I can't be depressed here, I can't possibly imagine what could possibly bring me down at this point.

June 1, 2007

Today was the best day I've had so far. It was definitely the kind of day I needed after yesterday. Everything that could have gone right went right, and nothing bad happened. I actually liked all three meals, and I was even able to make a trade for an oatmeal cream pie. I got mail, my mother came to visit, and to top it all off, it's Friday, which means we will be allowed out of our cells until midnight... definitely a good day!

Today was also the first time that I realized I'll be in jail on my first Father's Day...oh well. There's not much I can do about that now. The way I see it, that's a day for me, and nobody else cares, so it's all good.

There have been a lot of things about jail that I have avoided talking about because I don't want to explain it all the wrong way, but something just jumped out at me that describes this place perfectly. This place is JUST like church camp in so many ways that it's almost comical. The way the meals are served...the way the food even tastes... And here, you can meet someone on Monday and be best friends by Wednesday and then hate each other by Friday. That hasn't happened with me, and I don't expect it to, but that's just how the environment is. I'm with the same group of guys 24 hours a day, seven days a week, with no break other than when I'm in my cell.

Even still, I'm glad I'm here. I'm excited at what this all will most likely lead to. I can't imagine how odd (or even dumb) that might seem, but that's how I feel.

June 3, 2007

I don't know that I'll be able to remember much about the past (or next) couple of years. I feel like I've ruined what should have been the best years of my life. I know there are many good years to come, but I'll never have a second shot at life, and I really wish that wasn't the case.

My brain is starting to get out of control again, I think. I don't even know what the cause is, but I really feel like I'm losing touch (or focus) of what I'm even doing. I'm so tired of pouring my entire heart out onto paper and putting myself at such a big risk for a huge let-down, but at the same time, I want to convey every last thought I have onto paper. I have a feeling that I'll be glad I did, so I hope you're not throwing these letters away. Please keep them safe.

I didn't keep a journal in jail because inmates have no right to privacy there, and I hated the potential for a random cell check by a guard who had the absolute authority to simply thumb through my private things and potentially read anything I had written. Because of this, I simply used my letters to Candice as an equivalent to journaling. After all, she was the one person whom I knew would listen to everything I said without passing any sort of judgement on me. Often, I would simply blather on and unload my thoughts to paper, but I also sometimes wrote to her specifically.

June 4, 2007

It's hard to believe where we both were eight months ago. It was around this time when you and Jett were brought up to the hospital room. I might be remembering some things about that day out of order, but I definitely remember what happened that day all the way up to 8:54 p.m. when Jett was born, but the rest of the night (and pretty much the next eight months now) is a bit of a foggy memory.

My writing was rarely predictable, and I bounced between topics without warning or explanation.

The detectives from Rockwall came out to see me today. I was actually expecting them to be here sometime last week, but I'm not sure what took so long. There was a bank in Rockwall that I did last year just before Thanksgiving. I've kept that to myself until now because I wanted to wait and talk to them first. By the time you are reading this, you will probably know all about this, but in a nutshell, I came clean with them about that robbery, and I plan to talk to the FBI agents later this week about one other local bank robbery that I also did, and I should (hopefully) have a better idea about how much time I will be serving. It sure was a big relief talking to the detectives about the Rockwall bank today. I wish that would have happened sooner.

When I had first turned myself in, I had planned to discuss only my most recent crime. Without really understanding how the legal system worked, I was concerned that I would get a much larger prison sentence if I fessed up to every bank that I had ever done. Considering how poorly my last bank job had gone (and considering that it was the smallest take of all the ones I ever hit), it seemed most logical to only tell police about that last one. However, as I later came to find out, a good friend of mine had seen surveillance video from the Rockwall bank and had contacted police.

One detective from the Rockwall Police Department was the one who had contacted me several months before I turned myself in when I was doing my Hotel Jail experiment. Our face-to-face, as it were, finally happened in jail, as he would be one of the detectives who would interview me.

I'm not sure why, but I enjoyed speaking with law enforcement. It reminded me of all the times I had spent in the principal's office as a child, so the nostalgic vibes were impossible to ignore. I found regular police officers to be a bit annoying because they asked basic questions and didn't seem to know how to conduct an interview properly. Detectives were barely a step above that. Federal agents, on the other hand, were a completely different breed.

A couple of weeks before I'd written the previous letter to Candice, I'd had my first of two meetings with federal agents, and at that point, I was still a bit reserved with the amount of information I was willing to give. Sitting in my cell in Collin County one day, I received a call from the pod officer through the intercom. Walking out of my cell and over to the pod officer's desk, I saw two more detention officers who were there to escort me out of the pod, through the jail, and to an interview room where two men in black sat at a table. When I walked into the room, the two agents did that thing you see in the movies where they flash their unfolding-wallet-creds while simultaneously rattling off their names, positions, and ranks with the Federal Bureau of Investigation. I managed to contain my laughter, but it was definitely hilarious. I wondered which one was Mulder and which one was Skully, but that didn't make sense because they were two guys. They could have been Agent J and Agent K, except they were both white. As I sat down at a small table across from the talkative one, I wondered if they had one of those little red lights that every undercover cop in the 1980s Hollywood movies had. Thankfully, these ridiculous thoughts of mine subsided relatively quickly, and I managed to escape my fantasy without so much as a snicker.

When my two escorts left the interview room, they closed the door behind them and left me alone with the two federal suits. The room was smaller than a jail cell, if that's even possible. There was a single table dividing the room, and although I sat opposite of one agent, the other agent sat behind me in the corner. I figured he was the bad cop in this predictable setup, so I just let him sit there since I had no plan for them to really need to employ the whole good cop/bad cop routine.

With the exact professional tone you might expect a federal agent to have, the man in front of me began to thank me for my cooperation thus far with local authorities before going into a preliminary set of questions. Referencing the one bank I had confessed to, he asked for a detailed explanation of the entire crime to the extent that I was able to recall. I gave him the information that I deemed relevant—that I acted alone, that I had second thoughts, that the lady screamed her head off, and that the man at the front door lost his mind when the door locked behind me—but the agent scribbled at a much slower pace than I'd have thought necessary. I didn't know if he didn't believe me or if he just didn't care to rewrite the same details that were in the other police reports.

As he questioned me, he impressed me with how smoothly he transitioned from one inquiry to the next. His interviewing technique was considerably more thorough than that of the regular cops, but it was somehow less taxing on my psyche. It felt like I was chatting with a friend, yet he was robotic at the same time and showed no emotion—or sign of life, for that matter—as I explained my own process. When he was content with the information I had given him about the one bank I had robbed, he asked how many others there had been. It caught me by surprise that he skipped the part about asking *if* there were other banks. Instead, he just went forward as if I had already told him there were more banks. I feigned ignorance with little embellishment because I knew overreacting would be a dead giveaway. It didn't work because he directly, yet emotionlessly, told me that he didn't believe me. He backtracked as a matter of formality to acknowledge that he skipped the *if* on purpose before plainly asking if there were other banks. I answered with body language this time because I don't believe in repeating my answer to what was obviously the same question, but my shrug was not sufficient for the agent sitting behind me in the corner who had remained quiet until now.

"Okay, look," he said while stomping out of his chair, as if he had been in the conversation the whole time. "You and I both know this bank you told us about wasn't your first. I've seen the tapes. You ain't no rookie. You're not nervous. All hell breaks loose around you, and you just waltz out of there like it's no big deal."

He wasn't angry, but he definitely wasn't buying what I was trying to sell. I didn't say a word, and I didn't react. I just listened as he walked across the small room to the door and knocked as he continued talking. "So here's the deal. You have no criminal record, and you turned yourself in. Things are already working in your favor on this. I've only been doing this for about three decades, and I'm telling you right now you'll go to court and get 36 months. It doesn't matter if you only did one bank or five. You're still only going to get about three years either way, so there's no point in keeping this to yourself."

The door to the interview room had opened. The agent's knock had notified the detention officers in the hall that our meeting was over, but before leaving, he left me with a decision. "If you want to play dumb and basically call us idiots, then we'll have no choice but to find every unsolved bank job in America where the suspect fits your description, and we'll just say those were yours. That'll be a lot of work for us, but it ain't nothing compared to the amount of work you'll have to do to prove you didn't do them."

Somehow, I stayed calm and didn't react. He offered a second option. "Or you can tell us more and save us all a whole bunch of time. I promise you you're not going to do more time, but I understand you'll want to think about this, so just let us know when you're ready to talk again."

Before I could react, the meeting was over and the agents were gone. The two jailers escorted me back to my pod without a single word as if they hadn't just witnessed what was basically extortion. Everyone in that meeting knew that I was lying through my teeth when I said I had done only one bank, so it didn't bother me too much that they didn't believe my lie. What did bother me, however, was the overwhelming pressure I felt to succumb to that threat. It bothered me that I had no control in the matter. My only choice was whether or not I wanted to trust him. In my gut, I didn't believe he would really go through the trouble of pinning *every unsolved bank job in America* on me, but the risk was far too great. On top of that, I actually believed him when he said that a few more banks would not affect how much time I would eventually serve in prison.

When I got back to my pod, the dayroom was still open. There were guys playing chess at one table, cards at another table, and basketball outside. I zombie-walked straight to my cell and crawled into bed. I had a lot to think about, and it didn't seem wise to waste any time in figuring out exactly how I should proceed. I drifted in and out of consciousness before moving from my bed to the desk.

For quite a while now, I haven't felt like I could trust anyone, and that's the reason I've kept all this as much of a secret as I possibly could. One of these days, I hope I'm able to make sense of all this, but I'm sure it just seems like a big never-ending mess at the moment.

A better day is coming though. I promise!

It's almost comical how misunderstanding everyone is about my situation...especially here in jail. The guys I hang out with in here freaked out when I told them I'm adding two more banks to my list of charges. They absolutely trip out over my whole case really. Their lack of understanding is actually one of the things that make me feel better about my choice to be here. It's reassuring to know that these people can't relate to me, if that makes any sense.

I talked to the FBI today. It's so weird to be able to claim such a thing. It feels so wild...so unreal. The reality of it all is that I've made some extreme choices in my life, and everything is starting to pan out the way it never should have. My life should not be what it is today, and while I battle back and forth from time to time about who to blame, I realize that I'm where I am today because of decisions that I made on my own with the influence of no person or group of persons in my life, present or past.

With that said, it's very frustrating to look at my childhood and see so many "mistakes" that were made by those in charge of my development. I refuse to specifically blame my parents, and I won't even limit the list to my step-parents, aunts, or uncles. With such a large family, I was "raised" by a ton of people, so it's extremely tough for me to really point any fingers...as if it's even a relevant or legitimate thing to do anyway.

My frustration often becomes a very confusing mix of anger, sadness, and pure helplessness. Would it really have made much of a difference if I had been raised the specific way my mind required? Is there even such a thing, or am I just conceited and giving myself far too much credit for being anything out of the norm? After all, I barely made it through school, and I've failed every aspect of my life since. Then again, maybe all of this is the result of something far more integrated that I can't even understand.

The very words I use even bother me from time to time. When I go back to proofread my previous thoughts, I'm often embarrassed at the way I put my thoughts to paper. I cringe sometimes at the notion that I use a large vocabulary to hide an otherwise average intellect...convincing myself moments later that a "normal" person would never ponder such a thing, and the cycle continues.

Two weeks into my new life here, and I'm already noticing a trend that existed throughout my entire life in the free world. People mock me or make jokes about me being smart when we're in a group situation, but when I'm alone with someone, the mockery and jokes stop, and the genuine requests for help begin. Whether it's something as small as how to spell a word or something more intense like how to deal with a failing relationship, people ask for my advice. Why do people publicly hate me yet privately seek my thoughts?

It's all so confusing!

Meanwhile, I believe I was about to tell you about my talk with the federal guys...

Aside from the legal bonuses that were achieved by telling them about two more banks, I also felt a great peace and healthy pride of having done the right thing for once. Actually, instead of saying "for once" I can say "again."

For such a long time, I've felt like I was a person who lacked any sort of conscience and only made decisions out of personal desire, but I feel the urge to do the "right thing" lately, and even though I'm a bit hesitant to confidently note its origin, it's still a nice feeling.

MOVING FORWARD

June 6, 2007

I think about Jett more than I wish I did, but I can explain. Up to this point in his life, he has had no father. If I were to die tonight, he would never know the difference. The degree to which that bothers me is impossible to define by any form of explanation known to me. I've always wanted to be the irreplaceable father I felt I never had. I've always wanted to perfect all the imperfections that existed in the man that I haven't spoken to in six months. I still believe that I will be that man for Jett one day, but the bothersome fact still remains that I've never done a single thing for him up to this point.

While that thought bothers me, I still believe that this is what he needed—an absent father rather than a bad father. Maybe I'm wrong. Maybe he'll despise me despite anything I do once he knows that I wasn't around for his first...however many years this ends up being.

From the outside looking in, the average person would say that I couldn't care less for my son. I am pretty sure that some in my own family feel sorry that Jett's dad is such a piece of crap. In the end, I don't care what they think as long as my child and I have the relationship that he needs to have with his dad.

I'm still optimistic and convinced I've done the right thing in a bad situation.

June 7, 2007

Somewhere out there, there's a psychiatrist or psychologist who can help me better understand myself. I feel like that (the understanding itself) is the only medicine I'll ever completely need in order to be happy with myself.

❦ ❦ ❦ ❦ ❦ ❦

Those first two weeks in jail felt like an eternity. After being in custody a mere 17 days, I began to take an honest look at myself and figure out how much of my life had been affected by my own choices. Yes, my parents had divorced. Yes, I had bad teachers. Yes, the system failed me. But in jail, the system had failed everyone. I was surrounded by people who had life stories that made mine look like a walk in the park.

It wasn't long before I realized that I was locked up with a guy named Dee who had lived down the street from me for a few years when we were kids. Sitting in the dayroom playing cards one day, a few of us were comparing childhoods. Dee mentioned how cool my dad was when we were little. I laughed and said that everyone in my neighborhood only liked my dad because they didn't really know him. Sure, the boys on my street referred to my dad as Uncle Wayne, but I knew him as a power-tripping jerk whose main concern was to be in control. My friends knew him as the hilarious dad who had a ski boat and would take us joyriding in his pickup, but I dreaded when my friends weren't around because I thought my dad was mean.

"Mean?" Dee laughed because it was ridiculous, not because it was funny. "So your dad made you clean your room and cut the grass, and you call that *mean*? Man, my dad used to check my boxing game every day after school, and I lost every single one of those fights, trust me." To drive the point home, he showed a few shadowboxing moves before slapping the table and laughing because I'd said my dad was *mean*.

Dee went on to tell me his dad was an alcoholic who just loved to fight and beat up helpless people. I never knew those kinds of people actually existed because no matter how much I sometimes hated my home when I was a kid, at least nobody was throwing punches at me. My dad was quick to spank me with a belt, and I was constantly grounded for something, but I never actually feared for my physical safety, and I definitely didn't fear for my life.

Eventually, the conversation came back around to me, and when Dee asked me what I was doing in jail, I told him I was in for robbery. His eyebrows went up and he asked, "Oh yeah? Who you rob?"

With a bit of a chuckle, I said, "Chase." He asked who Chase was, and I busted out laughing. "You know…Chase! Like, *Chase Bank of Texas*."

Dee shook his head and stood up, "See, that's why you white folks be scaring me. I'm sitting here talking to some dude from my old neighborhood and thinking he's just here on some little dope charge or something, and now you wanna tell me you're a bank robber. What kinda shit is that, man? You crazy!"

I laughed even harder as he turned and walked across the dayroom back to his cell. I didn't believe he was really scared of white people. He was just being dramatic, and it was hilarious to me for whatever reason.

Left alone at the dayroom table, I grabbed my pen and paper again.

I need someone to write me. It's so lonely here. It's nearly two o'clock in the afternoon, so that's not late-night depression talking either. Being here has really magnified how many friends I don't have that I wish I did have.

I'm looking at these two pictures of Jett. I'm so glad to have these. It's hard to believe that's my son and that I'm missing so much of his life. Please record as much of his life as much as you can while I'm away.

I've wondered whether or not I should write to him while I'm here...not for his sake but for mine. There are going to be so many things that nobody can help him with other than me, and all those things are years and years away, so I'm optimistic knowing that this whole jail thing will be a distant memory by then.

When I thought about my son, I wondered what it would be like to be in his position. I wondered how it might affect him one day knowing that his father had gone to prison for the first few years of his life. I wondered if he would use that as an excuse to do bad stuff himself, and I wondered if he would blame me for all of his problems the way that I'd blamed everyone else for my problems.

I hated the idea of my son growing up and putting the blame on me for whatever choices he might make. I fantasized about the speeches I might give him about how his choices are his own and nobody else can take the blame for that. In those daydreams, I would have all the right words to say, and he would realize that I was right. In my fantasy, he would be accountable for his own choices, regardless of the outside circumstances.

Oddly, I had never fully considered that possibility for myself before jail. Consciously, I was aware that my choices were mine, but I still believed that I could have been much more successful in a better environment growing up. If only I had better parents...If only I had better teachers...If only the system had adjusted to me instead of me being required to adjust to the system...

But if I was going to give my son the accountability speech that I fantasized about, it only made sense for me to actually believe it and start living that way myself.

I experienced a noticeable growth based solely on the fact that I was willing to acknowledge that I had problems. I was clueless as to how I might identify and solve those problems, but there was great power in knowing that my problems began with the person in my mirror.

For far too many years, my identity had been defined by those around me. As a child in school, I had identified most with the kid inside me who constantly got in trouble. As a member of my family, I had identified most as the odd duck that didn't totally fit in. But being locked up in a world full of strangers forced me to really find myself.

❧ ❧ ❧ ❧ ❧ ❧

I returned to my cell and went deeper into my thoughts.

Initially, the mere idea of getting to know myself was exciting. The more time I spent alone in my cell reliving my past, the more I realized that I had never fully pursued my own personality.

> *Staying in my cell for nearly the entire day yesterday helped me analyze my situation for what it really is, and I feel that it's best for me to remain isolated as much as possible.*

As I wrote those words, it dawned on me that I had employed that strategy throughout my entire life and it had rarely produced a good result. Simple as it might seem, I decided that my path to change began with eliminating a few small habits.

Instead of spending the rest of the day to myself, I went back out into the dayroom and found a chess game to watch. At that point, I only knew enough about chess to understand what I was watching. I knew how the pieces moved, but I couldn't offer any competition to the guys playing. When they asked if I wanted to play, I declined.

Day after day, I wandered over to the chess table and simply watched. There never seemed to be any particular guy who dominated every game. It seemed to me that everyone was fairly equal in skill. It became my daily routine to watch those guys play chess all day. It was fascinating to me, and I wanted to learn more, but I never bothered asking questions. I knew how the pieces moved, but my knowledge of strategy was nonexistent. Instead of inquiring, I just watched and tried to figure it out for myself.

The jail in Collin County was a fairly civil environment, and it didn't seem to bother the chess guys that I just sat and watched without ever saying much. Eventually, I finally got the nerve to ask if I could play a game. I had been watching for hours each day, for weeks on end. I felt like I had grasped the concept enough to play and maybe even win.

Suffice it to say I did not win at all. Just a few moves into my first game, it was painfully obvious that I knew nothing about the game of chess other than how to set up the pieces and lose. It was somewhat embarrassing to be so terrible, and I wished I'd remained a spectator because there's no risk of losing on the sidelines. But those guys who played chess were cool. They didn't make me feel stupid or anything like that. They simply encouraged me to keep watching until I was ready to try again.

Between my fascination with chess and my hatred for jail food, all of my other problems soon began to disappear.

We have a three-week rotation of three meals per day that are served here for a total of only 63 different meals. I only eat 33 of them. To further break that down so you can realize how little I'm eating here, that basically equals one meal and one snack each day…a far cry from an unlimited amount of free casino food and going to Chili's every other day.

It's hard to imagine that I am still optimistic and confident in my choice to have my life put back together in jail. I don't feel crazy though. I feel fine. It's a nice feeling.

The routine of living in jail eventually normalized, and it no longer bothered me that I was woken up every morning an hour before breakfast just to stand at my cell door and show my arm band to a detention officer so he could verify that I hadn't escaped or died during the night. Never would I have expected that the same bracelet infants wear at birth would be the thing that jails used to ensure everyone stayed exactly where they were supposed to stay.

Instead of going back to sleep each morning after count time and risking missing breakfast, I usually sat at the desk in my cell and wrote.

All I really want is to repair all the things that I've broken and learn from my mistakes. I've screwed up SO many things in my life, but this is only the first of many steps to recovery…but I can't even define recovery. I can't tell you what that would even mean for me. From what am I trying to recover?

⁂ ⁂ ⁂ ⁂ ⁂ ⁂

Today was a pretty good day. First thing this morning at 4:00 a.m., the pod officer woke me up and told me that I had court. That was a surprise to me, and since I still don't have an attorney (and was told that I don't qualify for a court-appointed attorney), I was a little nervous about going to court. But the purpose of appearing in front of the judge was to determine whether or not I actually needed a court-appointed attorney. After a few quick questions, the judge appointed an attorney.

I got back to the jail from court just after lunch and was soon visited shortly thereafter by my newly appointed attorney who appeared dumbfounded and confused about my case. I like the guy, and I enjoyed our conversation.

The rest of my day was typical until around 9:00 p.m. when I met a guy who has been here since the day after I arrived. I've seen him around and knew he was different than everyone else, but I haven't had a reason to talk to him until he came over to me in the dayroom and started asking me a bunch of questions about how bank robbery cases are handled. Apparently he knew my charge and thought I could perhaps give him some advice since he's here for the same thing.

I wasn't much in the way of advice because, as I'm starting to learn, I'm quite ignorant on the whole judicial process. It's crazy how much I don't know. Before I came here, I just assumed my case would be a federal case and that the feds would just come take me and do their thing, but apparently the state can also charge me for the same crime. That's part of what my attorney discussed with me today.

> *He said the state will likely drop their case when the feds pick it up, but he also said the feds aren't likely to pick it up until the state drops it.*
>
> *Anyway, the guy who came over to talk to me in the dayroom is from Kenya. His English is perfect, and I found that impressive for some reason. His demeanor was similar to mine.*

I hadn't noticed just how much I was craving intelligent dialogue until I met the Kenyan bank robber. There were many types of people in prison, and it was quite sad to see just how low some people's lives could go. The detention officers didn't seem to help the situation either. Uniforms somehow gave guards absolute authority over the inmates, and rarely did those in charge seem to believe that inmates were humans at all.

I slowly realized, though, that I had been thinking of my fellow inmates as a group of people that somehow didn't include me. Even though I wore the same jumpsuit and was clearly locked up right alongside them, I somehow had subconsciously disregarded the fact that I was indeed one of them.

I didn't like that.

And it's not that I didn't like being *one of them* because facts are facts, and I'm okay with facts. What bothered me was that I clearly had a disconnection from reality. If my self-perception weren't based in reality, then what could it have possibly been based in? Furthermore, the mere possibility of being wrong about myself opened up an entire range of things that I was potentially wrong about. *What if there's actually nothing special about me? What if I'm actually not intelligent? What if I'm actually not in control? What if I'm actually just another criminal who got caught up in an unsustainable lifestyle?*

For the first time in my adult life—and likely the first time ever—I chose to contemplate what other people thought of me.

No, it wasn't literally the first time I had ever wondered how others perceived me, but it was definitely the first time I took their thoughts into consideration with regard to how I might need to adjust, or dare I say *change myself*, to the world around me. In fact, even that phrasing is inaccurate. There was no *world around me*. There was just a world, and I was part of it.

Like it or not, that was reality.

June 14, 2007

Once the legal dust has settled a bit and I'm in a long-term facility, I'm going to seek some serious help for myself. I think the biggest task ahead of me is identifying a starting point and a cause of all the things that make me who I am.

There was a sense of progress in simply being able to acknowledge that I needed help, but it wasn't that I wanted psychiatric treatment. I just needed help connecting the dots. When I thought about the way I went through life, it didn't make sense. Normal people respond to consequences and correct their mistakes, but I usually found joy in the consequences. Making mistakes was *more fun* than doing it right.

Not normal.

It wasn't that I necessarily wanted to be normal either. Frankly, that's still a terrifying thing to even consider. *Normal is average, and average is mediocrity. I'm comfortable being the extreme end of any spectrum, but I can't be in the middle. Being typical is for people who aren't special, and I'm not anything if I'm not special.*

But I began to wonder, *What's really so terrible about being normal? What's so awful about not being special?*

For the sake of being open minded, I considered what it might feel like to stroll through the dayroom, sit at a table with other people, and simply exist with them. Perhaps I could just exist in the conversation instead of sharing how much I knew. If they were playing a game, perhaps I could just play with them for the simple joy of playing a game rather than trying to destroy them with superior intellect, strategy, and tactic. Even at the chess table, where I was clearly inferior, perhaps I could *observe* rather than *study*. How hard could it be?

As a matter of fact, it wasn't hard at all.

It was impossible.

Chess—a game that I so desperately wanted to master—was not something I could simply sit and appreciate unless I was learning something. I didn't understand the social aspect of playing cards to pass the time. And I sure didn't see the benefit in staying quiet at a table where I was clearly the expert on whatever the topic of discussion was.

June 18, 2007

I'm trying to be realistic with myself in every way possible. I will admit to being a bit optimistic about a lot of things, but I think I've been fair with myself up to this point. My concern is that I will find myself several months (or even years) down the road second guessing all the "right choices" I've recently made. It's not that I exactly suspect when (or even if) I will somehow slip backwards, but it just bothers me that the potential is so strong.

I'll be glad when this is all behind me so I can move on. Of course, one thing that has helped me do so many bad things is the ability to ignore the present and only look to the future. Maybe I could just flip that around to use it in a good way.

It seems my perspective is changing, and I understand a lot of stuff that I don't think I understood before. One thing I don't really understand though is why everything has turned out the way it has. I mean, on the surface of it all, I understand. For example, man rob bank…man go to jail. That's the easy part, but what is so confusing to me is the deeper, less obvious cause to all the things that have come to happen in my life. Fortunately, it looks like I'll have plenty of time on my hands to figure it all out.

A lot of people ask me why I turned myself in. There is no single answer to that. There were several reasons I did the banks in the first place, and that's also very difficult to explain. But one of the main reasons for turning myself in was to just put a definite stop to my life as I was living it. The more time went by, the more I despised life itself. I had a bad feeling about how things would end up for me if I didn't go to jail soon. When I finally stopped fooling myself into thinking that I could get help from anyone in my family or my short list of friends, jail was the only feasible option left. Ironically, it seems that my bad choices (i.e. the bank stuff) are now serving as an escape route from the real world.

I feel like I have such a tendency to always go negative with my thoughts or outlook on things. But as I sit here right now, I have so many things that are good in my life. Okay, so I'm in jail while my wife sleeps soundly in the same room with my nine-month-old son who, by the way, is also sleeping soundly and completely unaware of how many things have been stripped from him because his father is…me.

…but it's all good! Right?

What am I supposed to think anymore? I had it all together when I decided to turn myself in. I had it all figured out. I knew how it would all go down. I knew so much about the outcome that I was comfortable, prepared...maybe even excited about the process.

Sometimes I wonder if my ability to articulate my thoughts properly only gets in the way. Other times, I am embarrassed about my own self-esteem. All I really need right now is someone who can do the math and tell me what is going on inside my head. I should have gone to school for psychiatry. I don't know that I would have made much of a psychiatrist, but I could have at least learned about myself.

I have so much useless information in my head, but I feel like I never quite realized the need to do the right thing. I don't blame anyone for that, but I wish I could do something that wasn't based in selfishness.

I'm so tired of writing, thinking, doubting, and not knowing. Why can't there just be one thing that I know for certain?

I wasn't supposed to grow up and be a criminal. Even my mother said she didn't even "know this man on the other side of the glass" during our last visit. Guess what... neither do I.

My emotions were unpredictable during those first several months in jail. I could go weeks on end without having a bad thought, but once the darkness crept in, it felt like my life could have ended at any moment. But the great thing about jail was that it offered a safe place to simply bunker down and wait for the storms to pass. If I stayed in bed for days on end, I didn't have to call and explain anything to a boss. I didn't require therapy to return to work. As long as I was alive and awake for count time, the jail could not have cared less about what was going on in my personal life.

In the free world, people cared when Clay wasn't doing so well. But in jail, nobody cared about Inmate #209135.

Somehow, that helped me.

FOR THE RECORD

Being reduced to a number might be humiliating for some, but it was necessary for me. As an inmate, the system doesn't recognize you as a person. Their job is to house you, feed you, and prevent you from killing yourself. Who you are as a person doesn't matter to them.

My identity was null and void.

Finding some level of humility in jail is really not that difficult if you allow yourself to be humbled. Narcissism completely consumed me for the majority of my life, and I wanted to find a way to control it. But there aren't many answers in jail except for the ones you search for on your own. Nobody comes along with a magical book of answers and helps you solve the mystery. Most prison programs are fundamentally flawed in that they don't push inmates to actually dive inward to figure out what's going on underneath the surface.

For the most part, your options are fairly limited as an inmate. I was mostly concerned with addressing my own behavior, and few programs offered practical answers about the inner workings of my mind itself. I was liable for my actions. My situation was the result of my choices, so that is what I wanted to explore.

In jail, I was surrounded by men who mostly blamed others for their troubles. Men who were there on DUI charges almost always claimed that legal limits were too low and that they weren't even drunk. Others there for domestic charges simply blamed their spouse for pushing their buttons. Even a cellmate of mine blamed his drug addiction for his crime. He carjacked a lady at gunpoint (completely sober, by the way) and still saw himself as a victim of his circumstances because he wouldn't have had to resort to crime if he had a better job.

I saw many men who so obviously needed to realize their own faults, and if jail taught me anything, it's that people who get out of jail almost always return eventually because they never addressed their own behavior. They simply got out, kept doing what they'd always been doing, and then came right back. It was always someone else's fault, of course. At worst, they were simply unlucky.

Yeah, right.

I didn't want to be *that guy*. Perhaps the fact that I'd turned myself in totally changed my perception. Who knows, maybe I'd have played the victim card too if I were going about my life and was suddenly plucked from society for a crime that was practically nothing more than accepting an invitation by the banks to come get free money.

Nonsense.

If I actually believed someone else was responsible for the choices that I made, then I would never be able to honestly teach my son the importance of making good decisions. I would never be able to tell my son that he controlled his own destiny if I seriously believed that other people could intervene and force him to make terrible choices. And what kind of father would I be if I taught my son something that I didn't believe in the first place?

Not every day in jail was spent contemplating the meaning of life though. There were plenty of days that served no purpose at all except to decompress and pass the time. By the end of my first year, I got pretty good at chess, and that became the thing that filled most of my free time. But no matter how many days passed without working on myself in any way, I almost never went to bed without wondering what it would be like when I made it back to the free world. I didn't know how long my prison sentence would be until January 2009, so in addition to wondering about life after prison, I also spent a great deal of time stressing over the fact that I really had no idea how far away my release date really was.

Within a few months of my arrest, I started getting letters from friends and family. Much to my surprise, they were most eager to simply let me know that they loved me and that they would do anything they could to support me. *Just let me know* became a common phrase from my family as a whole. If I needed money for commissary, stamps, pen and paper, extra food, or practically anything else, all I had to do was ask and they promised to be there for me.

Mail became a lifeline of sorts for me, and mail call was always the highlight of any day. Some of my relatives wrote to me as though I were in a land far away rather than acknowledging the fact that I was incarcerated. They told me they missed me and that they hoped I was doing okay *under the circumstances.* Others directly addressed the fact that I was in jail and even pressed me to use my time wisely in figuring out *what the heck is wrong with you*. Still, no matter how they chose to view my situation, they all had one definite thing in common. They loved me.

No matter what, they just loved me.

When my birthday rolled around about six weeks after my arrest, I got the same *Happy Birthday!* cards that I would have gotten if I hadn't been locked up. If the jail would have allowed it, they probably would have come and thrown me a party right there in the dayroom, too. Knowing how terrible I had been as a family member, it was bizarre seeing how forgiving they all were. It was easy to believe that they were sincere whenever they insisted *just let me know.*

In addition to friends and family who supported me early on, there were also people whom I hadn't seen in years who suddenly began writing to me as well. Some of them I hadn't seen in over a decade. On the flipside of that same coin were the many friends who didn't want anything to do with me at all. *Oh well*, I thought. *You win some, you lose some.*

All things considered, my first year in jail went by pretty fast. By the end of 2007, I still hadn't been to court to be sentenced, but that would come in due time. The important part to me is that I was holding up and constantly finding things about myself to work on. I found a book called *We're All Doing Time* by Bo Lozoff, and I read it cover to cover several times. The book itself was a little over my head at the time, but it at least supported my growing belief that I was ultimately in control of the manner in which I went through life.

Early in 2008, my divorce with Candice was final. We stayed in touch through the mail and visits. Thanks to her, Jett always knew exactly who I was even though I was nowhere to be found. Candice kept a picture book and taught Jett to say *Daddy*, and she also brought him to visit me whenever possible. Considering the situation as a whole, I considered myself incredibly lucky to have an ex-wife who didn't allow her feelings about me to get in the way of a relationship with my son. Even better than that, she was the one doing all the work to make sure Jett knew exactly who *Daddy* was.

The only bad thing about the visits in that first year or so was that they weren't contact visits. In the county jail, the visiting setup was the kind you see in jailhouse interviews on TV where two people are separated by a thick glass window as they speak to each other through a crappy phone. From the day of my arrest, it was nearly a year before I was transferred to a facility where I would be able to hold my son or hug my mother during our visits.

Otherwise, my life was still improving. I steadily searched for the missing piece that would tie everything together. But even on my worst days, I always had hope.

❧ ❧ ❧ ❧ ❧ ❧

Things started moving a little more quickly when the United States Marshals Service came to pick me up from the county jail. They transported me to the Earle Cabell Federal Building in downtown Dallas where a U.S. magistrate judge accepted my formality plea of not-guilty before sending me to the federal detention center in Seagoville, Texas.

Like the county jails I'd been to, Seagoville was also a direct supervision facility, but there was only one officer for about 160 inmates and the officer pretty much left everyone alone unless they absolutely had to get involved. The dayroom was too big to actually be called a dayroom. It looked like a food court in a hospital with tables fastened to the ground and chairs fastened to the tables. The building itself was elongated and had cell doors lining opposing walls—approximately 20 on each side. There was an identical upper tier accessible by two sets of stairs on opposite corners from each other. The walkway around the upper tier also doubled as a track where inmates walked for exercise if they wanted to. Most people seemed to agree that about 16 laps around that track equaled a mile.

Seagoville was way more laid back than any of the previous facilities where I'd been. In a county jail, the environment is more volatile because inmates are still adjusting to their new lives behind bars. It's the next step in the judicial process after being arrested, and some people take a while to acclimate to having lost their freedom. The tension is greater and inmates are more likely to fight over minor things. But in Seagoville, most of the inmates had been incarcerated long enough that the newness of it all had worn off. The inmates were also just different in the feds. It seemed like it was an older crowd, and everyone knew how to do their time. There weren't many fights, and things generally just seemed much more civil.

The guards were also different and the rules were less strict. They didn't seem as worried about the *do as I say, not as I do* type of mentality that I'd hated so much from my childhood.

One of the best things about the new facility was the number of decent chess players who were there. By then, my game had gotten good enough to compete with just about anyone I came up against, and I won considerably more than I lost. I'd yet to read any books about chess, and I certainly didn't study any particular strategies. I just tried stuff and then lost… and then tried other stuff and lost again…and then again, and again. To me, losing wasn't even a big deal because that's the best way to learn. Failure is comfortable territory for me because there really is no pure failure if the lessons learned are applied to future success.

There were probably a dozen decent chess players in my building, but only a couple of them were good enough to really challenge me. When you play chess for hours upon hours for days or even weeks at a time, you really get to know a lot about the kind of person you're up against. Likewise, they get to learn a lot about you.

Prison is funny. You can make eye contact and be fighting within seconds. But as with many other facets of life, Hollywood also tends to dramatize prison. Prison inmates don't just stalk around the yard looking for a fight. Most dudes just want to do their time peacefully and avoid losing commissary or visits. In actuality, it's not at all an aggressive move to walk by a guy sitting alone at a table with a chessboard setup and ask if he wants to play a game. Even if it's someone you've never met before, it's still cool. Hollywood might want you to think that *them is fightin' words,* but the more realistic response is probably something along the lines of *Right on, man. Let's see what ya got!*

There was one man in particular that I really liked playing with for several reasons. First of all, he was good. Second, he was a good sport. He didn't talk noise when he won, nor was he a sore loser. Mostly, he was just really cool and easy to chill out with all day. His style of play was pretty conservative but very difficult to beat.

We played several hours a day for at least two weeks before I actually knew his name—Smith. We played best-of-nine matches, so the first one to win five games won the match. Incarceration lends itself to extended matches like this, and we played countless matches over the year or so we were locked up together. One day, after losing to me in a game that was particularly complicated and fascinating, Smith finally asked me, "So what ya in for?"

I never understood why people got so bent out of shape when you asked them why they were in prison. It's almost always public record anyway. Besides, unless it's some type of sex-related offense, it's not like anybody else really cares. It never offended me when people asked me that. It might have annoyed me if they were just being nosy, but for the sake of simple conversation, it didn't bother me at all. "Robbery," I answered.

"Robbery?"

"Yep."

"Who'd you rob?"

"Well, this is the feds, so I'll let you figure that out," I answered with a bit of a laugh. He wasn't stupid, but it was a silly question. There's really only one type of robber you'll find in federal prison.

His eyebrows shot up. "You hit a bank?"

"Or two, yeah." I laughed again.

Setting up the chess pieces for the next game, Smith shrugged and muttered under his breath, "Well, that explains a lot."

"About what?" I asked. He wasn't being passive aggressive. He was just thinking out loud, and I had happened to hear him.

He half-laughed, "About the way you play chess, man. You send your pieces on a suicide mission." We both laughed while he added some historical references for color. "Like some

Kamikazes…or some Al-Qaeda or something." What he was saying wasn't nearly as funny as the way he delivered it. Still looking down at his pieces as he prepared for another game, he continued, "Dude be like 'Allahu Akbar' but then be like 'by the way, checkmate.'"

I was already laughing, but with his last line I totally lost it. It always feels good to laugh, but it was especially good in a place like that.

When we settled into the next game, we talked about all the different styles of chess, and he told me that there was a name for the style I preferred. I'd be lying if I said my pride wasn't at least a little bruised by that because I felt like I'd totally created the *Allahu Akbar Kamikaze Checkmate* style of play myself. If there was already an actual name for it, then that probably meant loads of other players had employed the same techniques. Smith might not have been as good of a chess player as I was, but he definitely knew more about the game away from the chessboard. I asked him to tell me more, so he did. "Yeah, man. They call it the romantic style, but I don't really know why. It's basically all about the style rather than whether you win or lose."

That made total sense to me. I would rather lose an exciting game than win a boring one. But the ultimate success was winning the exciting game.

His earlier comment was completely in context now.

Well that explains a lot.

It really did explain a lot. I would rather lead an exciting life and lose than lead a boring life and succeed. But the ultimate joy came from taking huge risks and still succeeding.

❧ ❧ ❧ ❧ ❧ ❧

My favorite part about Seagoville was the visits. It was within driving range of pretty much everyone in my family. My mother and Candice were on the approved visitors list to come see me, and I also added my stepdad and brother. There was a time when it seemed like I was getting visits nearly every weekend. It was nice sitting with my mother and talking about anything and everything. Those visits were in an actual visitation room with seats and vending machines and other families and pretty much just life in general. For two hours, I wasn't locked up at all.

Jett also started talking while I was at the unit in Seagoville. Whenever he came to see me, I could always count on him being excited and saying *Daddy! Daddy! Daddy!* while running straight for me the second I walked into the room. For a kid who never had a dad, he sure did love his. It was pretty freaking awesome, to say the least.

Things continued to improve for me the entire time I was in Seagoville. I played chess all day, I got a ton of mail, and people were coming to visit me. I dedicated myself to the simple things in life like honesty and integrity, and it generally just felt good to be a decent person. I still didn't really have a clear plan for the future, but I liked where things were headed.

My family stayed in touch with me and corresponded back and forth with me through the mail on a regular basis. And I'm not just talking about my immediate family either. I was getting letters from the same aunts and uncles and cousins whom I'd previously hoped to never see again. They were supporting me in every way imaginable. After a year of being nothing but a number, it was good to be Clay Tumey again.

It was a necessary evil to allow myself to be stripped of my identity because I wanted some distance between me and the person I had always been. For the duration of my first year in jail, I never once introduced myself to anyone as Clay. I always gave a different name or simply let them refer to me by my last name since that's what the guards always called out at mail call or something.

When you're locked up, you can be anybody you want to be. And by that, I just mean you can tell whatever story you want people to believe because nobody can verify or deny anything you're saying. If I told them my name was II (as in, the Roman numeral…short for Tumey), then that's what they would call me. When I was transferred to another tank, I introduced myself as Ross because that was my middle name. Everywhere I went, I picked a different name to give them, if any at all.

My favorite nickname was *Brain* because it was one of the names I hadn't given myself. The nickname was a result of a smart remark I'd made after destroying someone in chess. "You can't beat me," I boasted. "I'm basically just a brain with two feet." The few guys who were watching the post-match trash-talking session erupted in laughter, and they called me *Brain* for the next three months until I was transferred again.

In a way, I hated being called by something that wasn't my name, but it was also a constant reminder that my identity and my name were not one and the same.

My name didn't matter, but my character was everything.

Throughout my second year in prison, my attention was constantly drawn back to this thing about *character*. I don't even know where I first heard that term or why it was so prevalent in my conscious thoughts, but it was definitely there to stay. Much in the way that I was somehow biologically drawn to being a good father to my son, I was finding myself similarly drawn to simply being a good person.

I wasn't trying to satisfy an obligation to anyone or anything. I just wanted to be a respectable human being.

❧ ❧ ❧ ❧ ❧ ❧

On January 5, 2009, I was transported from Seagoville to Dallas to be sentenced. It had been over a year and a half since the date I was arrested, and I was finally about to find out just how much more time I would have to serve before returning to the free world with a second chance.

My attorney was a rock star in my opinion. He seemed to always know the precise answers to my precise questions, and he was one of those people that just seemed likeable. He wasn't bubbly or overly friendly or any of that nonsense. If anything he was robotic, but I couldn't have asked for a better attorney.

The feds do things a little bit differently when it comes to criminal procedure. With the state, you can negotiate a plea and come to an agreement before you actually fess up to anything. It's almost like buying a car, except you're negotiating the cost of your own freedom. With the feds, however, you simply enter a plea of guilty or not-guilty and then they respond accordingly. If you plead not-guilty, you go to trial. If you plead guilty, a judge sentences you to a term that he finds appropriate. There is no negotiation, and you have no say in the matter. As a defendant, you simply have two options: guilty or not-guilty.

By the time sentencing rolled around for me, I'd changed my plea to guilty for obvious reasons. There was no sense in going to trial for something that I had confessed to already. That would be madness even beyond my reach. But the sentencing process is a monster all on its own. First, a United States Probation Officer prepares a report for the judge that essentially answers every question imaginable regardless of whether or not the answer is relevant. Also included are relevant details such as how many banks I robbed and how much money I'll owe in restitution. The report will return a recommended sentencing range based on a very objective guideline that takes into account criminal history, severity of crime, and a host of other important information. For me, my range was 48 to 84 months.

As a defendant, it is normal—nearly standard procedure—to enter a motion for downward departure, which is legal speak for formally asking the judge to go easy on you and give a sentence that is actually lower than even the minimum recommended sentence. This seemed rather asinine to me, and I didn't want anything to do with it. I explained to my attorney that I simply wanted to take my sentence accordingly without requesting special treatment.

Another standard procedure at sentencing is to address the court—and the judge in particular—and discuss how sorry you are and how you've changed and how you'll never ever do it again. It's the adult version of *cross my heart, hope to die.* And I hated that even worse than asking for a downward departure. However, even though I didn't want to give the standard lying speech, I still wanted to address the court and put a few things on record.

Against my attorney's counsel, I did not write or even plan what I was going to say in court that day. There was no way in hell I was going to script that moment because I didn't want my brain to overpower my heart. I just wanted to stand before the court and be honest. It wasn't a plea for a smaller sentence, and it wasn't about promising I'd never do it again. For me, it was simply a crucial step into manhood, and I didn't want to write it out and rehearse it.

When it was my turn to enter the courtroom, a bailiff came and got me from a holding cell down the hall from the court. Before walking me back down the hall and into the courtroom, the bailiff reattached my leg irons and handcuffs.

Safety first.

It's hard to walk with a 12-inch chain attaching your ankles, but I penguin'd my way into the courtroom from a side door just to the left of the judge's bench. I wasn't really sure who all would be there, but I knew the judge would be the last to show, so it didn't surprise me to see his seat empty. I saw my attorney at the defendant's table, and I saw the prosecuting attorney at his table, and there was a lectern in between them. *I guess that's where all the action goes down.*

Behind them was a half-wall that divided the participators from the spectators, and behind that half-wall were a few rows of what looked like church pews. In those pews was a sea of familiar faces. I saw my mother first because that's the way it always is. And then I saw my uncle and aunt. They waved at me and fully smiled as though this were a college graduation ceremony instead of a freedom funeral. They were so happy to see me, and the feeling was mutual. I kept looking and saw another aunt and then a cousin. And another cousin and then a few friends.

If ever I needed proof that I had a living, breathing group of people ready to support me whenever I needed it the most, it was right there in that court room.

All I could do was smile.

When the judge came in, things moved along pretty quickly. The lawyers said their fancy phrases and the judge returned a few of his own. I don't have a clue what any of it was, but I didn't care. I was just waiting for my turn to talk.

There was a point when my attorney formally waived our right to move for downward departure, and I wanted to high-five him because that was pretty smart. He didn't have to say anything, but he was pointing out to the judge that his client specifically requested to not do all that *pretty please* nonsense.

For a moment, I imagined how it might have looked if I actually tried to high-five my attorney with my handcuffed wrists that were attached to the chain around my waist. *I bet they'd have all laughed.*

After a few more questions and answers from the judge and attorneys, it was finally my turn to speak.

Finally!

Over two years since the last time I'd left a bank as a bank robber, and I was now about to speak my piece before learning how much of my life it was all going to cost me.

I wiggled over to the lectern.

My mental checklist was short. I wanted to first make it clear that I was well aware of the choices I'd made, and I wanted to be clear that I made no excuses nor blamed anyone else. Those bad choices I made were definitely *me, myself, and I* types of choices, and nobody could accept any liability whatsoever except for Clayton Ross Tumey. That much I knew.

"But I don't want to stand here and pretend that I regret what I've done," I shared. "I know it was wrong, and I'll never do it again. That's for sure. But it's hard to regret what has turned into something so good."

I somehow managed to maintain my composure as I finished explaining how I was on my own and completely removed from my family for so long, yet there they were in court to support me when I didn't deserve it at all.

I wasn't asking for leniency. I just wanted to man up and accept the consequences for my actions.

❧ ❧ ❧ ❧ ❧ ❧

I don't experience fear very often. But I was definitely scared when the judge had heard everything from both sides and the only thing left was his decision. I knew I was getting at least four years because that's what the minimum was and we didn't ask for anything less. I was okay with four years, and I realistically expected something closer to five years. But there was still the off chance that I could get six years or seven years or even more than that.

When the judge came back and everyone rose to their feet, my whole body experienced anxiety. I could hear my heartbeat in my eardrum. The bones in my wrist were aching. Nothing in my body was exempt, and all I could think to do was continuously wring my hands behind my back to hopefully alleviate my nerves.

The judge began to speak, but I had no idea who he was talking to. He was telling me that I reminded him of a soldier, but I'd never been in the military. The soldier had PTSD and just wanted help, and I somewhat related to that *just wanted help* part. He'd robbed a bank and then walked across the street and bought a Slurpee from 7-Eleven where he just waited for the cops to show up.

"It was a cry for help," the judge said.

And with that, he began to explain what set me apart from regular criminals, and everything he said was definitely in my favor. He quoted scripture or federal law or something else that I definitely didn't understand before finally announcing my sentence: "36 months."

Three years?!

I was just a few months from finishing my second year already, which meant I basically had one more round of holidays and then I was going home.

I didn't even know where *home* was, but I was headed there the following year.

✤ ✤ ✤ ✤ ✤ ✤

When I got back to Seagoville, I kept to myself because you never know when someone might be having a super bad day, and I didn't want to put a target on my back by strolling back into the unit with a giant smile on my face because I'd just caught lightning in a bottle.

My cellmate saw me walking and met me just inside my door. He knew I'd been at court, and he knew I had gotten sentenced. Apparently I hid my emotions well until we got inside the cell because he thought I might have bad news.

He asked, "You all right, dude?"

"Man, you ain't gonna believe this!"

And with that, I happily recounted the entire day's events, right down to the very last thing that was said before court was adjourned. The prosecuting attorney understood why the judge did what he did, but as a formality, he still had to object. "Your honor, for the record, the government objects."

To which the judge replied, "For the record, overruled."

TYPE FIVE

After my sentencing, everything began to move a little more quickly than expected. There was still a year and a half left for me to serve in prison, but I felt like I needed to start getting things in order immediately.

I would need a job when I got out, but my driver's license had expired while I was in prison. I couldn't renew my license until I handled a few old traffic tickets that had turned to warrants. I couldn't pay those traffic tickets until I had a job, but I couldn't get a job if I didn't have a car. Even if I had a car, I didn't have a license to drive it.

It wasn't long before I realized that the revolving doors on prisons in America are there for a reason. Fortunately, I had a mother who was strong enough to get through all the crap that I'd caused yet still be there waiting to help me when I got my head on straight again. She contacted the various jurisdictions where I had warrants for unpaid tickets and told them I was in prison. A few of them allowed me to use my prison time to cover for the time I needed to serve with them, and aside from a few clerical fees, those tickets were as good as gone. For the few courts who wouldn't accept my time served, my mother handled those accordingly.

Then I started thinking about jobs. What exactly could I do with a felony on my record? It seemed like manual labor was my best bet, and since I was only going to be 31 years old when I got out, I would still be in fine physical condition to go swing a hammer or carry some lumber.

Before long, the technical aspects weren't much of a concern. Most things could be handled through the mail, and the rest could be dealt with as soon as I got out. But there was still the issue of me being me. Certainly I'd changed in the couple of years since my arrest, but everybody changes when they get to prison. I wanted to maintain that change when I got out.

In two years, I'd only rid myself of the person I was before prison, but I hadn't taken any steps to grow into anything else. I was just another numbered inmate floating around. It wasn't enough to get rid of the bad though. I still needed the missing piece that would push me to the next level.

Later that year, I caught my break. I had since been transferred back to the state prison system to finish my time there because, contrary to popular belief, you can be punished twice for the same crime in America. I had federal time and state time. Fortunately, they all ran concurrently, but I still had to be transferred from one jurisdiction to the next.

In October of 2009, I was sitting in the dayroom at a unit just south of Dallas when I was told to get dressed and go to the chapel. Church services were optional, and I hadn't planned on going that morning, so I wasn't quite sure what was going on. When I left my building and walked to the chapel, I saw a clean-cut, well-dressed man carrying a briefcase of some sort. He was headed to the chapel as well, so he was obviously the reason I'd been called to the chapel.

The man's name was Marcus Hill, and he was a recruiter for a non-profit prison program based in Houston. It was a business program, so that naturally caught my attention since I was going to be released in less than a year and I still didn't know what I was going to do for a job.

In the chapel, the first thing Marcus said was, "If you don't want to be here, you don't have to be. This is strictly voluntary, and I'm not mad at ya if you don't wanna be here. So if that's you..."

Marcus stopped talking as he pointed to the back door. He wasn't being a jerk. It was just his direct way of letting everyone know upfront that this meeting was not at all mandatory.

A handful of inmates stood and left, and the recruiter continued, "My name is Marcus, and I'm here to tell you about our entrepreneurship program." He went on to explain the training involved in the program and also played a short video on the chapel TV. Afterward, he told us that he would be back in a week to give us a preliminary test to see if we qualified.

As he gave us handouts of the material that would be on the test, he said, "If you don't want to be in the program, then don't study for this test. If you fail, you will not be accepted."

This was the tone of a man who gave this speech in prisons across Texas every...single...day. He continued, "If you make a perfect 100 on this test, that does not automatically mean you will be accepted. We'll go over that a little more next week."

As I took the handouts from him, I noticed that they were mostly about things I already knew. I kept my mouth shut.

When he returned the following week, I was ready for the test. I didn't have to study most of it, but I definitely made sure to study the factsheet about the program itself. They had something called the *10 Driving Values* that were basically the *Ten Commandments* for the program.

I completed the test several minutes before anyone else that day, and in addition to finishing first, I was certain my grade would be the highest.

A few candidates were dismissed based on their test scores and then Marcus began interviewing inmates one by one. When it was my turn, I told my story and talked about how my *change* had happened before I came to prison. I tried to market myself as if the program would be lucky to have me. It didn't dawn on me that I should worry about whether or not they'd even want me.

The conversation went well, and I genuinely liked Marcus. He was cool and easy to talk to.

In December of 2009, I was transferred to a private facility just outside of Houston where the program runs. It was nothing like anything I'd ever seen. It barely even felt like prison. The course itself was six months long, but graduates of the program stayed on the unit after graduation until their release, so an entire wing of the prison itself was steeped in this entrepreneurship program and its *10 Driving Values*, which included everything from love, integrity, and accountability to innovation, fun, and excellence.

It was weird, but it was cool.

After arriving at my new home, I unpacked and got situated in my new cell. Some of the guys from the program came and introduced themselves to me. The men used their real names and shook my hand. That alone felt odd, but I reflexively shook their hands in return and introduced myself as Clay.

No nicknames. Not my last name. Just Clay.

Shortly thereafter, one of the guards announced over the intercom system that it was time for class. I was too new on the unit to know where anything was, so I just followed the masses and trusted that I'd end up in the right spot.

There were about 150 inmates in the program, and it was wild walking into a classroom that we shared with no other class on the unit. Everybody in the room was all smiles and hugs, too. I'd never seen grown men hug like that before, yet there I was in a prison where hugging and being genuinely happy to see each other was somehow normal. It was more like a family event than a prison program.

I looked around and noticed the actual room itself was not at all typical. There were pictures on the walls and bright colors everywhere. It was reminiscent of the classroom at the church where I had spent so much of my time as a teenager. There were a few sofas, and the floor was even carpeted.

Carpet!

The ground was so soft and easy to walk on, and I really just wanted to take off my socks and shoes to feel the carpet with my bare feet. But my thoughts were interrupted by some dude named Roger who was way too friendly to not be on drugs, and he was hugging me and asking me what my name was. I don't know if he drugged me or infected me when he hugged me or what, but I wasn't even mad that he was in my space. I gladly told him my name and asked a lot of questions. He was quick to answer them, and he introduced me to as many guys as he could find. He was a graduate from a previous class, so he already knew most of the men there.

It didn't take long to realize that this was not a normal place, and I let down my guard almost immediately and appreciated the experience for what it was.

Amazing.

✥ ✥ ✥ ✥ ✥ ✥

After a few weeks in the program, I was already referring to my classmates as brothers. And it wasn't just a figure of speech. They were really good dudes who all had stories of their own, and most of those stories were not unlike my own. The details were different, of course, but the common thread among us was that we were leaving prison and doing something better with our lives soon.

The program itself was centered on business, but at the true core of it all was character building.

My name didn't matter, but my character was everything.

I loved going to class every day and hugging the requisite minimum of three classmates before the day began. I was actually making friends, and these people actually cared about me as a person. In the first month of class, we were going to have something called the Character Assessment. It was apparently a pretty big deal. I didn't quite understand what the assessment would evaluate, but I was all for it. That was the happiest I'd been in quite a while, and I was eager to hear all the great things my new friends thought of me.

The Character Assessment was literally just a sheet of paper with a bunch of blank lines on it, and each participant filled in the blanks and ranked their peers based solely on their character. We were also supposed to pick three words from a group of adjectives to describe each individual. Looking through the list, I wondered which ones I'd get the most. *Probably helpful or wise,* I thought.

When the time came to hear the results, we all went to the classroom where the chairs had been formed into a giant circle around the entire room. They called this the Confrontation Circle...because not only were the results of the Character Assessment going to be read in front of everyone, but other guys would have the opportunity to stand up and hold their brothers accountable for bad behavior. Everyone hated it, but I was so looking forward to it.

As the moderator began explaining how things would go, nobody in the room wasn't nervous. Except me. I just wanted to know how well I'd done. I was almost giddy. They do the results from lowest ranking to the top, so I knew it would be a bit before they got to me.

False.

I was actually pretty close to the bottom. And as the moderator began to read the words that people used to describe me, it wasn't at all what I'd expected. "Nearly half of your brothers say you're arrogant. Nearly 40% of them say you're condescending. About 25% of them say you're a know-it-all."

He went through the entire list, and I never heard a single good thing about me. And the fact that I knew everyone's intention made it even more painful. They weren't trying to be rude or hurtful. I could've dealt with that. They were just giving honest feedback, and I had no choice but to believe it. In January of 2010, I'd been working on myself for over three years but apparently had absolutely nothing to show for it.

I was devastated.

After the moderator finished his part and everyone else finished theirs, I was given the paper that had the results of my Character Assessment. There was no sense in running from tangible evidence that I had a lot of work to do on myself, so I wanted that printout as a reminder of how people perceived me on a daily basis.

I kept that small piece of paper on my desk and looked at it every single morning for the remainder of my time in prison. It was the width of a sheet of paper, but it was only about an inch in length. That was plenty of room to list all of those negative character traits people saw in me. Out to the side of each adjective was the number that represented how many people had made those observations.

Every morning I looked over that list one last time before leaving my cell, and every night I wondered if I'd been able to change my image. I was perfectly fine being a jerk back in the days when I didn't care, but to find out that I'm actually a jerk even when I don't want to be...

It was time to take a serious look at who I was and try to figure out how to stop being that person.

❧ ❧ ❧ ❧ ❧ ❧

About a week after the Character Assessment, we had a special teacher from California named Susan Olesek. She was an Enneagram teacher, but I didn't really know what an Enneagram was. I'd seen a book about it, but it really didn't look like anything I'd be interested in. Besides, the funky diagram on the front of our Enneagram book looked a bit Satanic to me, and I wasn't particularly interested in worshipping the devil any time soon.

I had been spending most of my free time obsessing over that little piece of paper that said all those bad things about me, so Susan Olesek and her Enneagram were of no concern really. However, I still had to go to class the day that she came and taught because it wasn't optional. It was part of the curriculum. It was right there on the syllabus: Enneagram Speaker 01/29 - 01/30.

Two days?

Walking into the classroom was really weird that day because she had these two easels at the front of the class and each had a big poster board of some sort. I couldn't really make out what they said, but I could definitely see the Enneagram shape on both of them, and it weirded me out. The entrepreneurship program was a faith-based program and we prayed every day before class, so I couldn't understand why they were letting this lady come teach this stuff to us.

Making my way to a chair, my eyes left the weird things on the easels and I saw Mrs. Olesek standing behind a lectern just watching us file in from the hallway. She had perfect posture and a smile that was far beyond the reach of any amount of skepticism I could conjure. I didn't know what she was about to teach, but I was going to listen.

She began by introducing herself and sharing a little about her personal life. That was a no-no in that line of work, but nobody else seemed to care. I jotted down notes just in case there was a pop quiz somewhere down the line, but I mostly found myself completely captivated by the ideas she was sharing with us.

She explained that the Enneagram was a system that suggests there are nine distinct personality types, and each of those types have variations and different subtleties about them. But mainly, there are the nine main types. I noticed *Types* was capitalized on her poster boards and in my book, so I adjusted my notes accordingly.

There are no good Types, and there are no bad Types. None are better than any others. They simply help define who we are as individuals.

The whole thing blew my mind because it didn't seem possible that the entire world fit into this simple Enneagram, but the more she spoke, the more sense it made. She started by discussing Type Eight. I knew people who sounded a lot like the Type she was explaining, and I immediately saw those people in a different light as I listened to the motivation and coping strategies of the Type. She made her way around the diagram until she landed on one that seemed to fit me: Type Five.

"Type Five," she explained, "is one of the three Head Types. They like to use mental intelligence to figure out the world. They're also withdrawn yet very competent and they tend to be known for some remote specialty that others might not even know exists."

The more Mrs. Olesek spoke, the more legitimate this Enneagram thing seemed to be. The symbol alone had spooked me, but the practical explanation of Types was downright fascinating. Even if the descriptions of the other eight personality styles were completely inaccurate, this Type Five thing was certainly resonating with me. She continued, "Fives have this need for privacy and they feel like the outside world is intrusive if not completely invasive."

It's worth noting, by the way, that Type Five is often also called The Investigator.

How appropriate.

And accurate.

Even in the way that I committed crime, my first course of action was to investigate. Before I turned myself in, I investigated. And as I sat in prison trying to escape my own destructive behavioral patterns, I was investigating.

If anything summarized my darkness before prison, it was the description of Type Five as they descend into their unhealthiest states of mind:

> Fives feel so small and helpless that almost everything becomes ominous to them. They are filled with dark fantasies and strange perceptions. They resist all help, shrinking away from people and into feverish nightmares and insomnia. They cannot stop their overheated minds. Feeling that they can no longer defend themselves from their pain and terror, unhealthy Fives want to escape from reality. In some cases, they attempt to accomplish this through psychotic breaks or schizoid withdrawal. They may also try to escape through suicide.[1]

Or prison, I thought.

Reading about Type Five felt like I was reading a biography about myself. It was vulnerable and empowering all at once. I'd stumbled my way through life for three decades without having the slightest idea that I was a *type* of anything. I always thought it was *my way or your way*. I didn't think there were other ways to go about life. But the more I read about this Enneagram stuff, the more I was convinced that I'd finally found the missing piece.

And as irony prevails, the missing piece was another puzzle.

The Enneagram was not merely a simple set of descriptions that were easily explained or understood after a weekend workshop. Sure, the basics were easy enough to grasp after a day or two, but the finer details were far too extensive to memorize right away. Learning the Enneagram on a deeper level would require dedication to both studying and practicing.

But even at its most fundamental level, it was still very interesting and captivating that there were all these different

1. Don Richard Riso and Russ Hudson, *The Wisdom of the Enneagram* (New York: Bantam, 1999), 216.

personality styles that somehow intertwined with each other. It was bizarre, and I couldn't stop thinking about it.

Blessed—not cursed, but definitely blessed—with an infinite curiosity, I always wanted to know more. But now there seemed to be an explanation for that curiosity. After all, I was a Type Five: The Investigator. So with an openness that I'd never experienced and an awareness that I'd never had, I began to take an honest look at myself. Thankfully, the pain of reality also provided an opportunity for healing.

I didn't immediately know all the answers, but I was on the verge of understanding truths about myself that I'd never allowed myself to even consider:

> Whenever Fives feel overwhelmed by people or circumstances, instantly and reflexively they detach from direct engagement with their senses and emotions and retreat into their minds.[2]

That was me. I did that! Except I'd always thought that was a *good* thing. I thought it was a natural gift to be able to remove myself from the real world and go inward. But in retrospect, I could see that this never produced anything good in my life, a simple truth that was no doubt punctuated by the fact that I was in prison.

However, while some might feel trapped by being systematically categorized as one of nine Types, it had the opposite effect for me. It was liberating. I felt as though someone finally understood me, which meant I was that much closer to understanding myself.

It gave me hope.

---

2. Ibid., 217.

❧ ❧ ❧ ❧ ❧ ❧

On the second day of the workshop, I decided that I was fully onboard with anything Mrs. Olesek was doing. Besides just being brilliant and otherworldly, if she was willing to fly all the way from California to Texas just to talk to a bunch of ex-cons, then that's the kind of person I needed in my life.

When the weekend was over, I couldn't help but smile at the timing of it all. Only a fool would believe that these things were all a series of coincidences. I had no business being in a state prison for a federal crime. It was a weird loophole that even allowed me to be at the previous facility where Marcus recruited me for his program in the first place. And the timing of the Character Assessment was perfect as it tore me open and forced me to see myself through the eyes of others.

And with Susan Olesek coming to Texas at just the right time with just the right tools to share with a lost soul…

Okay, God. I get it.

And thank you.

SECOND CHANCE

My first three years in prison seemed to take forever, but the last three months were just the opposite. I graduated from the entrepreneurship program in June of 2010, and my release was just two months away. I'd only recently learned about the different personality styles, and a couple of months just didn't seem like enough time to prepare for reentry into the free world.

After learning a little more about being a Five, I started looking for all the ways where I could apply this new information. In retrospect, there were obvious correlations between my Type and my behavior. Two and a half decades earlier, when my mother wrote that I sometimes thought my reasoning was better than an adult's, she was wrong. I didn't just *sometimes* think my reasoning was better; I *always* thought that. I was so fixated on my own perspective that it was impossible for me to even consider that someone else might have something worthy to say. But as I waited out those final few weeks in prison, it was pretty obvious that my old way of living certainly never did me any favors.

With my release date fast approaching, I began to study a book called *The Wisdom of the Enneagram* and found that my behavior, while unusual for most, was most certainly typical for people like me:

> While Fives' imaginations can be a source of creativity and self-esteem, living there almost exclusively fuels their anxieties about themselves and the world. It is not simply that young Fives see the world around them with startling clarity, they also elaborate on it in their minds—a faculty that will have profound repercussions later on, for better or worse.[3]

This made all the sense in the world. In reality, I saw things more clearly than others, but I also lost touch with reality once my imagination took over. I didn't think of myself as a rebel. To me, rebellion was about intentionally breaking the rules out of spite. It wasn't that I deliberately disregarded the rules; they just didn't exist to me. I thought of morality as some restrictive religion that kept people from thinking for themselves, and the last thing I wanted to do was give up my ability to think freely.

But in reality, I was wrong. That much was certain. For the first 30 years of my life, I was simply wrong.

Thankfully, *Wisdom* explained more than just the bad stuff about each Type. It also detailed the behaviors that exist during a potential descent, such as what I had experienced in the years leading up to my self-destruction.

> Fives worry that the needs of others will distract them from their projects, so they shut out "intrusions" by intensifying their mental activity. They minimize

3. Ibid., 211.

> their needs, becoming high-strung, cerebral, and secretive. They spend more time alone, speculating and elaborating on alternative realities.
>
> Fives fear that others will threaten the niche they have been creating, so they try to fend people off. They… enjoy subverting [other people's] beliefs. Their own ideas can be bizarre and disturbing, and they are scornful of those who cannot understand them.[4]

If ever there was an explanation of why I rejected my family and turned to my dream of being a poker player, this was it. I felt abandoned, but that was just a delusion. In actuality, my family cared a great deal about me and only wanted me to make the best choices for myself. From my point of view during the dark days, I was just *surrounded by idiots* who didn't understand.

But that wasn't true. That wasn't reality.

For me, isolation was a defense mechanism. But it wasn't just a physical isolation. Detachment from the emotional aspects of life gave me a false sense of protection from the world around me. I was only making my problems worse by losing that connection, so the obvious answer to me was to do the opposite if I wanted to improve things in my life. If my habit was to disappear into my own head, then I needed to make a conscious decision to stop doing that. And that's what everything really boiled down to for me: conscious decisions.

Self-awareness was my key to freedom because it forced me to take an honest look at myself and address my role in life. I had to realize that no matter what my circumstances were, my behavior was my own responsibility. But the Enneagram itself wasn't enough to solve my problems. I still had to actually do the work for myself and apply the things that I was learning. One very

4. Ibid., 216.

significant component for me was understanding and respecting the fact that all people approach life in their own specific way, and just because someone is different from me doesn't necessarily mean that they're wrong, ignorant, or even stupid. It just means that we're different.

After three years in prison, I began to feel like I was actually prepared to return to the free world with a new awareness. With the little bit of time I had left, I spent most of it simply trying to be mindful of my behavior. As it turns out, it's much easier to solve a problem when you know it exists.

When Mrs. Olesek had been in Texas teaching us about the different personality Types, she posed a question: *How did your Type contribute to your incarceration?* This was a great place for me to start.

For me, the answer to that question was a no-brainer. Throughout my life, my mind was in constant motion and wondering about the potential outcomes of the most bizarre scenarios. I detached from the world around me and looked at it as some sort of experiment. I didn't know how to exist in a world full of people who didn't understand me, and it was much easier to observe from a distance instead.

Much in the way I researched bank robberies, I looked back into my own past and sought out all the things I could have done differently. I wasn't trying to undo the past. I just wanted to learn from it.

The first thing that came to mind was my marriage. I loved my wife more than my behavior ever suggested. But with my natural detachment from emotions, I didn't feel the same kind of pain that she felt when things got bad. Even in our earliest years, I preferred disappearing into my own world. In my delusion, it was her fault for not knowing how to make me happy. But what could I have done differently? Above all, I could have stayed present instead of disengaging. That alone would have been enough for me to at least stay connected to her.

Communication was never my problem. My problem was that I wasn't present—spiritually, emotionally, or otherwise—to even have the conversation.

But now I was determined to never have that problem again.

☙ ☙ ☙ ☙ ☙ ☙

About a month prior to my release, the entrepreneurship program had another Character Assessment for current students and for graduates. As painful as my first one had been, I was still excited about doing it again. When managed properly, it can be a very useful tool. But I was also anxious to see if I'd improved any in the previous months. I knew I still rubbed a lot of people the wrong way because that's not just something you magically stop doing one day. But I was consciously trying to change my behavior, and I was aware of the things I was doing. I felt like that was enough to at least make a little bit of progress. If I improved in even one category, I would have considered that a success.

After our second Character Assessment, I was pleasantly surprised to see that only nine people said I was a jerk and only seven people said I was condescending. I say *only* because of how much worse it was just a few months earlier. Instead of focusing too much on the fact that 16 people still had a pretty critical view of me, I was happy to accept a move in the right direction.

There was still a lot of work to be done in my life, but at least I had the right idea of what to do and what to continue working on. By no means did prison fix me, and I definitely didn't fix myself. Even the Enneagram itself didn't change me or offer any sort of weird mystical power. It simply exposed me to a part of myself that I'd never dealt with appropriately. The work to become something better, however, was still my responsibility.

The first time I ever experienced freedom was in prison, and I'll never regret being blessed with the opportunity to make the most of a bad situation. As I told the judge at my sentencing, it's hard to regret something that had such a positive outcome. Many people misunderstand that sentiment and assume that I'm somehow proud of my criminal past, but I'm not. I can't change anything I've done, and retrospective hypotheticals are pointless. I can only learn from those mistakes and be thankful for second chances.

I was released from prison on August 31, 2010.

I was about to get my second chance.

HOMECOMING

Just a few minutes before being released from prison, I was given a $50 check and a voucher for a bus ride to anywhere in Texas. The rest was up to me.

The day I got out of prison was beautiful. The August heat in Texas is usually pretty unbearable for most, but I didn't even feel it. The sky was clear, and the birds were happy to see me. I knew so because they were singing a song just for me. I walked across the street and cashed my $50 check with my prison ID and bought my favorite soft drink—Tahitian Treat—and a pack of bubble gum.

Man, I really missed bubble gum!

The person picking me up was from the entrepreneurship program I'd graduated from on the inside. His name was Pat, and I'd never met him before. All I knew was that he was a really big dude driving a little tiny Scion, so I didn't think I'd have a problem finding him.

There was a park just across the street from the front door of the prison, and they had picnic benches and a pavilion and plenty of other places for people to sit and wait for their loved ones who were soon to be released from prison. I didn't have anyone there just yet, so I decided to sit at one of the picnic benches and enjoy my Tahitian Treat and bubble gum in solitude until I saw Pat. After a few minutes, a lady old enough to be my grandmother came over and sat across from me. The prison gave me regular clothes, and this old lady didn't realize that she was sitting across from a *violent offender*, as my paperwork had described me. I felt a little bad for how naïve she was for sitting next to me. I wasn't going to do anything to hurt her, of course, but I thought she'd be scared out of her mind if she knew who I was or what I'd done.

I hadn't been out of prison a full hour, but I was already within arm's reach of a normal person. She was perpendicular to me. She was sitting sideways facing the prison and using the table as an arm rest. I was facing the side of her head. It was weird. But it got even weirder when she spoke to me.

Without really looking at me, she asked, "Get out today?"

"Excuse me?" I heard her words clearly, but I was sure I'd misunderstood her question.

She chuckled and looked over at me, enunciating clearly to prove a point. "I said did you get out today."

I smiled and replied, "It's that obvious, huh?"

She hadn't offended me. She was a sweet old woman who just wanted to make me feel comfortable in a world where I obviously hadn't existed for quite a while, but it made me a little anxious that she could so easily tell that I'd just gotten out of prison. Thankfully, she obliged and answered the very question I was wondering. She held up her iPhone and said, "You're not playing on your phone. The only people who sit here without a phone are people who just got out."

She made a good point, and the humor was not lost on me. I was impressed by her observation, but I was mostly just happy to be having a conversation with someone who wasn't an inmate or a guard. It was nice, and I savored every second of it. It was also quite reminiscent of the old man who had sat next to me on the bus back to Texas the day I had turned myself in. She turned back to face the prison and went on to tell me that she was picking up her son. Again. This was his third time to prison, so she knew the routine pretty well by now. Without looking at me, she offered a quick piece of advice that was both unsolicited and completely welcome. "Now you stay away from this place, young man. This ain't the way to be."

"Yes, ma'am," I agreed and smiled along with her. She was mostly just making friendly chitchat, and I enjoyed it. After a few minutes of this, the conversation trailed off and we were left sitting there—her facing the prison and me facing the *Nutritional Facts* on my Tahitian Treat bottle. I'd never realized how much sugar was in those things. Then again, it probably wouldn't have mattered. Besides, my bubble gum was sugar free, so it probably all evened out anyway.

The old lady caught me daydreaming and interrupted by saying, "Would you like to call somebody?"

The thought had never crossed my mind a few minutes earlier when she'd mentioned me not having a phone and showing me hers. I wasn't worried about Pat. I knew he'd get there soon enough, and if I only had the chance to make one phone call, I'd preferred to call my mother anyway. "Yes, please. I live in Dallas though. Is that going to be long distance?"

"Oh, honey, you've been gone a while, huh? Long distance is free on these things." And with a friendly cackle, she took out her phone again and asked, "Who do you wanna call?"

"My mother, if that's okay."

She handed me her iPhone and said, "Sure thing. Go right ahead."

The iPhone came out in July of 2007, but I was arrested in May of 2007. I had only seen them on TV and in magazines. I'd never held one, and I definitely didn't know how to operate them. Before I had gone to jail, phones still had buttons. But this thing was little more than a rectangular piece of glass. Almost immediately, she realized her mistake and held out her hand to take the phone back. "Here, I'll dial it for you. What's her number?"

For the first time in well over three years, I was able to talk to my mother without being preempted every five minutes by a recording reminding both of us that *This call has been placed from a correctional institution.* When my mom answered the phone, I was all smiles.

"Hey, mom!"

"Hey, son!"

Just another reminder that I was free.

❧ ❧ ❧ ❧ ❧ ❧

Jett was just a month short of his fourth birthday when I got out of prison. To him, there never was a prison; it was just the blue chip store. He didn't know any better then, and I doubt he really cared. Those visits at the blue chip store were really our only times together for the first four years of his life.

There's no way to avoid the fact that I still missed those years with Jett, but when I got out of prison and started seeing Jett on a daily basis, I wasn't just some vaguely familiar guy popping back into his life. His mother made sure he knew who I was the entire time I was gone. If ever there was an example of a woman who put her child's needs before her own feelings, it was Candice. And while I was gone, Candice had remained a part of my family just the same. She'd gone to the birthday parties and the holiday parties and kept Jett in contact with my family just as much as her own.

My family planned a big *Welcome Home!* party for me long before I ever got out. It was a big deal to me, and it was by invite only because I wasn't ready to be swarmed by the whole world all at once. During my time away, many friends and family members were there to support me even though I didn't deserve it, and those were the people I wanted to see at my party.

One person I was particularly happy to see at my party was Marcus—the same man who had recruited me for the entrepreneurship program a year earlier. My time in that program was a large part of me getting my head on straight again—from the Character Assessment to the Enneagram and everything else—and I was delighted to introduce him to my family.

Also at that party was Candice. She brought Jett, of course, but it was also good to see her and just be in the same building with her. I was still convinced that I could be a good husband to her even though we were divorced. She'd made it clear that she wasn't interested in getting back together, so I left it alone for the time being. Besides, I knew it would take a while before she saw that I'd definitely changed since the last time she'd seen me, and I had no problem waiting that out.

During that first month, things were better than I had planned. I had a job almost immediately, and I loved being back in the real world. I woke up at 6:00 a.m. every morning and packed a lunch before heading to work. I only made $13 per hour at my new job, so I couldn't afford to go out to eat very often. But I didn't care about that. I was just happy to have a bed to sleep in and a place to earn a paycheck. And above all, I was thoroughly enjoying my new role as a there-every-weekend father to my son.

However, it was still a bit awkward being alone with Jett those first few visits. He was such an easy kid to take care of, and he was all kinds of fun to be around. But I'd never raised a child, and I wasn't sure how to go about it. Making snacks and playing outside are simple enough, but when he did something he wasn't supposed to do, I wasn't quite sure how to handle it.

Since I grew up in a culture where spanking children was the norm, it only made sense that I would discipline Jett the same. I hated it, but it was more effective than empty threats. Every time he got spanked, he cried. And it always reminded me of all the times I'd gotten spanked because I'd cried just the same. That never felt right to me though, and I was certain there was a better way. Until I found that better way, however, I had to go with what I knew.

Meanwhile, things with Candice were getting better. By that, I mean we were moving in the direction of us getting back together after all. At the time, it seemed to take forever, but in reality, we were back together by the end of my first month out. In a way, it was weird falling completely in love with my ex-wife, but that's what happened. And she fell in love with me just the same. The three of us together under one roof made all the sense in the world, and I couldn't have been happier. We talked about getting remarried on February 27, which was the date our divorce was final back in 2008. It seemed appropriate, and I loved the idea.

Sadly, our relationship fell apart months before February 27 ever rolled around. As with our first time separating, we never fought and things remained civil. People who knew both of us just couldn't understand why we were splitting up, and it reminded me of my own parents who'd gotten divorced then remarried to each other and divorced again when I was a child, except the difference in our situation was that we found out soon after our breakup that Candice was in fact pregnant with our second child. I was barely learning how to be a father to my first child, yet there was another on the way. Somehow, I was actually ready for that challenge.

❧ ❧ ❧ ❧ ❧ ❧

During my first 30 years, I'd always lived with someone—my parents, Candice, or friends who let me couch surf temporarily. But in the spring of 2011, I got my own apartment. It was the first time I'd ever actually lived on my own. I still went to Candice's on the weekends to see Jett, but during the week, I was alone in my apartment every day after work.

I enjoyed my job, but the pay was starting to be a problem. After paying my bills and child support, I didn't really have much money left over each month to have a life. Most of my evenings consisted of Facebook and Netflix, but even that gets old after a while. In a perfect world, Candice and I would have stayed together and raised Jett and our new baby together as one family unit, but we agreed that it wasn't smart to force our relationship just for the sake of the kids. I often wonder whether that was right or wrong, but regardless of what she and I decided on as a couple (or as two individuals), I was bent on providing the absolute best life possible for her and Jett and the baby on the way.

In September of 2011, she was eight months pregnant, and I was looking for a better job. My $13 per hour job was good for someone who'd just gotten out of prison, but I'd been out for a year at that point and was about to have more mouths to feed. In addition to Jett and the new baby, I was also determined to find a job making enough money so that Candice could quit her job and stay home fulltime. I don't know if I was trying to rectify how crappy I was during and after her first pregnancy, but I was motivated beyond measure to give her the life I felt she deserved regardless of whether or not she was my wife.

We had discussed the possibility of living together again for the sake of convenience and simply everyone together under one roof. It wasn't conventional, but it definitely beat trying to arrange schedules and ship kids around to see their parents. Candice moved into her new house during the middle of September that year, and I moved in shortly thereafter. Two weeks later, on September 27, 2011, our second son was born: Phoenix Ross Tumey. A week after that, Jett turned five years old.

Candice and I knew that there would be a bit of a gap during the time the baby was born and whenever I found a new job, so we just used credit cards to float us for a month or two until I found the big paying job I needed. I'd heard about a lot of the guys from the entrepreneurship program going to work in the oil fields after prison, and I knew the money was good in that industry. There was a bit of a boom going on in West Texas, so I started asking around trying to figure out how to get a job somewhere.

Anywhere.

There was one person in particular whom I knew would be able to help me if I could get in touch of him. His name was Roger, the same guy who was way too friendly to not be on drugs during my first day at the entrepreneurship program nearly two years earlier. I got his phone number through a mutual friend and gave him a call. He put me in touch with the right people, and my prospects were looking great. After a few more phone calls and a two-week notice at my current job, I was hired at one of the better drilling companies in the business and more than doubled my $27,000 salary to $60,000. Barely a year removed from prison, I was earning an honest living at a job that afforded me the opportunity to give Candice, Jett, and Phoenix the life that every man wants to give his family.

Life was good.

❧ ❧ ❧ ❧ ❧ ❧

Living with my ex-wife and our two children was unconventional, but I loved it. My work schedule meant that I was 400 miles away for two weeks at a time and then home for two weeks at a time. And my paycheck meant that Candice could stay home and live the life that she'd deserved for quite some time.

By 2012, Jett was ready to start kindergarten, but I wasn't the least bit worried about that. He was one of the sweetest kids I'd ever met—to the point that I was mostly concerned that he would get bullied by other kids—and he was smart enough that I wasn't worried about him struggling academically. The last thing I expected was for him to get into trouble or cause any problems. But within his first two weeks of school, his troubles were sudden and severe.

Jett didn't struggle to learn. He struggled to adhere to structure, and that was something I was all too familiar with, so

I wasted no time addressing his behavior at home after school. He hated being spanked, so I decided that was the thing he needed most. After all, if he hated it so much, maybe that would encourage him to correct his behavior at school.

But it only got worse.

Jett liked his teacher, but he wasn't nearly as fond of the assignments she gave. In fact, he really wasn't too keen on doing anything at school that involved sitting down and following orders. He was a sweet kid, so anger wasn't his driving force. Even in his insubordination, his manners persisted. You were more likely to hear a *no thank you* than a violent protest of any sort.

My son was much happier making his friends laugh or entertaining himself. He got along fine with the other kids, and he also liked his teachers. Jett just didn't see the need to *sit down, be quiet, and do as you're told.*

Every day Jett went to school, it was like rolling dice. Maybe he'd cause a riot. Maybe he wouldn't make a sound. There was no way to know, but I was on a first-name basis with the principal, assistant principal, counselor, and practically anyone who came in contact with Jett throughout any given day. Thankfully, my work schedule allowed for me to be completely accessible during my days off, but the downside to that was being gone for weeks at a time, which meant Candice was left to handle Jett on her own. Never mind the fact that she also had a baby to take care of, Candice just didn't understand *what's going on with Jett?* She'd always been the model student and had never caused any trouble. On top of that, Jett had never shown any signs of being a problem child. There was no explanation for his behavior, and she wasn't sure how to cope.

As his behavior got worse, so did the spankings. I didn't even realize I was repeating the same stupid cycle from when I was the kid being spanked by my dad, but that's exactly what was happening until one day when Jett screamed at me that I was hurting him.

"Yeah, that's kind of the point, Jett."

"But why?!"

"Because," I replied in a level, logical tone, "perhaps this will make you think twice about acting up at school."

As if I'd spoken a completely foreign language, his face contorted into an equal mixture of grimace and confusion as he shouted, "But you're HURTING me!"

Oh my god, you're right.

He meant that I was physically hurting him, and he was right. *Yeah, that's kind of the point, Jett.* But worse than that, I was actually hurting him in a way that wasn't physical at all. I was doing the same thing to my son that my dad had done to me. I was trying to punish away bad behavior instead of trying to find the cause of it. Had I not been through that myself, I probably would have never connected the dots.

I wasn't helping my son; I was hurting him. And that felt worse to me than all the years I'd spent in prison combined. This kind of thing was the very reason I used to think Jett was better off without me. When I was considering turning myself in several years earlier, I was convinced that I would do more harm than good if I stayed around because I just didn't know how to be a father, but I wasn't about to go disappear again. The worse Jett's behavior got, the more determined I was to be the perfect dad for my son. The whole thing was stressing Candice out, and I could tell. I felt bad for her, but I was also a bit excited to know that this was one thing where I could be useful as a father because of how much experience I had as the student in that situation. My child was struggling to find his place in school just like I had, and who better to guide him than me? *Nobody,* I thought. *This is my job.*

Throughout my life, I'd imagined the different scenarios that might present themselves with my future children. Sure, nearly 30 years had passed since I was in kindergarten, but I had vivid memories of wondering why no adults ever tried anything other than brute force punishment with me. Something I always hated about school as a child was the fact that educators handled all students the same. Students were clearly unique from each other, but that didn't seem to matter. Kids were expected to adapt to the system instead of the other way around. The correctional system in America is even worse in that regard. The focus is almost always on punishment rather than actual correction. However, while reading *Wisdom* in prison, I learned that there were no universal answers when it came to correcting bad behavior because the wide range of personalities that exist suggests that an equally wide range of solutions is necessary. What worked for one might not work for someone else, and that alone was a refreshing concept. It's not that I was unable to follow rules or obey instructions. I just wasn't presented with options that made sense to me.

My mother once asked me what she could have done differently as a parent. It was a difficult question to answer because it seemed to imply that she was somehow responsible for my behavior as a child and, ultimately, my incarceration. She simplified the question and said, "Well let me ask you this way. What would you do if that was your kid? How are you going to handle it if Jett goes to school and just decides to do whatever he wants?"

It was an interesting scenario to consider but certainly not one that I hadn't already thought about many times before. "Well," I said, "I can tell you what I *won't* do. I'm not going to keep doing anything that obviously doesn't work." It was a reference to the redundant punitive measures that persisted throughout my childhood.

I continued, "I'm not saying I'm not going to punish Jett or anything like that. If he needs discipline, then that's what he'll get. But if whatever I'm doing isn't working, then I'll try something different."

When my mother came to visit me in prison, our conversations had greater significance. I wasn't a fan of talking about what she could have done differently as my mother, but

I especially enjoyed discussing what I might do if Jett were to grow up and follow in my insubordinate footsteps. Talking this out with my mother helped prepare me to be a father because she had a long list of things that she would've done differently if given the opportunity.

"Spanking didn't work for you," she later told me. "And we knew that early on. I wanted you to go talk to someone—a counselor, a therapist, anyone—but your dad was against it."

Interestingly, my mother didn't even think my childhood behavior was my fault. "I never once attributed any of that to you," she said. "I thought it was our fault."

"I thought your behavior at school was some sort of an attempt to compensate for the divorce." My mom referenced the numerous occasions when my teachers moved my desk next to theirs, and she suggested that perhaps I was getting in trouble as a means of being closer to my teachers. It's an interesting theory, and when I think back to those years, nearly all of my teachers eventually placed my desk next to their own.

In my memory, their divorces weren't a big deal to me. Sure, there was the poem that I wrote in sixth grade, but nobody was ever supposed to know about that. My brother was particularly distraught about our parents being divorced, but it just didn't really matter to me. If anything, I enjoyed having two homes. Nevertheless, my mom's theory about why I was always in trouble was worth remembering in the event that my own child had his own troubles in school. No matter what, I wanted to always consider all possibilities and get to the root of *why* rather than trying to punish him into submission. I knew that my plan would always be to figure out the *why* before getting carried away with the punishment. After all, how could one possibly solve a problem that they haven't identified?

Ultimately, nothing seemed to work with Jett during his kindergarten year. He was two different people between home and school, and the school began to find themselves in a position where their only viable option was to keep sending him home over and over, especially on the weeks when I wasn't available. On the weeks when I was off work, I actually went and sat outside his classroom. All day. Every day. If he got out of line, I was there to intervene. That was rarely necessary, of course, but when I was out of town for work, the school reverted to sending Jett home when he began to act up again.

Eventually, we decided it would be best to pull Jett out of kindergarten and to seek some sort of professional help. Kindergarten wasn't a required grade, so that wasn't a concern. And his academics were fine, so we weren't worried about that either. The top priority was finding the root cause of Jett's behavioral issues and addressing it directly rather than trying to punish away his bad behavior. Even though I didn't have the answer, I felt like I'd accomplished something by continuing the search for the answer.

When I returned to work for my two-week shift, Candice began searching for doctors, therapists, and anyone else who could help our child. They ran their tests and began their play therapy sessions, but there was no way to really know if they were making progress until the following school year started back up. Jett's behavior at home was never the problem. It was only at school that he acted up.

The following summer, however, Jett returned to school as a first grader, and it seemed that most of his problems had disappeared. As parents, Candice and I couldn't have hoped for a better school for my son. Everyone from the school principal to Jett's teacher seemed prepared for Jett's return. Nobody held his previous year against him, and he started over with a clean slate. Most importantly—to me, at least—the educators at Jett's school understood that he was just unique and that they couldn't apply cookie-cutter discipline to his behavior. They wanted a specific plan in place based on the recommendation of his doctor and the school district's behavioral specialists. Of course, Jett didn't realize there was a team of people who were working to ensure he had a productive year in the first grade, nor did any of his classmates. But behind the scenes, great effort was given to the success of my son. It was a drastically different experience than mine from three decades earlier.

The Jett we all experienced during his kindergarten year never fully returned. Candice suggested that the biggest difference for Jett was that he knew what to expect when he returned to school, and I tend to agree with that. He was accustomed to staying home all day with his mother and baby brother, and school was a fairly new concept to him. However, when he started first grade, he at least had an idea of what school was going to be like, and he could adjust accordingly.

For me, of course, a key factor was that we pulled him out of school during kindergarten before he got too comfortable being in the principal's office several days per week. Academics took a backseat to behavioral issues, and we wasted no time in finding the professional help we thought he needed. For whatever reason, my dad was against that when I was a kid, but I made sure to end that cycle of ignorance with my own child. It certainly helped that Candice and I were on the same page and were willing to do whatever necessary to find the core problem.

Ultimately, only Jett knows exactly what his problems were during his first year in school. And only Jett knows why he decided to control himself the following year, but I definitely believe it was a conscious choice on his part to go to school and improve his behavior. I also believe that the adults in his life—the collective whole—are responsible for providing him the opportunity to find the right choices instead of punishing him into oblivion when he makes the wrong choices.

I try to avoid thinking much about how different my childhood might have been if the adults in my own life had searched a little deeper for answers instead of sticking with the *because I said so* mentality, but regardless of how terrible those years were for me, the fact remains that I was entering familiar territory when Jett began to follow in my footsteps.

Except this time, I was part of the solution.

Jett went on to complete first grade without incident, and he has since gone on to complete second grade just as well. He still gets into a bit of trouble here and there, but it seems like a normal, acceptable amount of trouble.

❧ ❧ ❧ ❧ ❧ ❧

My past helps me be a better father, and it's one of the reasons you'll never hear me say that I regret my past. Similarly, my time in prison also provides me the opportunity to have a voice to those who are currently incarcerated.

Not long after my release, I contacted Susan Olesek and thanked her for bringing her work with the Enneagram to prison. As it turns out, my class was only the second one she'd ever done behind bars, but she was working on an idea and would soon devote her life to prison work. The Enneagram Prison Project was the self-explanatory name for the program, and I was immediately on board—partly because I liked the Enneagram but mostly because I loved Susan.

In my personal life, however, things were becoming a bit mundane. Things were going great at work, and I enjoyed the steady income as well as the life it provided. I loved that Candice was staying home with our two very special children, and I was also thankful that we all lived under one roof, even if I wasn't there half the time. Still, work itself was becoming a drag, and I began to feel trapped. There was no way I could make that kind of money working anywhere else, so it no longer felt like a choice to work there. It was a necessity.

This was the very thinking that had gotten me into trouble so many other times, and I recognized that immediately. Being aware of the problem didn't fix anything, but it at least alerted me to the fact that there was a problem to be addressed.

By that point, my position at work had transitioned to one where I was mostly driving a pickup all day. I enjoyed the solitude, but the isolation was also doing me no favors. Knowing that I needed connection to others—but not fully knowing how to do that while driving a truck all day—I started searching for something on the radio to listen to. I'd always been a fan of talk radio, so I felt like there was a pretty good chance I could find something on the AM dial that might lift my spirits.

"This," I heard through the static of a choppy radio signal, "is The Dave Ramsey Show, where dad is dumb, tax is king, and the paid off home mortgage has taken the place of the BMW as the status symbol of choice."

Well that made absolutely no sense, I thought. But before I could change the channel, Dave was already taking phone calls.

"Hey, Dave. How's it going?"

"Better than I deserve," came Ramsey's reply. *Well, now there's a bit of positivity I could use!*

I didn't know anything about Dave Ramsey other than the little bit I learned after listening to him for a while that day. At the beginning of his second hour, I heard his introduction again and realized that he'd said debt was dumb and cash was king. That made a lot more sense because his entire show was about personal finance. I didn't know a thing about personal finance though and, quite frankly, didn't care to learn about it either. I just liked Dave's positive attitude and the way he was so willing to help an unending stream of strangers calling into the show asking for advice.

In addition to his willingness to help those in need, I also just thought Dave was a funny guy, and I soon found myself looking forward to the three-hour block on the radio when he came on. This was the break in my mundane days that I needed, and although I wasn't technically connecting with another person through mutual dialogue, it was the closest thing I could find after having spent all day in a pickup truck for days and even weeks on end.

Soon, I found myself knowing the answer to common questions from callers, and it became a game to me. I still didn't really care about anything Dave was teaching, but it was fun knowing what he would say before he even said it. As it turns out, people pretty much all call in with the same few problems, so anyone who listens regularly can quote Dave's perspective on pretty much anything. He's not wildly unpredictable or completely out of control with complicated theories. He teaches a very straightforward message that is easy to understand and retain.

And without even realizing it, I actually began learning about personal finance.

His biggest issue is debt. He hates it, and he thinks it's stupid. I'd always grown up thinking debt was just a way of life, but hearing him go on and on about how horrible it is, I started wondering if maybe I'd grown up with the wrong mindset toward it all. For kicks, I mentally went through all the things I currently owed money on. A few thousand here for the credit cards that carried us from when Phoenix was born until I got my new job making better money. A few more thousand on a credit card for tires. A couple more thousand here and a few more thousand there. When I actually added it all up, I owed over $44,000 to all of my creditors combined.

Insanity!

Only making $60,000 per year, I was certain there was no way I would ever pay off that much debt any time soon, but once an hour on The Dave Ramsey Show, they have a debt-free scream, which is really nothing more than a regular person calling in and talking about how much debt they paid off and how they did it. It wasn't gimmicky network marketing or anything else getting people out of debt either. They were simply cutting their lifestyle to a minimum and working overtime at work, delivering pizzas, and pretty much anything they could do to make extra money and pay down their debt to zero before going on the show and screaming at the top of their lungs, "Three. Two. One. I'm debt-free!"

Those calls were so inspiring, and I wanted to try it for myself. In addition to being a sound financial decision, the whole debt-free journey just seemed like another great way to prove to myself—and if I'm being honest, everyone else—that I was indeed a changed man who was capable of achieving great things.

Without knowing anything about budgeting, planning, or anything else related to personal finance, I knuckled down and took on the most insane work schedule I'd ever heard of. I worked over 90 hours per week for weeks on end without a day off. During one stretch, I worked 12 of 13 weeks and put every last extra dollar from my paycheck toward paying off my debt. It was crazy and probably a little bit unhealthy, but at the end of 16 months, I'd managed to pay down every last bit of my debt.

$44,000 in 16 months, in addition to the fact that I was still providing for Candice and our two sons. That journey was one of the greatest personal accomplishments of my life, and in August of 2014, I finally got my chance to go on The Dave Ramsey Show and share my story.

But my story wasn't just about working hard and paying off debt. In fact, the financial aspect of it all was almost secondary. The thing I wanted most to share with Dave and the eight million people who were listening that day was that my future is not defined by my past. And when I had decided to step up to the plate and take responsibility for all the crap that I'd caused, that's when I was able to sort through the mess and find a solution.

I was talking about money matters, but it was a metaphor for my entire life. It was a big deal for me to actually accomplish something good for my kids and for myself. Up to that point, I had felt as though my past were stamped across my forehead everywhere I went and that there was no escaping it.

All of this was playing through my mind as I stood in the studio. Shortly into the broadcast, Dave asked me, "How long were you incarcerated?"

I didn't like the question but answered it anyway. "About three and a half years," I said and almost immediately corrected myself. "A little over three years," I said. After a brief pause, I specified, "Three years, three months, and 10 days."

He gave a short laugh. "Okay. Yeah, give or take a minute," he joked. I laughed because I was nervous. Dave returned to a serious tone and added, "But it's all behind you now."

The weight of reality—this wonderful truth that the dark days were truly behind me—hit me hard, and my best effort at replying was a barely audible, "Every bit of it."

"Good for you," he said as he nodded slightly and continued. "Proud of ya, man. Very cool. Hard work, overtime, a goal, and a whole different kind of freedom when you yell *debt-free* today, huh? That's different than just paying off a little MasterCard." He laughed as I nodded in agreement. It was indeed a major weight off my shoulders to have paid my restitution in full, or as Dave put it, "That's a big monkey off the back."

"That's the nice way to put it," I said. He was right, but hearing him describe it that way made me wonder if I'd painted myself as the victim of some situation that I had actually created. I wasn't a victim, and I needed to be clear by delivering the main message that I'd wanted to share that day:

"But, ya know, I put myself in that position, so when you have to man up and take care of what you did, you just do it. It's not anybody's fault but mine...and to bring myself to be done with it is a big deal. "

It felt great to be able to step into a spotlight that big and take ownership for my biggest mistakes in life—not because I was proud of them but because I had dealt with them appropriately and successfully.

Dave's show is about *your life and your money*, as he often says. But when I did my debt-free scream that day, it represented so much more than a mere financial milestone.

It was closure.

It marked the end of my past and the beginning of my future.

AFTERWORD

Prison sucks. It worked for me because of me, not because of the system itself. If the message you get from this book is that jail is a place to go and solve your problems, then please allow me to clarify. *Do not try this at home.* Just as I did when I researched bank robbery to learn from the mistakes of others, please do the same with my story.

Freedom in Captivity was the working title of this book for the duration of my time writing it. I later changed the title because I didn't want *confinement* to be anyone's first thought whenever they saw the book. I chose *The Blue Chip Store* after I fell in love with the sentimentality of my son naming the book. Plus, I just think it's a cool title with a neat story behind it. But on my computer, the file where I saved the documents that eventually became the chapters of this book remained under the original working title because I never wanted to lose sight of the purpose of my work.

Your very existence is the reason I wrote this book in the first place, so it's with a bit of melancholy that I share with you a few more words before moving on to the next chapter of my life. Above anything else you might learn from me, I want you to see the truth in these closing thoughts.

I believe you have a purpose in this life. Not the generic plural version of *you* either. I mean you—specifically, you—the person reading this right now. You are valuable, and you have a role that nobody else can serve. I can't define that role for you, but I urge you to take a brutally honest look at yourself to understand what it is that makes you tick.

Confront yourself. Disconnect from the disguise you've been showing the rest of the world for so long and challenge the reality of who you are. *If you have to tell them who you are, it's probably because you're not.* Invite the insight of others, and don't make excuses for the image others have of you. Accept responsibility for who you are and address the things that you want to change in your life so that you can grow into a better version of yourself.

Choose hope. In my ignorance, I always believed that people used *hope* as a means of escaping pain. But in my darkest days, I realized that hope didn't help me *escape* the pain; it allowed me to believe that there was a way to get *through* the pain. As George Eliot said, *it is never too late to be what you might have been.* So no matter where you are in life, no matter your situation, choose hope.

⁂ ⁂ ⁂ ⁂ ⁂ ⁂

Freedom. Prison. Under normal circumstances, they are polar opposites. But my life isn't a series of normal circumstances, and I suspect the same can be said for you. I don't know what comes up for you in reading my story, but my hope is that you will identify the thing in your own life that is holding you captive so you can then begin your own journey to freedom.

The measure of intelligence is the ability to change.
—Albert Einstein

CPSIA information can be obtained at www.ICGtesting.com
Printed in the USA
LVOW11s0004241015

459602LV00005B/5/P